Imperial Eyes

Studies in colonial and exploration discourse have highlighted the great significance of travel writing as one of the ideological apparatuses of empire. However, the study of travel writing has tended to remain either naively celebratory or dismissive, treating texts as symptoms of imperial ideologies. By combining the study of genre with critique of ideology, *Imperial Eyes* offers a stronger, more textured approach.

The book shows how travel writing has produced "the rest of the world" for European readerships, and examines how metropolitan reading publics have been engaged with expansionist enterprises whose material benefits accrued mainly to the very few. These issues are approached through a two-pronged methodology that includes readings of particular corpuses of travel writing connected with particular historical junctures; and establishing connections from travel writing to forms of knowledge and expression that interact with it. The concept of transculturation is used to introduce questions about the ways in which modes of representation from the metropolis are received and appropriated by groups on the periphery – and how transculturation from the colonies to the metropolis takes place.

Imperial Eyes will appeal to readers interested in issues of colonialism and post-colonialism; in nineteenth-century British and Latin American literature; and in theories of discourse and ideology.

Mary Louise Pratt is Professor in the Departments of Spanish and Portuguese, and of Comparative Literature, at Stanford University, California.

Imperial Eyes

Travel Writing and Transculturation

Mary Louise Pratt

London and New York

First published 1992
by Routledge
11 New Fetter Lane, London EC4P 4EE

Simultaneously published in the USA and Canada
by Routledge
a division of Routledge, Chapman and Hall, Inc.
29 West 35th Street, New York, NY 10001

© 1992 Mary Louise Pratt

Set in 10/12pt Garamond by
Falcon Typographic Art Ltd, Edinburgh & London
Printed and bound in Great Britain by
T J Press (Padstow) Ltd, Padstow, Cornwall

British Library Cataloguing in Publication Data
Pratt, Mary Louise
  Imperial eyes: studies in travel writing
  and transculturation.
  I. Title
  820.9355

Library of Congress Cataloging in Publication Data
Pratt, Mary Louise
  Imperial eyes/Mary Louise Pratt.
  1. Europe – Relations – Latin America. 2. Europe – Relations –
  Africa. 3. Latin America – Description and travel. 4. Africa –
  Description and travel – to 1900. 5. Latin America – Historiography.
  6. Africa – Historiography. 7. Latin America – Relations – Europe.
  8. Africa – Relations – Europe. 9. Imperialism. 10. European prose
  literature – History and criticism. I. Title.
  D34.L29P73 1991
  940 – dc20   91–21435

ISBN 0–415–02675–X
ISBN 0–415–06095–8 pbk

To my sisters,
Sheila, Nora, Kathy,

and my great aunts,
Agnes, Mary, Lorna, Winifred,
Mary, Norma, Maude, and Pearl

You can observe a lot just by watching.
Yogi Berra

Contents

Illustrations

Preface

This book began in a course on travel writing and European expansion that my colleague Rina Benmayor and I taught together at Stanford University in the years 1978–81. She went on to other things, and I got stuck on the subject.

Work on the project has been supported by many sources. The initial course had the benefit of a National Endowment for the Humanities curriculum development grant through the International Relations Program at Stanford University. A year of primary research was made possible by an NEH Fellowship for independent research in 1982–3. Writing-up time in 1987–8 was provided by the Pew Foundation, a Guggenheim Fellowship, and the Stanford Humanities Center. I am grateful to all these sources for supporting my work.

This is a book marked by the global realignments and ideological upheavals that began in the 1980s and continue in the present. It was begun during the anguish of the Reagan–Thatcher years, when demystifying imperialism seemed more urgent than ever, and also more hopeless. It was interrupted by the outbreak of the intense institutional struggles now underway in most American universities over undergraduate humanities curricula – struggles, precisely, over the legacy of Euroimperialism, androcentrism and white supremacy in education and official culture. The writing of this book, then, has been accompanied by a continuing confrontation with the very ideologies whose workings are under study here. Its publication coincides, for better or worse, with the year of the Columbian quincentennial, an occasion in Europe and the Americas for a reconsideration of Eurocolonialism and its aftermaths. In the domains of official culture this conjuncture is chiefly providing an occasion to renovate celebratory narratives of European superiority. The indigenous nations of the Americas are finding in the quincentennial an opportunity to assert a counterhistory, revindicate their lifeways, and consolidate present day struggles for territory and autonomy. Intellectuals are called upon to define, or redefine, their relation to the structures of knowledge and power that they produce, and that produce them. In the midst of ecological catastrophe and continuing imperial adventurism, the quincentennial underscores what tremendous historical force has been wielded by the European idologies of territory and global possessiveness that are the critical focus of this book.

This is also a book by an Anglo-Canadian expatriate for whom the openings of the 1960s and 1970s coalesced in an attempt to sustain teaching, maternity, writing, parenting, institution-building, and domestic partnership in the United States. Many of the people to whom I owe my sanity, well-being, and such wisdom as has come to me in these years are people without whom this book would probably have been finished a lot sooner (to little advantage): graduate students in the Department of Spanish and Portuguese and the Program in Modern Thought and Literature at Stanford; colleagues in the Seminar on Women and Culture in Latin America and the Cultural Studies Research Group; my beloved and unsynthesizable children Sam, Manuel, and Olivia; my partner and most precious interlocutor, Renato Rosaldo. To Jean Franco, Kathleen Newman, Ed Cohen, Rina Benmayor, Nancy Donham, and Jim Clifford, I am thankful for conversation and comments on parts of this work, but above all for their abiding friendship. I am grateful to Harriet Ritvo and Vince Raphael for generously reading chapters and for many helpful comments. As research and editorial assistants, Judith Raiskin, Elizabeth Cook, and Dane Johnson worked harder and more imaginatively than I had any right to expect. I have appreciated their help.

While none of what follows has been presented previously in the form it has here, earlier versions of some sections have appeared in articles in *College Literature*, 8, 1981; *Escritura*, 7, 1979; *Georgetown University Roundtable in Language and Linguistics*, 1982; *Critical Inquiry*, 12, 1985; *Nuevo Texto Crítico*, 1, 1987; *Inscriptions*, 1, 1987; and essays in the collections *Writing Culture* (ed. James Clifford and George Marcus, Berkeley, California UP, 1986), *"Race," Writing and Difference* (ed. Henry Louis Gates, Chicago, Chicago UP, 1986) and *Literature and Anthropology* (eds Jonathan Hall and Ackbar Abbas, Hong Kong, Hong Kong UP, 1986).

Chapter 1

Introduction: Criticism in the contact zone

In Listowel, Ontario, the small Canadian farm town where I grew up, one corner of the main intersection was occupied by Livingstone's Drugstore, run by Dr. Livingstone. Dr. Livingstone was a real doctor turned druggist, but for children his store was above all the place where you could buy practical jokes, or have them played on you by Dr. Livingstone, especially if you went in on an afternoon when Mrs. Livingstone wasn't there. It was through Dr. Livingstone, for example, that I was introduced to the miracles of the dribble glass, the squirt ring, the Chinese handcuff, the phony pack of Juicy Fruit Gum that snapped down on your finger, and, around 1955, a horrifying new item Dr. Livingstone secretly sold my older brother and his friend: plastic vomit. I was therefore unsure if he really meant it the day he produced a discolored sheet of faded writing in a frame and said it was a letter written by a great uncle of his who had been a famous missionary in Africa. Only after consulting at Sunday school with Miss Roxie Ellis, herself a former missionary, did I take the story for true. "Our" Dr. Livingstone was a grand nephew of the "real" Dr. Livingstone in Africa. English Canada was still colonial in the 1950s: reality and history were somewhere else, embodied in British men.

The name on the faded letter followed me, trailing its colonial legacy. When they put in sewers in Listowel they decided to change all the street names, and ours was upgraded from Raglan Street to Livingstone Avenue. The town itself had been named a century before by the postmaster, in true colonial fashion, after his wife's birthplace in Listowel, Ireland. My sister met up with that piece of history in the mid-1970s in East Africa. In the lobby of the Nairobi YWCA she met Dame Judith Listowel, a wiry, penniless, and eccentric adventuress in her seventies, who was disgusted at the cost of hotels, and mildly interested to hear about the town that bore her name in Canada. A few years after that, when I was researching this book in California, I came across a book by Dame Judith which she must have just finished writing when my sister met her – it was a biography of David Livingstone. I don't know where Dame Judith is now, but my mother, who still lives in Listowel, recently moved into the former Livingstone mansion, now converted to a retirement home. "English-speaking peoples of the world, unite!" All his life my father held passionately to that nostalgic, neoimperial call. Even after they changed his street name and my sister came back with her story from Nairobi, he never conceded that they already were united, or at least stuck together, all across the globe, with words.

Redundancy, discontinuity, and unreality. These are some of the chief coordinates of the text of Euroimperialism, the stuff of its power to constitute the everyday with neutrality, spontaneity, numbing repetition (Livingstone, Livingstone . . .). In recent years that power has become open to question and subject to scrutiny in the academy, as part of a large-scale effort to decolonize knowledge. This book is part of that effort. The effort must be, among other things, an exercise in humility. For one of the things it brings most forcefully into play are contestatory expressions from the site of imperial intervention, long ignored in the metropolis; the critique of empire coded ongoingly on the spot, in ceremony, dance, parody, philosophy, counterknowledge and counterhistory, in texts unwitnessed, suppressed, lost, or simply overlain with repetition and unreality. It calls for the story of another letter.

In 1908 a Peruvianist named Richard Pietschmann was exploring in the Danish Royal Archives in Copenhagen when he came across a manuscript he had never seen before. It was dated in Cuzco in the year 1613, some four decades after the final fall of the Inca Empire to the Spanish, and signed with an unmistakably Amerindian, Andean name: Felipe Guaman Poma de Ayala. (*Guaman* in Quechua means "falcon" and *poma* means "leopard.") Written in a mixture of Quechua and rough, ungrammatical Spanish, the manuscript was a letter addressed by this unknown Andean to King Philip III of Spain. What stunned Pietschmann was that the letter was twelve hundred pages long. There were nearly eight hundred pages of written text and four hundred elaborate line drawings with explanatory captions. Titled the *New Chronicle and Good Government and Justice*, the manuscript proposed nothing less than a new view of the world. It began by rewriting the history of Christendom to include the indigenous peoples of America, then went on to describe in great detail the history and lifeways of the Andean peoples and their leaders. This was followed by a revisionist account of the Spanish conquest, and hundreds of pages documenting and denouncing Spanish exploitation and abuse. The four hundred illustrations followed the European genre of the captioned line drawing but, as subsequent research revealed, they deployed specifically Andean structures of spatial symbolism (see plates 1 and 3.) Guaman Poma's letter ends with a mock interview in which he advises the King as to his responsibilities, and proposes a new form of government through collaboration of Andean and Spanish elites.

No one knew (or knows) how this extraordinary work got to the library in Copenhagen, or how long it had been there. No one, it appeared, had ever bothered to read it, or even figured out how to read it. Quechua was

1 Guaman Poma de Ayala's drawing of biblical creation. The caption reads
"El primer mundo/Adan, Eva," "The first world/Adam, Eve." The drawing is
organized according to Andean symbolic space, with Adam and the rooster
on the "male" side of the picture under the male symbol of the sun and Eve,
the chickens and children on the female side, marked by the moon. The two
spheres are divided by a diagonal, here marked by Adam's digging stick, a
basic tool of Andean agriculture. The Inca empire was likewise laid out in
four kingdoms divided by two diagonals intersecting at the city of Cuzco.

not known as a written language in 1908, or Andean culture as a literate culture. Pietschmann prepared a paper on his find which he presented in London in 1912. The reception of his paper, by an international congress of Americanists, was apparently confused. It took another twenty-five years for a facsimile edition of Guaman Poma's work to appear in Paris; the few scholars who worked on it did so in isolation. It was not until the late 1970s, as positivist reading habits gave way to interpretive studies and Eurocentric elitisms gave way to postcolonial pluralisms, that Guaman Poma's text began to be read as the extraordinary intercultural *tour de force* that it was.[2]

To be read, *and to be readable*. The readability of Guaman Poma's letter today is another sign of the changing intellectual dynamics through which colonial meaning-making has become a subject of critical investigation. His elaborate inter-cultural text and its tragic history exemplify the possibilities and perils of writing in what I like to call "contact zones," social spaces where disparate cultures meet, clash, and grapple with each other, often in highly asymmetrical relations of domination and subordination – like colonialism, slavery, or their aftermaths as they are lived out across the globe today.

Perhaps these two letters – the seemingly inevitable monolingual page from an Englishman in Africa to his nephew, yellowing on the wall of a rural Canadian drugstore, and the seemingly incredible twelve hundred bilingual pages from an unknown Andean to the King of Spain, lost in an archive in Copenhagen – can serve to suggest the vast, discontinuous, and overdetermined history of imperial meaning-making that is the context for this book. Its main, but not its only subject is European travel and exploration writing, analysed in connection with European economic and political expansion since around 1750. The book aims to be both a study in genre and a critique of ideology. Its predominant theme is how travel books by Europeans about non-European parts of the world went (and go) about creating the "domestic subject"[3] of Euroimperialism; how they have engaged metropolitan reading publics with (or to) expansionist enterprises whose material benefits accrued mainly to the very few. Several chapters of the book take up such questions through readings of particular corpuses of travel accounts connected with particular historical transitions. One chapter, for example, looks at eighteenth-century European writings on southern Africa in the context of inland expansion and the rise of natural history. Others study the emergence of sentimental travel writing through materials from the Caribbean and the early British exploration of West Africa (1780–1840). Others examine discursive reinventions of South America during the period of Spanish American independence (1800–40). Another traces continuities and mutations in the imperial imaginary from the Victorians in Central Africa (1860–1900) to postcolonial travelers of the 1960s and 1980s.

These case studies are shaped by a number of shared questions. How has travel and exploration writing *produced* "the rest of the world" for European readerships at particular points in Europe's expansionist trajectory? How has it produced Europe's differentiated conceptions of itself in relation to something it became possible to call "the rest of the world"? How do such signifying practices encode and legitimate the aspirations of economic expansion and empire? How do they betray them?

The book also undertakes to suggest connections from travel writing to forms of knowledge and expression that interact or intersect with it, outside and inside Europe. Chapter 2, for example, considers how travel writing and enlightenment natural history catalyzed each other to produce a Eurocentered form of global or, as I call it, "planetary" consciousness. The classificatory schemes of natural history are seen in relation to the vernacular peasant knowledges they sought to displace. Scientific and sentimental travel writing (chapters 3 through 5) are discussed in complementary fashion, as bourgeois forms of authority that displace older traditions of survival literature. Within the sentimental mode, relations are drawn between travel narrative and slave autobiography, which appear at about the same time and act upon each other. Chapter 7 emphasizes determinations of gender in some early nineteenth-century travel writing, focusing on a rather unpredictable division of labor between female and male writers. In chapter 9 the writings of what Teddy Roosevelt called "hyphenated Americans" are examined in terms of challenges they posed to the British explorer tradition; postcolonial travel writing of the 1960s is read in relation to tourist propaganda on the one hand and contestatory genres like *testimonio* and oral history on the other. Here too the enactment of race and gender relations is at issue.

At a number of points the book leaves both Europe and travel literature behind, to examine instances of non-European expression developed in interaction with European repertoires. Here the materials are from South America. Chapter 8 looks at how Spanish American writers in the early nineteenth century selected and adapted European discourses on America to their own task of creating autonomous decolonized cultures while retaining European values and white supremacy. It is a study in the dynamics of creole self-fashioning. Elsewhere, instances from the history of Andean indigenous expression (like Guaman Poma's letter) are introduced to suggest the dynamics of self-representation in the context of colonial subordination and resistance. While the representational practices of Europeans remain the chief subject of the book, then, I have sought ways to mitigate a reductive, diffusionist perspective.

I have also sought ways to interrupt the totalizing momentum of both the study of genre and the critique of ideology. These projects are both anchored, as I am, in the metropolis; to concede them autonomy or completeness would reaffirm metropolitan authority in its own terms – the very thing travel writers are often charged to do. In writing this book I have tried to avoid simply reproducing the dynamics of possession and innocence whose workings I analyze in texts. The term "transculturation" in the title sums up my efforts in this direction. Ethnographers have used this term to describe how subordinated or marginal groups select and invent from materials transmitted to them by a dominant or metropolitan culture.[4] While subjugated peoples cannot readily control what emanates from the dominant culture, they do determine to varying extents what they absorb into their own, and what they use it for. Transculturation is a phenomenon of the contact zone. In the context of this book, the concept serves to raise several sets of questions. How are metropolitan modes of representation received and appropriated on the periphery? That question engenders another perhaps more heretical one: with respect to representation, how does one speak of transculturation from the colonies to the metropolis? The fruits of empire, we know, were pervasive in shaping European domestic society, culture, and history. How have Europe's constructions of subordinated others been shaped by those others, by the constructions of themselves and their habitats that they presented to the Europeans? Borders and all, the entity called Europe was constructed from the outside in as much as from the inside out. Can this be said of its modes of representation? While the imperial metropolis tends to understand itself as determining the periphery (in the emanating glow of the civilizing mission or the cash flow of development, for example), it habitually blinds itself to the ways in which the periphery determines the metropolis – beginning, perhaps, with the latter's obsessive need to present and re-present its peripheries and its others continually to itself. Travel writing, among other institutions, is heavily organized in the service of that imperative. So, one might add, is much of European literary history.

In the attempt to suggest a dialectic and historicized approach to travel writing, I have manufactured some terms and concepts along the way. One coinage that recurs throughout the book is the term "contact zone," which I use to refer to the space of colonial encounters, the space in which peoples geographically and historically separated come into contact with each other and establish ongoing relations, usually involving conditions of coercion, radical inequality, and intractable conflict. I borrow the term "contact" here from its use in linguistics, where the term contact language refers to improvised languages that develop among speakers of different native languages who need to communicate with each other consistently, usually in context of trade. Such languages begin as pidgins, and are called creoles when they come to have native speakers of their own. Like the societies of the contact zone, such languages are commonly regarded as chaotic, barbarous, lacking in structure. (Ron Carter has suggested the term "contact literatures" to refer to literatures written in European languages from outside Europe.[5]) "Contact zone" in my discussion is often synonymous with "colonial frontier." But while the latter term is grounded within a

European expansionist perspective (the frontier is a frontier only with respect to Europe), "contact zone" is an attempt to invoke the spatial and temporal copresence of subjects previously separated by geographic and historical disjunctures, and whose trajectories now intersect. By using the term "contact," I aim to foreground the interactive, improvisational dimensions of colonial encounters so easily ignored or suppressed by diffusionist accounts of conquest and domination. A "contact" perspective emphasizes how subjects are constituted in and by their relations to each other. It treats the relations among colonizers and colonized, or travelers and "travelees," not in terms of separateness or apartheid, but in terms of copresence, interaction, interlocking understandings and practices, often within radically asymmetrical relations of power.[6]

A second term I use often in what follows is "anti-conquest," by which I refer to the strategies of representation whereby European bourgeois subjects seek to secure their innocence in the same moment as they assert European hegemony. The term "anti-conquest" was chosen because, as I argue, in travel and exploration writings these strategies of innocence are constituted in relation to older imperial rhetorics of conquest associated with the absolutist era. The main protagonist of the anti-conquest is a figure I sometimes call the "seeing-man," an admittedly unfriendly label for the European male subject of European landscape discourse – he whose imperial eyes passively look out and possess.

A third and final idiosyncratic term that appears in what follows is "autoethnography" or "autoethnographic expression." I use these terms to refer to instances in which colonized subjects undertake to represent themselves in ways that *engage with* the colonizer's own terms. If ethnographic texts are a means by which Europeans represent to themselves their (usually subjugated) others, autoethnographic texts are those the others construct in response to or in dialogue with those metropolitan representations. Guaman Poma's review of Inca history and customs in his *New Chronicle*, and his appropriation of the Spanish chronicle form to do so, constitute a canonical instance of autoethnographic representation (see plates 2 and 3). Autoethnographic texts are not, then, what are usually thought of as "authentic" or autochthonous forms of self-representation (such as the Andean *quipus*, which stored much of the information Guaman Poma wrote down). Rather autoethnography involves partial collaboration with and appropriation of the idioms of the conqueror. Often, as in the case of Guaman Poma, the idioms appropriated and transformed are those of travel and exploration writing, merged or infiltrated to varying degrees with indigenous modes. Often, as with Guaman Poma's letter, they are bilingual and dialogic. Autoethnographic texts are typically heterogeneous on the reception end as well, usually addressed both to metropolitan readers and to literate sectors of the speaker's own social group, and bound to be received very differently by each. Often such texts constitute a group's point of entry

2 Autoethnographic depiction from Guaman Poma's *Nueva coronica y buen gobierno*, from a series of representations of Andean agriculture. Caption reads "Trabaxa/Zara, papa hallmai mita" meaning "Work [in Spanish]/corn, time of rain and banking up [in Quechua]." The small writing under the caption reads "enero/Capac Raymi Quilla" meaning "January [in Spanish]/month of great feasting [in Quechua]. The man on the left is identified as a "labrador, chacarq camahoc," "laborer [in Spanish], in charge of sowing [in Quechua]."

into metropolitan literate culture. Though I have been unable to pursue the matter here, I believe that autoethnographic expression is a very widespread phenomenon of the contact zone, and will become important in unraveling the histories of imperial subjugation and resistance as seen from the site of their occurence.

The outlines of this study are intentionally broad, but they open out from a point of departure that is quite specific. It is marked in the mid-eighteenth century, by two simultaneous and, as I argue, intersecting processes in Northern Europe: the emergency of natural history as a structure of knowledge, and the momentum toward interior, as opposed to maritime, exploration. These developments, as I suggest in the following chapter, register a shift in what can be called European "planetary consciousness," a shift that coincides with many others including the consolidation of bourgeois forms of subjectivity and power, the inauguration of a new territorial phase of capitalism propelled by searches for raw materials, the attempt to extend coastal trade inland, and national imperatives to seize overseas territory in order to prevent its being seized by rival European powers. From this point of departure, the book moves in a roughly chronological order.

The geographical parameters I have chosen are historically determined as well. At the end of the eighteenth century, South America and Africa,

3 Contemporary autoethnographic representation, by painters from the Andean town of Sarhua, State of Ayacucho, Peru. The caption, "Tarpuy" means "sowing" in Quechua. These paintings, a unique creation of the artists of Sarhua, often include much longer captions explaining in Spanish the custom named in Quechua.

long linked with Europe and each other by trade, became parallel sites of new European expansionist initiatives arising precisely from the new momentum for interior exploration. The "opening up" of Africa began haltingly in the 1780s with the founding of the African Association (see chapter 4). Simultaneously in Spanish America, independence movements that would open the South American continent to the same expansionist energies were beginning to consolidate themselves, also haltingly (Francisco Miranda first sought revolutionary support from England in the 1780s). Much of the momentum on both continents was British, as are many of the writers I discuss here. In 1806 Britain invaded both the Rio de la Plata and the Cape of Good Hope – using some of the same officers in both places. But the players were by no means entirely British. In 1799, the German Alexander von Humboldt and the Frenchman Aimé Bonpland were preparing to join a trip up the Nile, when they were thwarted by Napoleon's invasion of North Africa. They transposed their itinerary to South America and went up the Orinoco instead (see chapter 6). In the 1960s and 1970s, decolonization movements in Africa and national liberation movements in the Americas shared ideals, practices, and intellectual leadership. In the same period, not coincidentally, both continents became the object of the grumpy metropolitan discourse I discuss in chapter 9 as the "third-world blues."

Readers of European travel books about Europe have pointed out that many of the conventions and writing strategies I associate here with imperial expansionism characterize travel writing about Europe as well. As I suggest at several points in the discussion, when that is so, related dynamics of power and appropriation are likely to be found at work as well. The discourses that legitimate bourgeois authority and delegitimate peasant and subsistence lifeways, for example, can be expected to do this ideological work within Europe as well as in southern Africa or Argentina. The forms of social critique through which European women claim political voice at home make similar, though not identical, claims abroad. The eighteenth century has been identified as a period in which Northern Europe asserted itself as the center of civilization, claiming the legacy of the Mediterranean as its own.[8] It is not surprising, then, to find German or British accounts of Italy sounding like German or British accounts of Brazil.

I described this book earlier as a study in genre as well as a critique of ideology. Scholarship on travel and exploration literature, such as it exists, has tended to develop along neither of these lines. Often it is celebratory, recapitulating the exploits of intrepid eccentrics or dedicated scientists. In other instances it is documentary, drawing on travel accounts as sources of information about the places, peoples, and times they discuss. More recently, an estheticist or literary vein of scholarship has developed, in which travel accounts, usually by famous literary figures, are studied in the artistic and intellectual dimensions and with reference to European existential dilemmas. I am doing none of these things. With respect to genre, I have attempted here to pay serious attention to the conventions of representation that constitute European travel writing, identifying different strands, suggesting ways of reading and focuses for rhetorical analysis. The book includes many readings of quoted passages. I hope that some of the readings and ways of reading I propose will be suggestive for people thinking about similar materials from other times and places. The study of tropes often serves to unify corpuses and define genres in terms, for example, of shared repertoires of devices and conventions (and yet it is, of course, the corpuses that create the repertoires). My aim here, however, is not to define or codify. I have sought to use the study of tropes as much to disunify as to unify what one might call a rhetoric of travel writing. I have aimed not to circumscribe travel writing as a genre but to suggest its heterogeneity and its interactions with other kinds of expression.

Part I

Science and sentiment, 1750–1800

Chapter 2

Science, planetary consciousness, interiors

[He may] make a tour of the world in books, he may make himself master of the geography of the universe in the maps, atlasses and measurements of our mathematicians. He may travell by land with the historians, by sea with the navigators. He may go round the globe with Dampier and Rogers, and kno' a thousand times more doing it than all those illiterate sailors.

(Daniel Defoe, *The Compleat English Gentleman* (1730))

Verses are hardly fashionable any longer. Everybody has begun to play at being the geometer and the physicist. Sentiment, imagination, and the graces have been banished. . . . Literature is perishing before our very eyes.

(Voltaire, Letter to Cideville, 16 April 1735[1])

The European part of this story starts in the European year 1735. At least that is where the narration is going to begin – the story takes another twenty or thirty years to really get underway. In that year 1735, two rather new and deeply European events took place. One was the publication of Carl Linné's *Systema Naturae* (*The System of Nature*), in which the Swedish naturalist laid out a classificatory system designed to categorize all plant forms on the planet, known or unknown to Europeans. The other was the launching of Europe's first major international scientific expedition, a joint effort intended to determine once and for all the exact shape of the earth. As I propose to argue, these two events, and their coincidence, suggest important dimensions of change in European elites' understandings of themselves and their relations to the rest of the globe. This chapter is about the emergence of a new version of what I like to call Europe's "planetary consciousness," a version marked by an orientation toward interior exploration and the construction of global-scale meaning through the descriptive apparatuses of natural history. This new planetary consciousness, I will suggest, is a basic element constructing modern Eurocentrism, that hegemonic reflex that troubles westerners even as it continues to be second nature to them.

Under French leadership, the international scientific expedition of 1735 set out to resolve a burning empirical question: Was the earth a sphere, as Cartesian (French) geography said, or was it, as (English) Newton had hypothesized, a spheroid flat at the poles? It was a question highly charged by the political rivalry between France and England. One team of scientists and geographers, led by the French physicist Maupertuis, was sent north to Lapland to measure a longitudinal degree at the Meridian. Another headed for South America to take the same measurement at the Equator near Quito. Nominally led by the mathematician Louis Godin, this expedition has gone down in history under the name of one of its few survivors, the geographer Charles de la Condamine.

The La Condamine expedition was a particular diplomatic triumph for the European scientific community. Spain's American territories were strictly closed to official travel by foreigners of any kind, and had been for more than two centuries. The Spanish court's obsession with sealing its colonies off from foreign influence and foreign espionage was legendary. After losing control over the slave trade to Britain in 1713, Spain had become more fearful than ever of inroads into its economic and cultural monopolies. The more the international contacts of the creole elites in its colonies broadened, the more fearful Spain became. "The policy of the Spaniards," wrote the British pirate Betagh in the 1720s, "consists chiefly in endeavoring, by all ways and means possible, to restrain the vast riches of those extensive dominions from passing into other hands."[2] Knowledge of those riches, said Betagh, and of "the great demand for European manufactures among the Americans has excited almost every nation in Europe." Military installations in Spanish American ports and mining operations in the interior were the two colonial constructions most carefully shielded from outside eyes, as they were the most assiduously sought out by Spain's rivals. In 1712, for instance, the King of France hired a young engineer named Frézier to travel the coasts of Chile and Peru posing as a trader, "the better to insinuate himself with the Spanish Governors, and to have all the opportunities of learning their strength."[3] Obsessed with mines, Frézier never managed to lay eyes on one. Yet even the hearsay he reported was avidly devoured by readers in France and England. In the absence of new writings on South America, the compiler of Churchill's collection of voyages in 1745 translated an account of Chile written a century earlier by the Spanish Jesuit Alonso de Ovalle.[4] As regards the interior of Spanish America, even such dated accounts were more to be relied upon than contemporary conjectures, like Betagh's report of an earthquake in the interior that had "lifted up whole fields and carried them several miles off."[5]

In the case of the La Condamine expedition, the Spanish crown set aside its legendary protectionism. Eager to build its prestige and live down the "black legend" of Spanish cruelty, Philip V seized the opportunity to act as an enlightened continental monarch. Conditions on the expedition's scope were agreed on, and two Spanish captains, Antonio de Ulloa and Jorge Juan, were sent along to ensure scientific inquiry did not give way to espionage – which it promptly did. Just about everything else went wrong, too. So trying an enterprise was the La Condamine expedition that over sixty years would pass before anything like it was attempted again.[6] Rivalries within the French contingent rapidly overcame collaborative bonds. International cooperation gave way to endless bickering with local colonial authorities over what could or could not be seen, measured, drawn, or sampled. At one point, the entire expedition was held up in Quito for eight months, accused of plotting to plunder Inca treasures. The foreigners, with their odd-looking instruments, their obsessive measurings – of gravity, the speed of sound, heights and distances, courses of rivers, altitudes, barometric pressures, eclipses, refractions, trajectories of stars – were the object of continual suspicion. In 1739 the group's surgeon was murdered after getting caught up in a dispute between two powerful families at Cuenca in Ecuador; La Condamine barely escaped the same fate. A court battle was fought for more than a year over whether the French *fleur de lys* could be placed on the expedition's triangulation pyramids (the *fleur de lys* lost). Interior exploration was proving to be an even greater political nightmare than its maritime antecedent.

The logistical nightmares of interior exploration were also new, and the La Condamine expedition was spared none of them. The rigors of Andean climate and overland travel produced continual sickness, damaged instruments, lost specimens, wet notebooks, agonizing frustration and delay. In the end, the French group disintegrated completely, each person left to find his own way home or remain stranded in South America. Though the South American expedition had set out a year before its Arctic counterpart, nearly a decade passed before the first survivors began straggling back to Europe. The question of the earth's outlines had long since been put to rest (Newton won).

In addition to information on other subjects, what the South American group brought home were discomfiting lessons in the politics and (anti-) heroics of science. Mathematician Pierre Bouguer returned first and won the glory of reporting to the French Academy of Science. La Condamine arrived in 1744 via the Amazon and won acclaim for his unprecedented Amazon journey. Through an aggressive campaign against Bouguer, La Condamine managed to make himself the chief spokesperson for the expedition all over Europe. Meanwhile, Louis Godin, the nominal leader, was slowly working his way home. Arriving in Spain in 1751, he was denied a passport to France through the machinations of Bouguer and La Condamine. The naturalist Joseph de Jussieu continued his research in New Spain till 1771, when he was sent back from Quito, completely insane. The young technician Godin des Odonnais made his way to Cayenne, where he waited eighteen years for his Peruvian wife to join him, returning to France at last in 1773. (More on her story below.) Others were never heard of again.

Spain's cooperation with the La Condamine expedition was striking evidence of the power of Science to raise Europeans above even the most intense national rivalries. La Condamine himself celebrated this continental impulse in the preface to his travel account, where he congratulated Louis XV for supporting scientific cooperation with his fellow nations even while simultaneously at war with them: "Whilst his Majesty's armies flew from one end of Europe to the other," said La Condamine, "his mathematicians, dispersed over the surface of the earth, were at work under the Torrid and Frigid Zones, for the improvement of the sciences, and the common benefit of all nations."[7] One cannot help noticing the conspicuously nationalist ring of La Condamine's sentiment here, however: the French scientist proudly congratulates his own king on his enlightened cosmopolitanism. In a similarly double-edged spirit, both the British Royal Society and the French Academy of Science rewarded the Spaniards Juan and Ulloa with honorary memberships – transnational gestures not unrelated to the intense national rivalries between Britain and France and their competing interests in Spanish America. Such gestures sum up the ambiguous interplay of national and continental aspirations that had been a constant in European expansion, and was to remain so in the age of science. On the one hand, dominant ideologies made a clear distinction between the (interested) pursuit of wealth and the (disinterested) pursuit of knowledge; on the other hand, competition among nations continued to be the fuel for European expansion abroad.

There is one respect in which the La Condamine expedition was a real success, namely, as writing. The tales and texts it occasioned circulated round and round Europe for decades, on oral circuits and written. Indeed, the body of texts that resulted from the La Condamine expedition suggests rather well the range and variety of writing produced by travel in the mid-eighteenth century, writing that in turn produced other parts of the world for the imaginations of Europeans. A brief catalogue of writings from the La Condamine expedition may help suggest what it means to talk about travel, writing, and contact zones at this moment in history.

The mathematician Bouguer, the first to return, expanded his report to the French Academy of Sciences in 1744 into an *Abridged Relation of a Voyage to Peru*. Initially in this account the voice of the scientist predominates, structuring the discourse around measurements, climactic phenomena, and so forth. As his travels turn inland, however, Bouguer's scientific narrative becomes interwoven with a story of suffering and hardship that even today makes for stirring reading. As the expedition camps out atop the frigid Andean cordillera to do its triangulations, anecdotes of bleeding chilblains and Amerindian slaves dying of cold are interspersed with physiological speculations on the retention of body heat. Of mines, Bouguer reports only hearsay, noting that "the impenetrable nature of the country" makes new ones hard to find, and also that "the Indians are wise enough not to be very aiding in these sort of researches," for "should they succeed, they

4 The La Condamine expedition taking measurements. From Charles de la Condamine, *Mesure des trois premiers degrès du Méridien dans l'Hémisphère Austral (Measurement of the Three First Degrees of the Meridian in the Southern Hemisphere),* Paris, Imprimerie Royal, 1751.

would be opening a career of labour painful to excess, which themselves alone would bear the weight, and with but little portion of the profits."[8] Bouguer also produced a technical book on the expedition called *La Figure de la terre*.

La Condamine also published his report to the French Academy as *Brief Narrative of Travels through the Interior of South America* (1745). It was read and translated widely. Perhaps because Bouguer had already spoken for the Andean part of the mission, La Condamine's account relates mainly his extraordinary return journey down the Amazon and his attempts to map its course and its tributaries. The account is written mainly not as a scientific report, but in the popular genre of survival literature. Alongside navigation, survival literature's two great themes are hardship and danger on the one hand, and marvels and curiosities on the other. In La Condamine's narrative the drama of sixteenth-century expeditions in the region – Orellana, Raleigh, Aguirre – is replayed with all its mythic associations. Entering the jungle, La Condamine finds himself "in a new world, far from all human commerce, upon a sea of fresh water. . . . I met there with new plants, new animals, and new men."[9] He speculates, as had all his predecessors, on the location of El Dorado and the existence of the Amazons, who, though they may well have existed, most probably "have now laid aside their ancient customs."[10] The jungle remains a world of fascination and danger.[11]

While the 1745 *Brief Narrative* is certainly the best known of La Condamine's writings, he published copiously in other genres as well, all based on his American travels. His "Letter on the Popular Uprising at Cuenca" appeared in 1746, followed by a *History of the Pyramids of Quito* (1751), and a report on the *Measurement of the First Three Degrees of the Meridian* (1751). For the rest of his life he engaged in research and polemics on a range of America-related scientific issues, including the effects of quinine, smallpox vaccination (widely used by Spanish missionaries), the existence of the Amazons, the geography of the Orinoco and the Rio Negro. He wrote about rubber, which he introduced to European scientists, curare poison and its antidotes, and the need for common European standards of measurement. La Condamine's specialized scientific writings suggest the extent to which science came to articulate Europe's contacts with the imperial frontier, and to be articulated by them.

It was the two Spanish captains Juan and Ulloa who produced the one full-length account of the expedition. Authored by Ulloa at the request of the King of Spain, their *Voyage to South America* appeared in Madrid in 1747, and its English translation by John Adams went through five editions. Neither science nor survival literature, Ulloa and Juan's account is written in a mode I like to call "civic description." Virtually devoid of anecdote, the book is an enormous compendium of information on many aspects of Spanish colonial geography and of Spanish colonial life – except, of course, mines, military installations, and other strategic information. It is a "statistical" work, in the earliest sense of the term, in which statistics meant "an inquiry into the state of a country" (*Oxford English Dictionary*). Adams praised the account for its reliability in contrast with the "pompous describers of wonderful curiosities,"[12] an allusion to survival literature in general, and probably to La Condamine in particular.

Juan and Ulloa also addressed to their king a second, clandestine volume titled *Noticias secretas de América (Secret News of America)*, which reported critically on many aspects of Spanish colonial rule and, as one commentator puts it, explained "much left unsaid in the works of the French Academicians."[13] Not till the first years of the nineteenth century, when the Spanish Empire was in its final collapse, did this work fall into the hands of the English and become public.

Alongside the catalogue of texts that got written from the La Condamine expedition, there is a catalogue of texts that did not. It includes, for example, the work of Joseph de Jussieu, the naturalist who remained behind in South America, where he continued to exercise his profession for another twenty years. When he eventually lost his mind and had to be sent back to France from Quito, the friends who packed him off seem simply to have lost track of the trunk containing his lifetime of research. Only one study, on the effects of quinine, did get published – under La Condamine's name! The rest may still turn up one day in Quito.

The most riveting and enduring story that arose from the La Condamine expedition was an oral one that made it into print only vestigially. It is a survival story whose hero is not a European man of science, but a Euroamerican woman, Isabela Godin des Odonais, an upper-class Peruvian who married a member of the La Condamine expedition, with whom she bore four children. After the break-up of the scientific party, her husband made his way to Cayenne, where he spent eighteen years trying to arrange passports and passage to France for himself and his family. After the heartbreaking death of her fourth and last child, Mme. Godin, now in her forties, made a daring decision. Accompanied by a party that included her brothers, nephew, and numerous servants, she set out to join her spouse by traveling over the Andes and down the Amazon by the same route that made La Condamine a hero. Disaster ensued. Threatened by smallpox, so the story goes, her indigenous guides deserted the party, and all, including her brothers, nephew, and servants, died of exposure after languishing for days in the jungle. Mme. Godin, wandering deliriously, gradually made her way alone back to the river, where she was rescued by indigenous canoeists who took her to a Spanish missionary outpost. Haggard, her hair turned white, the story continues, she emerged on the Guyanese coast to be taken off to Europe by her ever-devoted spouse.

Mme. Godin's romantic and spine-chilling story was written down in 1773 – not by her, but by her husband, at the request of La Condamine, who appended it to editions of his own narrative.[14] Even today, the tale

5 Natural phenomena of South America, as seen by the La Condamine expedition. At bottom left stands the volcano Cotopaxi, snow-covered and erupting; bottom right depicts the "phenomenon of the arc of the moon" projected on the mountainsides; upper right depicts the "phenomenon of the triple rainbow, seen for the first time in Pambamarca and later in various other mountains." From Jorge Juan and Antonio de Ulloa, *Relación histórica del viaje a la América meridional*, Madrid, Antonio Marín, 1748.

is thoroughly compelling, its complexities irresistible, as they often seem to be wherever women protagonists appear in the lore of the colonial frontier. Mme. Godin's story is a replay of the great Amazon quest, carried out by the female Amazon herself – or a near thing to it. Love, loss, and jungle transform the creole woman from a white aristocrat into the combative woman warrior that Europeans had created to symbolize America to themselves. At the same time, it destroys her as a sex object: Mme. Godin emerges as a real-life version of Candide's ruined princess Cunégonde. Symbolic reversals abound in the story. The exchange of gold reverses direction, for example. At one point, Mme. Godin gives two of her gold chains to the two Indians who had saved her life in the jungle, turning the paradigm of conquest back on itself. To her fury, the gifts are immediately taken away by the resident priest and substituted with the quintessential colonizing commodity, cloth. With such delicious ironies, it is no wonder Mme. Godin's Amazon descent lived and thrived all over Europe for more than fifty years. Her husband's twenty-page letter represents a meager trace of a vital existence in oral culture.

THE CARPET BEYOND THE SELVAGE

Oral texts, written texts, lost texts, secret texts, texts appropriated, abridged, translated, anthologized, and plagiarized; letters, reports, survival tales, civic description, navigational narrative, monsters and marvels, medicinal treatises, academic polemics, old myths replayed and reversed – the La Condamine corpus illustrates the varied profile of travel-related writing on the frontiers of European expansion at mid-eighteenth century. The expedition itself is of interest here as an early, and notoriously unsuccessful, instance of what was shortly to become one of Europe's proudest and most conspicuous instruments of expansion, the international scientific expedition. In the second half of the eighteenth century, scientific exploration was to become a magnet for the energies and resources of intricate alliances of intellectual and commercial elites all over Europe. Equally important, scientific exploration was to become a focus of intense public interest, and a source of some of the most powerful ideational and ideological apparatuses through which European citizenries related themselves to other parts of the world. These apparatuses, and particularly travel writing, are the subject of what follows.

For the purposes of this study, the La Condamine expedition has a more specific significance as well. It is an early instance of a new orientation toward exploring and documenting continental interiors, in contrast with the maritime paradigm that had held center stage for three hundred years. By the last years of the eighteenth century, interior exploration had become the major object of expansionist energies and imaginings. This shift had significant consequences for travel writing, demanding and giving rise to new forms of European knowledge and self-knowledge, new models for European contact beyond its borders, new ways of encoding Europe's imperial ambitions. In 1715 the French spy Frézier deemed interior exploration in Peru impossible because "Travelers must carry so much as their very Beds, unless they will comply to lie like Natives on the Ground, upon Sheeps Skins, with the Sky for their Canopy."[15] For the English prefacer to Ulloa's account thirty years later, interior exploration is the essential next step: "What idea can we form of a Turkey carpet," he asks, "if we look only at the border, or it may be, at the selvage?"[16] By 1792 the French traveler Saugnier saw it as a matter of global fairness: the interiors of Africa "deserve the honor" of European visitation as much as the coasts.[17] In 1822, Alexander von Humboldt affirmed, "It is not by sailing along a coast that we can discover the direction of chains of mountains and their geological constitution, the climate of each zone, and its influence on the forms and habits of organized beings." For his English translator the issue was an aesthetic one: "In general, sea-expeditions have a certain monotony which arises from the necessity of continually speaking of navigation in a technical language. . . . The history of journies by land in distant regions is far more calculated to encite general interest."[18]

As travel, then, the La Condamine expedition marks the onset of an era of scientific travel and interior exploration that in turn suggests shifts in Europe's conception of itself and its global relations. In its calamitous failures, the expedition stands as a precursor. As writing, it exemplifies configurations of travel writing which, as bourgeois forms of authority gained momentum, would be thoroughly reorganized. (The next chapter will examine these transformations in travel writing on southern Africa.) In the second half of the eighteenth century, many traveler-writers would dissociate themselves from such traditions as survival literature, civic description, or navigational narrative, for they were to be engaged by the new knowledge-building project of natural history. The emergence of that project is marked by the second event of 1735 that I promised to discuss, the publication of Linnaeus' *System of Nature*.

THE SYSTEM OF NATURE

While the La Condamine expedition was making its way across the Atlantic in the name of science, a 28-year-old Swedish naturalist was ushering into print his first major contribution to knowledge. The naturalist was named Carl Linné or, in Latin, Linnaeus, and the book was called *Systema Naturae* (*The System of Nature*). Here was an extraordinary creation that would have a deep and lasting impact not just on travel and travel writing, but on the overall ways European citizenries made, and made sense of, their place on the planet. To a contemporary reader *The System of Nature* seems a modest and in fact rather quaint achievement. It was a descriptive system designed to classify all the plants on the earth, known and unknown, according to the characteristics of their reproductive parts.[19] Twenty-four (and later twenty-six) basic configurations of stamens, pistils, and so forth were identified and laid out according to the letters of the alphabet (see plate 6). Four added visual parameters completed the taxonomy: number, form, position, and relative size. All the plants on the earth, Linnaeus claimed, could be incorporated into this single system of distinctions, including any as yet unknown to Europeans. Born out of earlier classificatory efforts by Roy, Tournefort, and others, Linnaeus' approach had a simplicity and elegance unapproached by his predecessors. To combine the ideal of a unified classificatory system for all plants with a concrete, practical suggestion of how to construct it constituted a tremendous breakthrough. His schema was perceived, even by its critics, as making order out of chaos – both the chaos of nature, and the chaos of earlier botany. "The Ariadne thread in botany," said Linnaeus, "is classification, without which there is chaos."[20]

As it turned out, the 1735 *System* was only a first run. While La Condamine fought his way around South America, Linnaeus fine-tuned his system, giving it its final shape in his two definitive works, the *Philosophia Botanica* (1751) and the *Species Plantarum* (1753). It is to these works that European science owes the standard botanical nomenclature which assigns plants the name of their genus followed by their species, followed by any other differentiae essential to distinguish them from adjacent types. Parallel systems were also proposed for animals and minerals.

The Linnaean system epitomized the continental, transnational aspirations of European science discussed earlier in connection with the La Condamine expedition. Linnaeus deliberately revived Latin for his nomenclature precisely because it was nobody's national language. The fact that he himself was from Sweden, a relatively minor player in global economic and imperial competition, undoubtedly increased continent-wide receptivity to his system. Competing paradigms, produced in particular by the French, were equally continentalist in scope and design. Linnaeus' system alone launched a European knowledge-building enterprise of unprecedented scale and appeal. His pages of Latin lists might look static and abstract, but what they did, and were conceived to do, was to set in motion a project to be realized in the world in the most concrete possible terms. As his taxonomy took hold throughout Europe in the second half of the century, his "disciples" (for so they called themselves) fanned out by the dozens across the globe, by sea and by foot, executing what Daniel Boorstin has called a "messianic strategy."[21] Arrangements with the overseas trading companies, especially the Swedish East India Company, gave free passage to Linnaeus' students, who began turning up everywhere collecting plants and insects, measuring, annotating, preserving, making drawings, and trying desperately to get it all home intact. The information was written up into books; the specimens, if dead, were mounted into natural history collections which became serious hobbies for people of means all over the continent; if alive, they were planted in the botanical gardens that likewise began springing up in cities and private

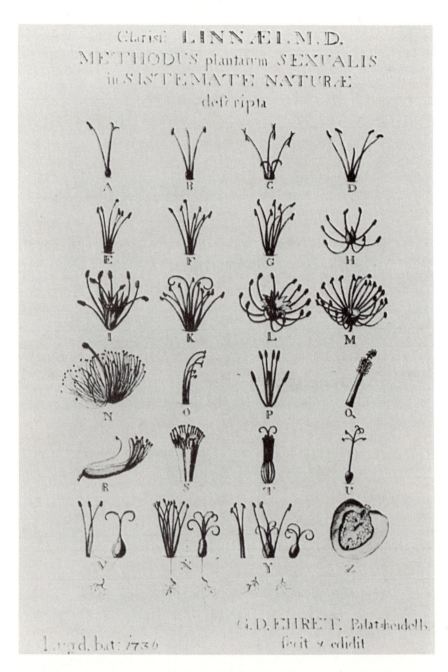

6 Linnaeus' system for identifying plants by their reproductive parts. This illustration by Georg D. Ehret first appeared in the 1736 Leiden edition of his *Species Plantarum*.

estates all over the continent. Linnaeus' pupil Kalm went to North America in 1747, Osbeck to China in 1750, Lofling to South America in 1754, Forsskal to the Near East in 1761, while Solander joined Cook's first voyage in 1768, Sparrman his second in 1772 (see chapter 3 below), and so on. Linnaeus' own words to a colleague in 1771 convey the energy, excitement, and global character of the enterprise:

> My pupil Sparrman has just sailed for the Cape of Good Hope, and another of my pupils, Thunberg, is to accompany a Dutch embassy to Japan; both of them are competent naturalists. The younger Gmelin is still in Persia, and my friend Falck is in Tartary. Mutis is making splendid botanical discoveries in Mexico. Koenig has found a lot of new things in Tranquebar. Professor Friis Rottboll of Copenhagen is publishing the plants found in Surinam by Rolander. The Arabian discoveries of Forsskal will soon be sent to press in Copenhagen.[22]

It is as if he were speaking of ambassadors and empire. What I want to argue is, of course, that in quite a significant way, he was. As Christianity had set in motion a global labor of religious conversion that asserted itself at every point of contact with other societies, so natural history set in motion a secular, global labor that, among other things, made contact zones a site of intellectual as well as manual labor, and installed there the distinction between the two. At the same time, the Linnaean systematizing project had a markedly democratic dimension, popularizing scientific inquiry as it had never been popularized before. "Linnaeus," as one present-day commentator puts it, "was above all a man for the non-professional." His dream was that "with his method it would be possible for anyone who had learned the system to place any plant anywhere in the world in its right class and order, if not in its right genus, whether the plant was previously known to science or not."[23]

Travel and travel writing would never be the same again. In the second half of the eighteenth century, whether or not an expedition was primarily scientific, or the traveler a scientist, natural history played a part in it. Specimen gathering, the building up of collections, the naming of new species, the recognition of known ones, became standard themes in travel and travel books. Alongside the frontier figures of the seafarer, the conqueror, the captive, the diplomat, there began to appear everywhere the benign, decidedly literate figure of the "herborizer," armed with nothing more than a collector's bag, a notebook, and some specimen bottles, desiring nothing more than a few peaceful hours alone with the bugs and flowers. Travel narratives of all kinds began to develop leisurely pauses filled with gentlemanly "naturalizing." Descriptions of flora and fauna were not in themselves new to travel writing. On the contrary, they had been conventional components of travel books since at least the sixteenth century. However, they were typically structured as appendices or formal digressions from the narrative. With the founding of the global classificatory project, on the other hand, the observing and cataloguing of nature itself became narratable. It could constitute a sequence of events, or even produce a plot. It could form the main storyline of an entire account. From one angle, what is told is a story of urbanizing, industrializing Europeans fanning out in search of non-exploitive relations to nature, even as they were destroying such relations in their own centers of power. As I will try to show in the next chapter, what is also told is a narrative of "anti-conquest," in which the naturalist naturalizes the bourgeois European's own global presence and authority. This naturalist's narrative was to continue to hold enormous ideological force throughout the nineteenth century, and remains very much with us today.

Linnaeus' system is only one instance of the totalizing classificatory schemas that coalesced in the mid-eighteenth century into the discipline of "natural history." The definitive version of Linnaeus' system appeared alongside equally ambitious undertakings like Buffon's *Histoire naturelle*, which began to appear in 1749, or Adanson's *Familles des plantes* (1763). While these writers proposed competing systems that differed from Linnaeus' in substantive ways, the debates among them remained grounded within the totalizing, classificatory project that distinguishes this period. The schemas constituted, as Gunnar Eriksson puts it, "alternative strategies for realizing a project common to all eighteenth-century natural history, the faithful representation of nature's own plan."[24] In his classic analysis of eighteenth-century thought, *The Order of Things* (1970), Michel Foucault describes the project thus: "By virtue of structure, the great proliferation of beings occupying the surface of the globe is able to enter both into the sequence of a descriptive language and into the field of a mathesis that would also be a general science of order."[25] Speaking of natural history as undertaking "a description of the visible," Foucault's analysis stresses the verbal character of the enterprise, which, as he puts it,

> has as a condition of its possibility the common affinity of things and language with representation; but it exists as a task only in so far as things and language happen to be separate. It must therefore reduce this distance between them so as to bring language as close as possible to the observing gaze, and the things observed as close as possible to words.[26]

An exercise not only in correlation but also in reduction, natural history

> reduces the whole area of the visible to a system of variables all of whose values can be designated, if not by a quantity, at least by a perfectly clear and always finite description. It is therefore possible to establish the system of identities and the order of differences existing between natural entities.[27]

Though natural historians often thought of themselves as engaged in discovering something that was already there (nature's plan, for example), from a contemporary standpoint it is rather a question of "a new field of visibility being constituted in all its density."[28]

While natural history was unquestionably constituted in and through language, it was an undertaking that was realized in many aspects of social and material life as well. Europe's growing technological capacities were challenged by the demand for better means of preserving, transporting, displaying, and documenting specimens; artistic specializations in botanical and zoological drawing developed; printers were challenged to improve reproduction of visuals; watchmakers were in demand to invent and maintain instruments; jobs came into being for scientists on commercial expeditions and colonial outposts; patronage networks funded scientific travels and subsequent writing; amateur and professional societies of all kinds sprung up locally, nationally, and internationally; natural history collections acquired commercial as well as prestige value; botanical gardens became large-scale public spectacles, and the job of supervising them a naturalist's dream. (Buffon became keeper of the King's garden in France, while Linnaeus devoted his life to his own.) No more vivid example could be found of the way that knowledges exist not as static accumulations of facts, bits, or bytes, but as human activities, tangles of verbal and non-verbal practices.

Of course the scientific enterprise involved all manner of linguistic apparatuses. Many forms of writing, publishing, speaking, and reading brought the knowledge into being in the public sphere, and created and sustained its value. The authority of science was invested most directly in specialized descriptive texts, like the countless botanical treatises organized around the various nomenclatures and taxonomies. Journalism and narrative travel accounts, however, were essential mediators between the scientific network and a larger European public. They were central agents in legitimating scientific authority and its global project alongside Europe's other ways of knowing the world, and being in it. In the second half of the century scientific travelers would work out discursive paradigms that sharply distinguished themselves from the ones La Condamine inherited in the first half of the century.

The systematizing of nature, I am suggesting, is a European project of a new kind, a new form of what one might call planetary consciousness among Europeans. For three centuries European knowledge-making apparatuses had been construing the planet above all in navigational terms. These terms gave rise to two totalizing or planetary projects. One was circumnavigation, a double deed that consists of sailing round the world then writing an account of it (the term "circumnavigation" refers either to the voyage or the book). Europeans have been repeating this double deed almost continually since it was first accomplished by Magellan in the 1520s. The second planetary project, equally dependent on ink and paper, was the mapping of the world's coastlines, a collective task that was still underway in the eighteenth century, but known to be completable. In 1704 it was possible to speak, in the words of one editor of travel books, of the "Empire of Europe" as extending "to the utmost bounds of the earth, where several of its nations have conquests and colonies."[29] Circumnavigation and mapmaking, then, had already given rise to what one might call a European global or planetary subject. Its profile is sketched with ease and familiarity by Daniel Defoe in the passage providing the first epigraph to this chapter. As Defoe's terms make clear, this world historical subject is European, male,[30] secular, and lettered; his planetary consciousness is the product of his contact with print culture and infinitely more "compleat" than the lived experiences of sailors.

The systematizing of nature in the second half of the century was to assert even more powerfully the authority of print, and thus of the class which controlled it. It seems to crystallize global imaginings of a sort rather different from the older navigational ones. Natural history maps out not the thin track of a route taken, nor the lines where land and water meet, but the internal "contents" of those land and water masses whose spread made up the surface of the planet. These vast contents would be known not through slender lines on blank paper, but through verbal representations in turn summed up in nomenclatures, or through labeled grids into which entities would be placed. The finite totality of these representations or categories constituted a "mapping" not just of coastlines or rivers, but of every visible square, or even cubic, inch of the earth's surface. "Natural history," wrote Buffon in 1749,

taken in its full extent, is an immense History, embracing all the objects that the Universe presents to us. This prodigious multitude of Quadrupeds, Birds, Fish, Insects, Plants, Minerals, etc., offers a vast spectacle to the curiosity of the human spirit; its totality is so great that it seems, and actually is, inexhaustible in all its details.[31]

Alongside this totalizing embrace, how timid seems the old navigational custom of filling in the blank spaces of maps with iconic drawings of regional curiosities and dangers – Amazons in the Amazon, cannibals in the Caribbean, camels in the Sahara, elephants in India, and so on.

Like the rise of interior exploration, the systematic surface mapping of the globe correlates with an expanding search for commercially exploitable resources, markets, and lands to colonize, just as navigational mapping is linked with the search for trade routes. Unlike navigational mapping, however, natural history conceived of the world as a chaos out of which the scientist *produced* an order. It is not, then, simply a question of depicting the planet as it was. For Adanson (1763), the natural world without the scientist's ordering eye is

a confused mingling of beings that seem to have been brought together by chance: here, gold is mixed with another metal, with stone, with earth;

there, the violet grows side by side with an oak. Among these plants, too, wander the quadruped, the reptile, and the insect; the fishes are confused, one might say, with the aqueous element in which they swim, and with the plants grow in the depths of the waters. . . . This mixture is indeed so general and so multifarious that it appears to be one of nature's laws.[32]

Such a perspective may seem odd to late twentieth-century western imaginations trained to see nature as self-balancing ecosystems which human interventions throw into chaos. Natural history called upon human intervention (intellectual, mainly) to compose an order. The eighteenth-century classificatory systems created the task of locating every species on the planet, extracting it from its particular, arbitrary surroundings (the chaos), and placing it in its appropriate spot in the system (the order – book, collection, or garden) with its new written, secular European name. Linnaeus himself took credit for adding 8,000 new items to the corpus during his lifetime.

Analyses of natural history, such as Foucault's, do not always underscore the transformative, appropriative dimensions of its conception. One by one the planet's life forms were to be drawn out of the tangled threads of their life surroundings and rewoven into European-based patterns of global unity and order. The (lettered, male, European) eye that held the system could familiarize ("naturalize") new sites/sights immediately upon contact, by incorporating them into the language of the system. The differences of distance factored themselves out of the picture: with respect to mimosas, Greece could be the same as Venezuela, West Africa, or Japan; the label "granitic peaks" can apply identically to Eastern Europe, the Andes, or the American West. Barbara Stafford mentions probably one of the most extreme instances of this global resemanticizing, a 1789 treatise by German Samuel Witte claiming that all the pyramids of the world, from Egypt to the Americas, are really "basalt eruptions."[33] The example is a telling one, for it suggests the system's potential to subsume culture and history into nature. Natural history extracted specimens not only from their organic or ecological relations with each other, but also from their places in other peoples' economies, histories, social and symbolic systems. For La Condamine in the 1740s, before the classificatory project had taken over, the naturalists' knowledge existed in parallel with even more valuable local knowledges. Noting prophetically that "the diversity of plants and trees" on the Amazon "would find ample employment for many years, for the most laborious botanist; as it would also for more than one designer," he goes on to add a thought that by the end of the century would, in scientific contexts, have become nearly unthinkable:

I speak here only of the labour it would require, to make an exact description of these plants, and to reduce them into classes, and range each under its proper genus and species. *What would it be, if we comprehend herewith, an examination into the virtues ascribed to them by the natives*

*of the country? An examination, which is undoubtedly the most attractive
of our attentions, of any branch of this study.*[34]

Natural history as a way of thinking interrupted existing networks
of historical and material relations among people, plants, and animals
wherever it applied itself. The European observer himself has no place
in the description. Often the Linnaean project is figured in the image of
Adam in the Garden of Eden. For Linnaeus, says Daniel Boorstin, "nature
was an immense collection of natural objects which he himself walked
around as superintendent, sticking on labels. He had a forerunner in this
arduous task: Adam in Paradise."[35] While invoking the image of primordial
innocence, Boorstin, like many other commentators, does not question it.[36]
Questioning it, one can see why from the very beginning, human beings,
especially European ones, posed a problem to the systematizers: could
Adam name and classify himself? If so, was the naturalist supplanting
God? Linnaeus early in the game seems to have answered yes – he is
once supposed to have said that God had "suffered him to peep into His
secret cabinet."[37] To the acute discomfort of many, including the Pope, he
eventually included people in his classification of animals (the label *homo
sapiens* is his). Their descriptions, however, are rather different from those
of other creatures. Initially, Linnaeus posited among the quadrupeds a single
category *homo* (described only by the phrase "Know thyself") and drew
a single distinction between *homo sapiens* and *homo monstrosus*. By 1758,
homo sapiens had been divided into six varieties, whose main features are
summarized below:

a. Wild Man. Four-footed, mute, hairy.
b. American. Copper-colored, choleric, erect. Hair black, straight, thick;
nostrils wide; face harsh; beard scanty; obstinate, content, free. Paints
himself with fine red lines. Regulated by customs.
c. European. Fair, sanguine, brawny; hair yellow, brown, flowing; eyes
blue; gentle, acute, inventive. Covered with close vestments. Governed
by laws.
d. Asiatic. Sooty, melancholy, rigid. Hair black; eyes dark; severe, haughty,
covetous. Covered with loose garments. Governed by opinions.
e. African. Black, phlegmatic, relaxed. Hair black, frizzled; skin silky; nose
flat, lips tumid; crafty, indolent, negligent. Anoints himself with grease.
Governed by caprice.[38]

A final category of the "monster" included dwarfs and giants (the giants
of Patagonia were still a firm reality), as well as man-made "monsters" like
eunuchs. The categorization of humans, you will notice, is explicitly comparative. One could hardly ask for a more explicit attempt to "naturalize"
the myth of European superiority. Except for the monsters and wild men,
the classification exists barely modified in some of today's schoolbooks.

7 Linnaeus' four types of anthropomorpha, from left to right the troglodyte, the tailed man, the satyr, and the pygmy. Originally appeared in Linnaeus-Hoppius, *Anthropomorpha* (1760).

Navigational mapping exerted the power of naming as well, of course. Indeed, it was in naming that the religious and geographical projects came together, as emissaries claimed the world by baptizing landmarks and geographical formations with Euro-Christian names. But again, natural history's naming is more directly transformative. It extracts all the things of the world and redeploys them into a new knowledge formation whose value lies precisely in its difference from the chaotic original. Here the naming, the representing, and the claiming are all one; the naming brings the reality of order into being.

From another perspective, however, natural history is not transformative in the least. That is, as it understands itself, it undertakes to do virtually nothing in or to the world. The "conversion" of raw nature into the *systema naturae* is a strangely abstract, unheroic gesture, with very little at stake – certainly not souls. In comparison with the navigator or the conquistador, the naturalist-collector is a benign, often homely figure, whose transformative powers do their work in the domestic contexts of the garden or the collection room. As I will be illustrating further in the next chapter, the naturalist figure often has a certain androgyny about it; its production of knowledge has some decidedly non-phallic aspects, perhaps alluded to by Linnaeus' own image of Ariadne following her thread out of the labyrinth of the Minotaur.

Here is to be found a utopian image of a European bourgeois subject simultaneously innocent and imperial, asserting a harmless hegemonic vision that installs no apparatus of domination. At most naturalists were seen as handmaidens to Europe's expansive commercial aspirations. Practically speaking, in exchange for free rides with trading companies and so forth, they produced commercially exploitable knowledge. "It is chiefly from the natural history," said one writer in a 1759 preface, "that we collect the value and importance of any country, because from thence we learn its produce of every kind."[39] Introducing a new compendium of travels in 1756, De Brosse praised the new capacity "to augment the earth with a new world, to enrich the old world with all the natural production and serviceable customs of the New."[40] In 1766 the reviewer of a book of travels by one of Linnaeus' students declared the travels of "men of science" as superior to those of "men of fortune" on both literary and commercial grounds:

> The researches of the naturalist, in particular, are productive of no less advantage to others, than delight himself; especially those of the BOTANIST, whose discoveries and acquisitions are often of the utmost consequence to the trading and commercial interest of his country. Nay, the celebrated Linnaeus has even ventured to assert, that the knowledge of plants is the very foundation of the whole public economy; since it is that which feeds and clothes a nation.[41]

At the same time, the interests of science and commerce were carefully held distinct. Expeditions mounted in the name of science, like Cook's to the South Seas in the 1760s and 1770s, often went under secret orders to look out for commercial opportunities and threats. That the orders were there, yet were secret, suggests the ideological dialectic between scientific and commercial enterprises. On the one hand commerce was understood as at odds with the disinterestedness of science. On the other, the two were believed to mirror and legitimate each other's aspirations. "A well regulated commerce," said Linnaeus' pupil Anders Sparrman, "as well as navigation in general has its foundation in science . . . while this, in return derives support from, and owes its extension to the former."[42]

Commercial prospects placed science arguably within the general public interest, though in fact the benefits of mercantile expansion and imperialism accrued overwhelmingly to small elites. Yet, at the level of ideology, science – "the exact description of everything," as Buffon put it – created global imaginings above and beyond commerce. It operated as a rich and multifaceted mirror onto which all Europe could project itself as an expanding "planetary process" minus the competition, exploitation, and violence being carried out by commercial and political expansion and colonial domination.

Indeed, when it came to plants, animals, and minerals, though not to people, the systems applied themselves identically to Europe as to Asia, Africa, and the Americas. The systematizing of nature represents not only a European discourse about non-European worlds, as I have been discussing, but an urban discourse about non-urban worlds, and a lettered, bourgeois discourse about non-lettered, peasant worlds. The systems of nature were projected within European borders as well as beyond them. The herborizers were as happy in the countryside of Scotland or southern France as they were in the Amazon or southern Africa. Within Europe, the systematizing of nature came at a time when relations between urban centers and the countryside were changing rapidly. Urban bourgeoisies began to intervene on a new scale in agricultural production, seeking to rationalize production, increase surpluses, intensify exploitation of peasant labor, and administer the food production on which the urban centers utterly depended. The enclosure movement was one of the more conspicuous interventions, which threw many peasants off the land and into cities or squatter communities. Attempts to improve breeding in domestic animals and crops scientifically began at this time.[43] Subsistence societies of any kind appeared backward with respect to surplus-oriented modes, and as in need of "improvement." In 1750 the French commentator Duclos in his *Considerations on the Customs of This Century* found that "those who live a hundred miles from the capital, are a century away from it in their modes of thinking and acting," a view today enlightenment scholars often unquestioningly reproduce.[44]

As differences between urban and rural lifeways widened, European peasantry came to appear only somewhat less primitive than the inhabitants of the Amazon. Likewise the system of nature overwrote local and peasant ways of knowing within Europe just as it did local indigenous ones abroad. Sten Lindroth associates Linnaeus' documentary, totalizing approach with forms of state bureaucracy that were particularly highly developed in Sweden, notably record-keeping apparatuses which elaborately documented and classified individual citizens. By the mid-eighteenth century, says Lindroth, "no other nation in Europe had a more thorough knowledge of its population than the Swedes; the one and a half million Swedish citizens were all annotated in the proper statistical columns as born, dead, married, sick, and so on."[45] Indeed, the Linnaean genus and species labels look remarkably like the given and family names required of citizens – Linnaeus referred to generic names as "the official currency of our botanical republic."[46] Although the systematizing of nature preceded the onset of the Industrial Revolution, Lindroth observes "striking similarities between [Linnaeus'] way of writing and the principles which emerged in manufacturing."[47] Standardization and serial manufacturing, for instance, had already made their way into production, notably in the making of interchangeable parts for firearms. Other analogies emerge from the area of military organization, which at precisely this period began standardizing uniforms, exercises, discipline, and so forth.

Such analogies become even more suggestive when one recalls that bureaucracy and militarization are the central instruments of empire, and control over firearms the single most decisive factor in Europe's subjection of others, right down to the present day. (As I wrote this chapter, and perhaps still as you read it, in Soweto and on the West Bank of the Jordan, stones were being thrown at armored cars by subjugated peoples with no weapons.) Academic scholarship on the Enlightenment, resolutely Eurocentered, has often neglected Europe's aggressive colonial and imperial ventures as models, inspirations, and testing grounds for modes of social discipline which, imported back into Europe in the eighteenth century, were adapted to construct the bourgeois order. The systematization of nature coincides with the height of the slave trade, the plantation system, colonial genocide in North America and South Africa, slave rebellions in the Andes, the Caribbean, North America, and elsewhere. It is possible to reverse the direction of the Linnaean gaze, or that of Defoe's armchair traveler, to look out at Europe from the imperial frontier. Other genealogies for Enlightenment processes of standardization, bureaucracy, and normalization then come into view. For what were the slave trade and the plantation system if not massive experiments in social engineering and discipline, serial production, the systematization of human life, the standardizing of persons? Experiments that proved profitable beyond any European's wildest dreams. (The wealth that fomented the French Revolution was created in Santo Domingo, which by the 1760s was the most productive place the earth had ever seen.) Plantation agriculture stands out clearly as a crucial setting for the Industrial Revolution and the mechanization of production. Similarly, even by the early seventeenth century, there were no bureaucracies like colonial bureaucracies, for which Spain had set an elaborate example.

Economic historians sometimes call the years 1500–1800 the period of "primitive accumulation," in which through slavery and state-protected monopolies, European bourgeoisies were able to accumulate the capital that launched the Industrial Revolution. One wonders indeed what was so primitive about this accumulation (as one wonders what is so advanced about advanced capitalism), but accumulation it was. In the sphere of culture the many forms of collection that were practiced during this period developed in part as the image of that accumulation, and as its legitimation. The systematizing of nature carries this image of accumulation to a totalized extreme, and at the same time models the extractive, transformative character of industrial capitalism, and the ordering mechanisms that were beginning to shape urban mass society in Europe under bourgeois hegemony. As an ideological construct, it makes a picture of the planet appropriated and redeployed from a unified, European perspective.

In Europe, as on the frontiers of expansion outside it, this production of knowledge does not express connections with changing relations of labor or property, or with aspirations of territoriality. It is a configuration commented on indirectly, however, in contemporary theorizing about the structure of the modern state. The state, argues Nicos Poulantzas, always portrays itself "in a topological image of exteriority," as separate from the economy: "As an epistemological object, the State is conceived as having immutable boundaries fixed through its exclusion from the atemporal domain of the economy."[48] As the momentum of European expansion turns inland toward the "opening up" of interiors, such conceptions come into play within Europe and on the frontiers of its expansion. The chapters to follow will suggest more fully how they are deployed and challenged in the literature of travel and exploration.

Chapter 3

Narrating the anti-conquest

At times indeed the Company officials allowed the main slave depot in Cape Town to be used as a sort of brothel.

> (Philip Curtin et al., *African History* (1978))

It is a relief to turn from these scenes of contention and disorder to notice the efforts that were made at this time [1793] by several colonists to improve the domestic animals of the country.

> (George M. Theal, *A History of Southern Africa* (1907))[1]

The previous chapter introduced the eighteenth-century systematizing of nature as a European knowledge-building project that created a new kind of Eurocentered planetary consciousness. Blanketing the surface of the globe, it specified plants and animals in visual terms as discrete entities, subsuming and reassembling them in a finite, totalizing order of European making. Perhaps one should be more specific about the terms: "European" in this instance refers above all to a network of literate Northern Europeans, mainly men from the lower levels of the aristocracy and the middle and upper levels of the bourgeoisie. "Nature" meant above all regions and ecosystems which were not dominated by "Europeans," while including many regions of the geographical entity known as Europe.

The project of natural history determined many sorts of social and signifying practices, of which travel and travel writing were among the most vital. For the purposes of this book, what is of chief interest is the mutual engagement between natural history and European economic and political expansionism. As I suggested above, natural history asserted an urban, lettered, male authority over the whole of the planet; it elaborated a rationalizing, extractive, dissociative understanding which overlaid functional, experiential relations among people, plants, and animals. In these respects, it figures a certain kind of global hegemony, notably one based on possession of land and resources rather than control over routes. At the same time, in and of itself, the system of nature as a descriptive paradigm was an utterly benign and abstract appropriation of the planet. Claiming no transformative potential whatsoever, it differed sharply from overtly imperial articulations of conquest, conversion, territorial appropriation, and enslavement. The system created, as I suggested above, a utopian, innocent vision of European global authority, which I refer to as an *anti-conquest*. The term is intended to emphasize the *relational* meaning of natural history, the extent to which it became meaningful specifically in contrast with an earlier imperial, and prebourgeois, European expansionist presence.

This chapter undertakes to illustrate more concretely the impact of natural history and global science on travel writing. Through a set of examples, I aim to suggest how natural history provided means for narrating inland travel and exploration aimed not at the discovery of trade routes, but at territorial surveillance, appropriation of resources, and administrative control. This discussion is intended to be read in conjunction with two subsequent chapters, which take up sentimental travel writing, the other main form of anti-conquest in this period. In travel literature, I argue, science and sentiment code the imperial frontier in the two eternally clashing and complementary languages of bourgeois subjectivity.

In what follows I examine a sequence of four North European travel books on southern Africa written across the eighteenth century and spanning what I have been calling the Linnaean watershed: Peter Kolb's *The Present State of the Cape of Good Hope* (Germany, 1719); Anders Sparrman's *Voyage to the Cape of Good Hope* (Sweden, 1775); William Paterson's *Narrative of Four Voyages in the Land of the Hottentots and the Kaffirs* (Britain, 1789), and John Barrow's *Travels into the Interior of Southern Africa* (Britain, 1801). My aim here is not to survey the extensive literature of travel on southern Africa in this period; rather, I have selected four texts that particularly illustrate the discursive impact of natural history and the new planetary consciousness. (A contrasting instance of southern African travel writing is taken up in the next chapter.) My observations coincide at a number of points with those of J. M. Coetzee in his 1988 study *White Writing: On the Culture of Letters in South Africa*. The opening chapters of this valuable book focus heavily on eighteenth- and nineteenth-century travel writing on South Africa, including the writers discussed here. Coetzee goes on to examine how European problematics of representation carry forward into nineteenth- and twentieth-century literature in South Africa, as I have tried to do for Spanish America in chapter 7 below.

The literature on the Cape of Good Hope is a particularly fruitful one for studying the discursive shifts in travel writing, for the Cape was one place where scientific travel, the momentum for inland expansion, and the shifting relations of contact these engendered, played themselves out conspicuously and dramatically. The "great age" of scientific travel is usually associated with the South Sea expeditions of Cook, Bougainville, and others, first organized around the transit of Venus in 1768. These maritime expeditions indeed inaugurated the era of scientific travel, and scientific travel writing. But at the same time, they marked an end: the last great navigational phase of European exploration. Cook discovered and mapped the shores of the last uncharted continent, Australia. In a way, he set the stage for the new phase of inland exploration. The Cape of Good Hope was one of the few places in Africa where Northern Europeans had access to the continental interior. It was a magnet both for settlers and for explorers eager to make their mark. It was a place where interior colonization broke into open conflict with sea-oriented mercantilism, where competition among European nations was played out as warfare. In the early decades of the nineteenth century, as inland expansion proceeded, southern Africa was also to become a canonical test site for the civilizing mission in the labors of the London Missionary Society and their unmanageable star, David Livingstone.

Established in 1652 by the Dutch East India Company as a supply port for commercial ships, the Cape Colony proved a vital stopping-off point for European travelers of all kinds. Fresh meat was available from the indigenous Khoikhoi ("Hottentot")[2] population, while the Company grew fresh vegetables to combat scurvy, provided leisure, cared for sick sailors, supplied ships with healthy crewmembers, and so on. Vulnerable to attack and dependent on the indigenous cattle-herding population for fresh meat, the Company initially took pains to minimize its encroachment on the region and its exploitation of indigenous labor. A proposal to attempt enslaving the Khoikhoi in 1654 was rejected; slaves were procured initially from West Africa, then from Malay and Ceylon. Nevertheless, frontier conflict was immediate and constant (the first cross-racial murder recorded was in 1653), and intensified greatly in the 1670s as interior colonization by Europeans expanded as well.

Within a few years of founding the Cape Colony, the Dutch East India Company reluctantly agreed to grant a portion of the inhabitants the status of "free burghers," or independent farmers, and to allow them to wrest grazing and farming lands from the cattle-rearing indigenous peoples. This population of independent colonists grew slowly, largely out of the ranks of Company workers, stranded sailors, and African or Euroafrican women. (Till 1685 there were no racial prohibitions on marriage; in 1685 marriages were outlawed between Europeans and Africans, but not between Europeans and persons of mixed blood.) The settlers' numbers were substantially increased in 1689 by 150 Huguenot dissenters from Holland, who brought with them the Dutch Reformed Church. In 1699 the free burgher (Boer) population, the ancestors of today's Afrikaners, numbered just over 1,000 men, women, and children, owning an unspecified number of slaves. A century later, they were 17,000 plus 26,000 slaves. Today they number two million.[3]

The outlines of today's Afrikaner agro-pastoral society – and today's South African race war – were thus already in place by 1700. The prison at Robben Island, where Nelson Mandela and the founders of the African National Congress were held during the 1960s, was established in 1657 for Hottentots "who assaulted or robbed a burgher."[4] Largely outside the control of Company administration, and often at odds with the Company's interests, free burgher society developed along its own expansive lines, pressing its way inland, usually in conflict and occasionally in alliance with resident Khoikhoi chiefdoms. By force of horses (which indigenous Africans were forbidden by law to own), firearms (which European settlers were required by law to own), and strategic alliances among rival groups, the Europeans gradually overcame indigenous control and broke up local socioeconomic structures. Smallpox epidemics in 1713, 1755, and 1767 weakened the indigenous position. Gradually more and more Khoikhoi were forced into the role of subsistence laborers, herding the Boers' cattle rather than their own. By 1778 the new governor Von Plattenburg reported finding no autonomous Khoikhoi communities in the Cape Colony. Which is not, of course, to say that indigenous society and indigenous resistance to colonization ended here; both continued in forms which I will discuss further below.

From the beginning of their presence, Europeans in the Cape periodically mounted expeditions to explore the interior. One early object of interest, typical of the seventeenth century, was a mythical, gold-producing empire known as Monomatapa, akin to the El Dorado so long sought in the Americas.[5] These early expeditions were not seen as having produced any discoveries of value; nor, in the era of navigational narrative, did they result in travel books. Not till the early eighteenth century did a European literature on southern Africa begin in earnest, one of the first major contributions being Peter Kolb's *The Present State of the Cape of Good Hope*.

PETER KOLB AND THE REVINDICATION OF THE HOTTENTOTS

Published in German in 1719, Kolb's book was translated into Dutch (1721), English (1731), and French (1741), and remained one of the main print sources on southern Africa through the first half of the century.[6] Trained as a mathematician, Kolb was sent to the Cape in 1706 by a Prussian patron to carry out astronomical and meteorological research.

Though his mission was scientific, Kolb's account, like that of La Condamine in South America, was not. His book, like La Condamine's, contrasts in a number of respects with writings on the other side of the Linnaean watershed. It is devoted mainly, as the title page puts it, to "A Particular ACCOUNT of the several NATIONS of the *HOTTENTOTS*: Their Religion, Government, Laws, Customs, Ceremonies, and Opinions; Their Art of War, Professions, Language, Genius, &c together with A Short ACCOUNT of the DUTCH SETTLEMENT At the *CAPE*." Kolb's account consists in the main of vivid ethnographic description of Khoikhoi society and lifeways in the traditional mode of manners and customs description. While his account is based on what

L'HISTOIRE se prépare à écrire ce que lui apprend L'EXPERIENCE, qui se présen-
te à elle avec sa Pierre de touche, & sa Devise Rerum Magistra. On voit dans
le lointain, la Baie du Cap de Bonne-Espérance; & sur un nuage, les Armes
de la Compagnie des Indes Orientales, soutenues par le Dieu du Commerce.

8 Frontispiece, French edition of Peter Kolb's *Present State of the Cape of Good Hope* (*Description du cap de Bonne-Esperance*, Amsterdam, Jean Catuffe, 1741). "History," says the caption, "prepares to write what she is taught by Experience, who presents herself with her touchstone and her motto *Rerum Magistra*. In the background appears the Bay of the Cape of Good Hope; and on a cloud, the insignia of the East India Company, held up by the god of Commerce."

Kolb describes as years of contact with many different groups of Hottentots, this contact itself is not narrated, nor are Kolb's travels in the interior. Kolb was writing before narrative paradigms for interior travel and exploration emerged in the last decades of the century. In 1719 navigational paradigms still prevailed: the only part of his experience Kolb does present as narrative is his six-month sea voyage to arrive at the Cape. In keeping with the conventions of navigational narrative, the trip is told as a survival story complete with storms, sickness, brackish water, and threat of attack on the high seas.

As its title promises, Kolb's account includes chapters on Khoikhoi forms of government, religion, ceremonies, domestic economy, cattle management, medicine, and so on. It is easy to vouch for the vividness of the description, but less easy to speak for its accuracy. Kolb declares he "made it a Rule not to be believe any Thing I did not see of which a Sight could be had," but in the very next sentence confirms having seen "that *Negroes* are born White"[7] and change color several days later! Nevertheless, his account is undeniably the most substantive source on the indigenous people of the Cape in this period. Here is a representative passage, to give something of the flavor of his writing:

> For the making of Butter, they use, in the Place of a Churn, a Wild Beast's Skin, made up into a Sort of Sack, the hairy Side inward. Into this Sack they pour so much Milk as will about half fill it. They then tie up the Sack; and Two Persons, Men or Women, taking Hold of it, One at one End, the Other at the other, they toss the Milk briskly to and fro' till it becomes Butter. They then put it in Pots, either for Anointing their Bodies and *Krosses*, or for Sale to the *Europeans*; for the *Hottentots*, unless in the Service of *Europeans*, eat no Butter.[8]

The last sentence is a telling one, for it locates "the Europeans" in the same frame as "the Hottentots," in the kind of everyday interaction that goes on all the time in contact zones. Such interaction would have little place in writers to follow. Kolb's observation about the butter reverses usual directions of Eurocolonial exchange and cultural value. Here it is the Europeans who consume a substance the Africans reject as inedible; the Europeans are buying a manufactured product from the Africans, not selling one to them. Who are the barbarians and who the civilized? Who are the market and who the marketers?

One can probably attribute such manipulations of perspective to Kolb's polemical intent, which is to revindicate the Khoikhoi from negative stereotypes laid down by earlier writers. Kolb attacks his predecessors for "their Wantonness and Precipitation in the Characters they have drawn of the *Hottentots*, whose Minds and Manners, tho' wretched enough, are not so wretched as they have made 'em."[9] With a humanism not found in later writers, Kolb affirms the Hottentots above all as cultural beings. He is acutely critical of European claims that they lack the capacity for religious belief, claims made, of course, by Christian writers seeking to explain the complete failure of missionization in the Cape. In response Kolb emphasizes the depth of the Khoikhoi's commitment to their own religion – in other words, he insists they be understood by Europeans in the same terms Europeans understand themselves. Without denying the repugnance to Europeans of many Khoikhoi practices, he rejects paradigms of essential difference that make it "natural" for Europeans to deal with the Africans differently from the ways they deal with each other. The passage quoted above on butter-making, for example, goes on to condemn the "nastiness" of the product and the filthy conditions of its production – but the paragraph after that similarly condemns the Europeans at the Cape, who buy it in large quantities. Strange and often revolting, the Khoikhoi are not a conquered people in Kolb's portrayal, nor does he advocate their conquest. In fact, when he describes their relations with the Dutch settlers, he paints an idealized picture of two nations which after initial confrontations entered into "the most solemn Engagement" to fight no further, but to exist as a Confederacy and defend each other against common enemies.

In keeping with its interactive perspective, Kolb's account, especially in comparison with subsequent ones, is strikingly dialogic in character. Khoikhoi persons are often quoted (though never in their own language), or represented speaking for themselves in response to the author's questions about their actions or customs; indeed, Kolb exhibits a particular fascination for the complexities of interaction in the contact zone. Early in his account he establishes what one might call a contact perspective through a lengthy anecdote about a talented Khoikhoi entrepreneur named Claas who became a broker between Europeans and indigenous inhabitants, eventually falling foul of both. Another early anecdote tells of an indigenous boy raised by the Dutch and sent abroad, who returned to rejoin indigenous society.

Kolb's insistence on the commensurability of Khoikhoi and European societies constitutes the very limitation of his approach. His strategy for revindicating the Khoikhoi is not to show that they are equal to Europeans (this he does not believe), but to show that they are full-fledged anthropological beings in European terms. Contrary to the claims of their detractors, they can in fact be described in terms of the full array of categories through which Europeans recognize other societies as real and human: religions, government, laws, professions, and so on – the whole catalogue from Kolb's title. These are also the categories through which Europeans define and value themselves, and compare themselves with others. Kolb's revindication of the Khoikhoi obviously involves assimilating them to European cultural paradigms. Differences that fall outside the paradigms are inaccessible to the discourse or can be expressed only as absences and lacks. So it is, as J. M. Coetzee suggests, that the most fundamental differences between Khoikhoi and European society can be more clearly present, albeit in perverse form, in the discourse of their detractors. Coetzee attributes the widespread vilification of the "Hottentots" in the writings of seventeenth- and eighteenth-century Europeans to frustration at the Khoikhoi failure to fulfill anthropological and economic expectations. From their first contact with the Cape, as Coetzee documents, Europeans criticized the "Hottentots" incessantly for their idleness and sloth – that is, their failure (refusal) to respond to the opportunity (demand) to work for material reward. What is missing, Coetzee argues, is recognition of the internal values of Khoikhoi society and its subsistence lifeways. "The moment when the travel-writer condemns the Hottentot for doing nothing marks the moment when the Hottentot brings him face to face (if he will only recognize it) with the limits of his own conceptual framework."[10] Both Peter Kolb's account and those he was writing against exhibit this profound limitation.

By the end of the eighteenth century, as modern racist categories emerged, as European interventionism became increasingly militant, and as Khoikhoi society was broken up and indentured by colonists, Kolb's humanist stance disappeared as a discursive possibility. The "Hottentots" ceased to be described, or even describable, by Europeans in terms of categories like government, professions, opinions, or genius (as in Kolb's title). Indeed, Linnaeus' 1759 classifications of humans (see p. 33) erased those very categories with the derogatory phrase "governed by caprice." As other commentators have pointed out, even European philosophies that valorized non-European lifeways in this period tended to share this reductive attitude: in European constructions, American noble savages and paradisiacal Polynesians were valued precisely for their supposed *lack* of government, professions, laws, and institutions.[11] Kolb wrote before this global reduction of subsistence societies to nature had taken hold.

Finally and predictably, the treatment of land and space in Kolb's account contrasts sharply with subsequent writings. In retrospect, what was to become landscape and natural history is conspicuous in Kolb's account by its absence. When it does turn up, the terms of presentation are very different from those of the classificatory, post-Linnaean writers. The following description of the interior of the Cape, for instance, celebrates variety but shows no sign of a differentiating, classificatory impulse:

> The Plains and Valleys are all lovely Meadow-Lands, where Nature appears in such a Profusion of Charms as to ravish the Eye that beholds her. They everywhere smile; are everywhere adorned with beautiful Trees, Plants and Flowers, some of them so singular and of so attractive a Shape and Beauty, all of them so fragrant, that they fill the Eye with incredible Delight, and the Air with the sweetest Odours. Among these are the *Aloe*, and other curious medical Trees, with Herbs of medical Qualities in Abundance.[12]

The language bears out James Turner's characterization of seventeenth-century landscape description as "composite," "not a portrait of an individual

Maniere dont les Hottentottes portent leurs Enfans, leur donnent le sein, & les accoutument au Tabac.

Tom. I. pag. 270.

9 "How the Hottentots carry and nurse their babies, and the accoutrements of tobacco-smoking," from 1741 French translation of Peter Kolb's *Present State of the Cape of Good Hope* (*Description du cap de Bonne-Esperance*, Amsterdam, Jean Catuffe, 1741).

Villages & Huttes des Hottentots.

Tom. I. pag. 288.

10 "Villages and Huts of the Hottentots," from 1741 French translation of Peter Kolb's *Present State of the Cape of Good Hope* (*Description du cap de Bonne-Esperance*, Amsterdam, Jean Catuffe, 1741).

place, but an ideal construction of particular motifs. Its purpose is to express the character of a region, or a general idea of the good land."[13] As in La Condamine's account, particular flora and fauna are pointed out in Kolb's account for their curiosity, their medicinal potential, or their place in indigenous lifeways. For example, the two most elaborate botanical portraits Kolb includes, complete with drawings, are of substances the Khoikhoi themselves particularly prize, the *dacha* (cannabis) leaf, and the *Kanna* (ginseng) root. Europe's totalizing descriptive project is not in evidence.

While Kolb rejects essential distinctions between Africans and Europeans, another line of hierarchy does cut deeply through his humanist world, and that is slavery. While combating reductive stereotypes of the Khoikhoi (who were not owned as slaves), Kolb manifestly writes from within a pre-abolitionist world. His description of the Cape Colony begins with houses and churches, and ends with slave lodges and stables. It is slaves who continually drive the society, and Kolb's discourse, into disorder. Describing the West African slaves at the Cape as "the most untractable, revengeful, cruel Wretches that I ever heard of," Kolb ends his first volume with a spine-chilling relation of "an Execution or Two." One of the anecdotes involves the fate of a group of slaves who attempted to escape and in the process murdered a European, "ript up his Belly, tore out his Entrails, and hung 'em upon the next Bushes." Captured and convicted, they are tortured to death:

> Four of the Men were broke alive: The Queen Elect was hang'd. The Rest stood at the Executions with Ropes about their Necks; and afterwards were severely whipt with split Canes, and branded with a red hot Iron. The Four, who were broke alive, shew'd no Manner of Concern when they were stretch'd upon the Wheel. Nor did they, while their limbs were breaking by the most violent Blows the Executioner could give, cry, any of 'em, so much as *Oh!* or shew any other Token of Complaint . . .[14]

and so forth for another gory half-page. Readers of Michel Foucault's study of corporal punishment *I, Pierre Rivière . . .*[15] will recognize here the sensuous, sensationalist discourse of torture that predated the coalescence in Europe of institutional forms of social control such as prisons, clinics, schools. Kolb expresses no discomfort with that discourse here, yet the sensationalist anecdotes of slave torture truly do interrupt – erupt in – his text. The dialogic dimension vanishes; it is not the words, but the silent non-screams of the tortured slaves that are recorded. In Kolb's world, slavery seems to be a disturbance, an occasion for the sensational, but also a contained or normalized one. It would, of course, become less contained and normalized in the latter decades of the century. In the scientific travel writers who follow, sensationalism and slavery virtually disappear, as does most social drama of any kind. On the other hand, as I will be showing in the next chapter, both eventually find a new home in sentimental travel writing, much of which was allied with the abolitionist cause. There, the sensationalist language of pain that Kolb uses to reassert slavery is strategically transformed into an intense rhetoric of protest.

In sum, Kolb's account, like much of the literature of the La Condamine expedition, predates both the System of Nature and the normalizing of inland exploration and travel on the frontiers of European expansion. It also represents a particular moment in South African history. By Kolb's time, sixty years of continuous European presence had not produced a local conquest, and indigenous hegemony still held. European domination was nevertheless on the agenda, notably of the books Kolb was writing against, which advocated the outright subjection of the Khoikhoi. Within the ideological circle of those books, the Khoikhoi's very resistance to Christianity, for example, counted as evidence of intrinsic inferiorities which further justified conquest. In this context, Kolb's affirmation of the Khoikhoi as cultural, political, religious, and social beings is perhaps not a naive egalitarian gesture, but a critical one in which European superiority (to which Kolb is certainly committed) does not naturally imply subjugation. Sixty years later, discourses are in place which make such a gesture obsolete, and virtually impossible.

NATURALIZING THE CONTACT ZONE: ANDERS SPARRMAN AND WILLIAM PATERSON

The end of the eighteenth century was a time of crisis and upheaval in the Cape of Good Hope. As the European colony grew, local impatience with the protectionist policies of the East India Company intensified, a process occurring at the same time in the Americas. In Capetown a revolt of the colonists erupted in 1779. In the interior, the expansionist agrarian energies of the Afrikaners brought them into intense, endemic conflict with both the mercantile interests of the Company and the resident indigenous peoples. In 1778 Company officials attempted to establish the Fish River as the inland limit for burgher encroachment, beyond which everything was to continue in the hands of independent, indigenous Nguni (Bantu-speaking, "Kaffir") societies. Needless to say, this declaration did not succeed in stabilizing the situation, nor was the Company prepared to make the extensive commitment that would have been required to enforce it. The "embryonic Afrikaner people," as Curtin et al. describe them, continued to pursue their own interests and construct their own society. Pass laws like those suspended in South Africa in 1987 were already in force in the 1770s. Nguni groups continued to oppose the Afrikaner incursion from across the river, and the Afrikaners continued to be harassed by indigenous groups in their midst, notably the !Kung (Bushmen). They were also troubled by another phenomenon of the contact zone, so-called "mixed bands" of Khoikhoi, !Kung, escaped slaves, Euroafricans, and the occasional renegade white person.[16]

Despite the upheavals of the period, by the late eighteenth century, the spread of settler society was making interior travel in southern Africa increasingly feasible for Europeans. The flowering of natural history made it increasingly desirable, and the emergence of new narrative paradigms made such travel increasingly writable and readable. These changes register clearly in the writings of two travelers of the 1770s, the Swede Anders Sparrman and Englishman William Paterson.

A pupil of Linnaeus, Sparrman was sent to southern Africa in 1772 as a naturalist who would make his living as a private tutor. Late that year he joined Cook's second expedition around the world, resuming his work at the Cape two years later, and remaining until 1776. Regarded as "the first full-length personal account of travels in the far interior of Southern Africa,"[17] Sparrman's much-cited *Voyage to the Cape of Good Hope*[18] was published in Swedish in 1783, with a German translation appearing in 1784, followed by four editions in English starting in 1785, and Dutch and French translations in 1787.

Paterson was the son of a Scottish gardener and was sent to the Cape as a botanical collector by the Countess of Strathmore. He was described as "the first to write and publish in English a book entirely devoted to a description of experience at first hand of travel in South Africa"[19]; his *Narrative of Four Voyages in the Land of the Hottentots and the Kaffirs*[20] appeared in English in 1789, with French and German translations and a second English edition appearing the following year. In 1781, now a British Lieutenant, Paterson participated in a British attack on the Cape Colony, leading to accusations that his travels had been motivated by espionage. It is certainly likely that the British benefited from his strategic knowledge.

In the prefaces to their books, both Sparrman and Paterson are explicitly identified as inaugurating a new era of interior exploration and scientific travel, particularly as regards Africa. Writing his own preface, Paterson defines himself over and against conquerors and commercial travelers, neither of whom, he says, have been able to appreciate Africa:

> If ambition never instilled in the conquerors of the world the desire to extend their empire to the deserts of Africa, if commerce has not tempted men to examine a country whose outer appearance could never seduce anyone whose sole object is to increase his wealth . . . nevertheless there exist men who, despite all the terrors of these countries find them objects capable of adding to their satisfactions.[21]

These new men are of course the naturalists. Sparrman's English prefacer likewise identifies him as an innovator, noting that "in fact the account given by him of the whole face of the country, may be considered, in a great measure as new," since sea-travelers "could not possibly be expected" to provide such information.[22]

Not surprisingly, both these writers distance themselves clearly from the anecdotal literature of survival and the sensationalist discourse of monstrosities and marvels. In fact, they stake their authority on that contrast. Paterson's preface gravely announces that his book "is not a novel under the guise of a travel book," while Sparrman warns the reader that "a great many prodigies and uncommon appearances, about which I have frequently been asked . . . are not to be found in my journal." Although "men with one foot, indeed, Cyclopes, Syrens, Troglodytes, and such like imaginary beings have almost entirely disappeared in this enlightened age," Sparrman notes, his predecessors have been guilty of "tales almost as marvellous," particularly as regards the Hottentots.[23] (The barb here is aimed mainly at Peter Kolb.)

For both these Linnaean emissaries, the narrative of travel is organized by the cumulative, observational enterprise of documenting geography, flora, and fauna. The encounter with nature, and its conversion into natural history, forms the narrative scaffolding. The procedure seems so obvious that it is hard to think of it as an innovation. As one might expect, landscape in these books is no longer emblematic or composite, but highly specific and differentiated. The following passage illustrates how the system of nature generates the substance of Paterson's travel account:

> When the heat of the day had passed, we made our way east-north-east, through an extremely arid country, leaving the immense chain of mountains to our right: forty miles away we observed another chain of mountains to our left. Though this country has an extremely arid appearance, it nevertheless abounds in plants of the euphorbe class, in *orpin*, mezembryanthimum, and several species of geranium.[24]

The language is strongly visual and analytic. Linnaean italics sprinkle the pages, though never so many as to disconcert the uninitiated. Here in a similar vein is Sparrman:

> Very late in the evening we arrived at our driver's farm, which was very pleasantly situated on the other side of Bott River. This river was beset at small intervals with pretty high mountains, the peaks and ridges of which delightfully varied the scene. In the declivities of some of them caverns and grottos were seen, which certainly did not exist from the beginning, but were produced by the vicissitudes and changes to which all natural objects are subject.[25]

Several pages of such benign proceedings are enough to call up again the image of the naturalist as Adam alone in his garden. Where, one asks, is everybody? The landscape is written as uninhabited, unpossessed, unhistoricized, unoccupied even by the travelers themselves. The activity of describing geography and identifying flora and fauna structures an asocial narrative in which the human presence, European or African, is absolutely marginal, though it was, of course, a constant and essential aspect of the traveling itself. In the writing, people seem to disappear from the garden as Adam approaches – which, of course, is why he can walk around as he pleases and name things after himself and his friends back home. At one point, on a deserted islet, Sparrman describes himself "a-botanizing . . . in the same dress as Adam wore in his state of Nature." As embodied in the naturalist, European authority and legitimacy are uncontested, a vision undoubtedly appealing to European readers.

For the most part, the human world is naturalized, functioning as a backdrop for the naturalist's quest. As is usually the case, in the accounts of both Sparrman and Paterson, the traveling party provides a microcosm of colonial relations, seen in occasional passing glimpses. Out of the corner of the landscanning eye, Khoikhoi servants move in and out on the edges of the story, fetching water, carrying baggage, driving oxen, stealing brandy, guiding, interpreting, looking for lost waggons. Referred to simply as "a/the/my Hottentot(s)" (or not at all, as in the eternal "our baggage arrived the next day"), all are interchangeable; none is distinguished from another by a name or any other feature; and their presence, their *disponibilité*, and subaltern status, are now taken for granted. (Paterson: "The next morning, having found a Hottentot kraal two miles away, I took one of the inhabitants as a guide."[26])

Apart from their ghostly presence as members of "the party," the Khoikhoi inhabit a separate textual homeland in these books, where they are produced as objects of formal ethnographic description. Sparrman allocates them a thirty-page descriptive digression in the middle of his book, while Paterson puts them in a fourteen-page footnote to his first chapter, between shorter notes on the hartebeest and the zebra. These post-Linnaean ethnographic portraits of the Khoikhoi contrast with Peter Kolb's description in ways that express schematically the advance of colonialist interests. Quite simply, while Kolb wrote the Khoikhoi primarily as cultural beings, these two texts of the 1780s produce them above all as bodies and appendages. Kolb's ethnographic question-and-answer is replaced in Sparrman and Paterson by visual scrutiny as the means of knowledge. Sparrman's portrait of the Hottentots begins with five pages devoted to body parts, especially genitals,[27] four to clothing, three to ornaments. Kolb, too, wrote about bodies and genitals, yet the bodies in his discourse were entities shaped or, in modern parlance, inscribed on by culture. Describing, for example, a ceremony by which young boys (supposedly) had a testicle removed and substituted with a ball of sheep's fat, Kolb's main reaction is to remark repeatedly on the fineness and precision with which the operation *is carried out*. Sparrman, on the other hand, *observes* that Hottentot men *have* two testicles, and on the basis of his observation denies the existence of the procedure Kolb described. The effect is to deculturate the increasingly subjugated Africans. Needless to say, the dialogic dimension of Kolb's account contrasts with static descriptive apparatuses in Paterson and Sparrman. Indigenous voices are almost never quoted, reproduced, or even invented in these late eighteenth-century accounts; the intellectual and spiritual attributes Kolb elaborated on are denied almost point for point. When Sparrman comments on cannabis, he pointedly aims not to discuss its place in indigenous mores but to suggest that colonists "work it up into sheeting, sacking, sail-cloth, cordage, and other articles."[28]

In the midst of current scholarly critique of colonialist discourses, contemporary readers can scarcely fail to link this creation of a speechless, denuded, biologized body with the deracinated, dispossessed, disposable work force European colonialists so ruthlessly and tirelessly fought to create in their footholds abroad. One might want to argue that Sparrman's and Paterson's accounts simply reflect changes the Khoikhoi peoples themselves had undergone during the five decades of colonial intervention since Kolb. Their traditional lifeways had after all been permanently disrupted. Yet the complicity of these texts begins in the fact that they portray the African peoples not as undergoing historical changes in their lifeways, but as having no lifeways at all, as cultureless beings (*sans mœurs*, in the French version of Paterson). Whatever changes might have been taking place tend not to be expressed *as changes*, but are "naturalized" as absences and lacks. Sparrman's description presents itself as timeless truth and simply challenges the veracity of Kolb's earlier account when it conflicts. As the Khoikhoi are deterritorialized – extracted from the landscape in which they still live – they are thus taken out of economy, culture, and history too. These are moves the natural history enterprise is designed to make easy, and in fact obligatory. So does the anti-conquest "underwrite" colonial appropriation, even as it rejects the rhetoric, and probably the practice, of conquest and subjugation.

While rigidly circumscribing African indigenous peoples, Sparrman, in particular, often dramatizes his interactions with Afrikaner (Boer) settlers, on whose assistance he also depends. Here the word that glosses, and idealizes, relations between settlers and travelers is "hospitality." The traveler's encounters with the Afrikaners are regularly measured up against the beloved bourgeois scenario of the rough and humble peasant gladly sharing his subsistence with the enlightened man of the metropolis whose essential superiority is accepted, though his dependencies are held in contempt. Sparrman and Paterson scarcely if ever mention the practices of exchange which structured their relations with the settlers most concretely. Custom had it, for instance, that the assistance of Afrikaner settlers – food, lodging, oxen, servants – was paid for in powder and shot, substances hard to store and difficult to obtain in remote areas; substances upon which the settler invasion utterly and systematically depended. In the travel accounts, this exchange is not mentioned, perhaps for the same reasons that so little is said about the uses to which the ammunition is being put.

The complexities of life in the contact zone similarly show up only in glimpses. The poverty of Afrikaner settlers often confuses categories – both Sparrman and Paterson recount approaching African huts only to find

11 Frontispiece, 1785 English translation of Sparrman's *Voyage to the Cape of Good Hope* depicting the "Prospect of the country at the Cape of Good Hope."

they are the homes of European settlers. In the remotest areas, itinerant European loners are encountered moving from place to place across the lines of difference. Both writers report on transracial sexual alliances and intermarriages – not just the common case of European men and African concubines, but also a tale of a European woman bearing a child by an African lover; of a European man who marries a tribal woman out of true love. The violence and destruction of the contact zone are glimpsed too, but only in their aftermath, in traces on bodies or in anecdotes: a woman wounded years ago by a Bushman arrow, a man whose wife and children were murdered, a chief who has had his land taken from him. Conflict and tensions between indentured African laborers and their European masters are offstage, referred to at times, but not dramatized, elaborated, or witnessed. For example, in Sparrman's account the genocidal campaign underway against the !Kung ("Bushmen") is represented through a dispassionate, recipe-like description of how the Boers organize a Bushman hunt.[29]

In Sparrman's book, encounters with settler hospitality often enact an ideological drama essential to the authority of the naturalist, that of validating his way of knowing over others that precede it. Sparrman's interactions with the Afrikaners often dramatize clashes between peasant knowledge and science. Pointedly, Sparrman imposes the term "peasant" on the Afrikaners in general, even the well-to-do, who would certainly not apply the term to themselves. In many anecdotes the Afrikaners are condescended to or made fun of specifically as peasants. One amusing chain of anecdotes foregrounds the contrast between settler views of nature and those of the naturalist. On a particularly fruitful day of collecting, Sparrman finds his insect box is full, and he is "obliged to put a whole regiment of flies and other insects round the brim of [his] hat."[30] In search of a place to stay, he is directed to the house of "a rich and infirm widow of fifty-two years of age." On arriving, Sparrman attempts to conceal his bug-festooned hat in order not to alarm his hostess. He is betrayed at dinner, however, by the servants, one of whom whispers to her mistress that his hat "was full of little beasts (*kleine bestjes*)." Sparrman rises to the occasion:

> It was now necessary for me to cease eating a while, for fear of being choked with some of the big words and long Dutch phrases, which I was obliged to coin on the spot, in order to convince her of the great utility of understanding these little animals for medical and oeconomical purposes, and at the same time to the glory of the great Creator.[31]

By quoting the Afrikaner phrase *kleine bestjes* Sparrman underscores the verbal substitution that constitutes his naturalist's mission. He will supply the "correct" names. The heteroglossia is powerful, for the Afrikaner phrase aligns the Afrikaner mistress with her African servant in the category of the scientifically uninitiated. As the anecdote goes on, Sparrman's explanation succeeds, but a repeat performance is called for shortly after when a large group of the widow's friends and relatives arrive. Again, the distance between lay and professional knowledge is humorously played out: "They had seen an insect hunter before, but when they looked into my collection of herbs, and found it to contain not only flowers, but likewise grass and small branches of shrubs and trees, they could not forbear laughing at a sight so unexpected."[32]

Sparrman is unmistakably mocking himself in this anecdote as well as primitivizing his hosts. This self-mockery is in keeping with the relation these two post-Linnaean writers establish between themselves and their readers. When he does appear, the self-effacing protagonist of the anti-conquest is often surrounded by an aura not of authority, but of innocence and vulnerability. Sparrman's anecdote about the widow is revealing in this respect. Pushing aside the conventional erotic potential of the scene (young bachelor/rich widow), the writer turns it into a parodic Oedipean drama. Infantilizing himself, Sparrman de-eroticizes the widow, commenting on her infirmity and stating, rather than finessing, her age. Struggling not to talk with his mouth full, the boychild-Sparrman tries to possess the mother-widow through words, specifically through the discourse of natural history. The moment is interrupted, of course, by other people with claims on her, people whom Sparrman is able neither to frighten nor impress. Socially, and sexually, too, Sparrman carries out an anti-conquest.

None of which is terribly serious, for the person who really matters is the father back in Sweden awaiting the son's return. Unlike such antecedents as the conquistador and the hunter, the figure of the naturalist-hero often has a certain impotence or androgyny about him; often he portrays himself in infantile or adolescent terms. The naturalist's production of knowledge has some decidedly non-phallic aspects, perhaps alluded to by Linnaeus' own image of Ariadne following her thread out of the labyrinth of the Minotaur (see p. 33 above). Meandering through country-sides, looking, gathering, improvising, reacting to whatever turns out to be there, Linnaeus' disciples do not wholly resemble Dr. Frankensteins or fire-stealing Prometheuses. (Rousseau's *Memoirs of a Solitary Walker* includes a famous portrait of the author herborizing in a long Turkish robe.[33])

The naturalist-heroes are not, however, women – no world is more androcentric than that of natural history (which is not, of course, to say there were no women naturalists). The paternal structure of discipleship is overwhelmingly evident. While Linnaeus the father/king presides at home over the garden/kingdom, the sons range over the world for the missing pieces that will complete it. The image of Adam in the primordial garden is an image of Adam before the very creation of Eve. As the prefaces of their books often suggest, the desire that takes the Linnaeans abroad involves a choice, like Dr. Frankenstein's, against heterosexual conjugal life and women. Eve's absence is undoubtedly a precondition for Adam's infantility and innocence.

Within its innocence the naturalist's quest does embody, as I suggested earlier, an image of conquest and possession. Eve is the garden whom he in his unobjectionable way plunders and possesses. "We paused to rest," says Paterson again and again, "and I added several specimens to my collection." But unlike the conquistador's, his booty is not taken from anyone else. The dried little specimens have no value of their own – they are merely instances of themselves, tokens of their genus and species. Paterson's preface highlights the contrast between conquest and the anti-conquest of science. Simultaneously, it reveals their connection. In the "wilds" of Africa, he writes,

> The naturalist will find a vast field for his observations, and there he will discover objects capable, by their immense variety, of satisfying all his tastes; there he will see all the simple objects in the state of nature, and will contemplate in the savage Hottentot the virtues that he has perhaps vainly wished to find in civilized societies. Penetrated by such sentiments, and greatly excited by the perspective of a land whose products are unknown to us, I left England with the resolution to satisfy a curiosity *which, if it is not seen as useful to society, is at least innocent* (my italics).[34]

What an ideological tangle there is in these few sentences! On the one hand, the claim to innocence and disinterestedness, and, on the other, the vocabulary of ego-centered lust and desire. On the one hand, a demanding (masculine) self with needs to be met, and, at the same time, a receptive (feminine) self penetrated by sentiments. The accumulative, differentiating project of science lines up explicitly with that other form of differentiation and accumulation which is called Taste. Knowledge gets identified with consumption (like Sparrman at the widow's dinner table) and as the satisfaction of a self-contained desire.

In the literature of the imperial frontier, the conspicuous innocence of the naturalist, I would suggest, acquires meaning in relation to an assumed guilt of conquest, a guilt the naturalist figure eternally tries to escape, and eternally invokes, if only to distance himself from it once again. Even though the travelers were witnessing the daily realities of the contact zone, even though the institutions of expansionism made their travels possible, the *discourse* of travel that natural history produces, and is produced by, turns on a great longing: for a way of taking possession without subjugation and violence. Such longings reach something of an extreme in the final South African account I propose to consider: John Barrow's *Travels into the Interior of Southern Africa in the Years 1797 and 1798*. The book appeared in London in 1801.

SCRATCHES ON THE FACE OF THE COUNTRY, OR WHAT MR. BARROW SAW IN THE LAND OF THE BUSHMEN

Barrow's travels in the interior of the Cape Colony were occasioned by a period of explosive breakdowns in the internal relations among East India Company, Afrikaner settler society, and indigenous chiefdoms, along with increasing external aggression from France and Britain. The attempt to contain European expansion at the Fish River did not succeed, and the Afrikaners continued to expand inland onto territory controlled by Nguni peoples. They also continued to resent deeply the Company's reluctance to support them. In 1786 the Company sent a *landrost* or administrator to contain the increasingly militant Afrikaners. He lasted only a few months, and, shortly afterward, an Afrikaner attack against the Nguni provoked an unprecedented general uprising of Africans against Europeans.[35] Indentured Khoikhoi and enslaved !Kung rebelled in large numbers and joined the Nguni, providing precious horses and guns stolen from their European masters. These were turned devastatingly against the Afrikaner colonists, whom the colonial government did little to protect. The Afrikaners retaliated against the colonial administration and in some areas proclaimed independent republics.

Uncertainty and violence prevailed for many years, at a time when the Dutch East India Company's financial troubles limited its ability to respond. In 1795, the Cape Colony was taken by Britain (on the pretext that it was in danger of falling to the French, who under Napoleon had just overrun the Netherlands). British colonists (the English South Africans of today) began to arrive, decidedly unwelcomed by the Afrikaners. The Colony was returned to the Dutch in 1803, retaken by Britain in 1806, and confirmed under British rule in 1815. John Barrow, a young career diplomat, went to the Cape during the first period of British control as personal secretary to the new colonial governor, Lord George McCartney. McCartney appointed Barrow as his representative to the interior, requiring Barrow's several lengthy journeys there. His job was to explore the grievances between settlers and Company officials, to establish a sense of the British presence among both Afrikaner and indigenous populations, and to document the "face of the country" further.

Unlike Kolb, Paterson, or Sparrman, Barrow was traveling officially in the name of a Eurocolonial territorial enterprise. In his account of his travels, the naturalist's rhetoric of anti-conquest comes close to taking on the role of an official discourse, aimed at legitimating the British takeover of the Cape. In what might seem a paradox, Barrow's narrative makes only very limited reference to the military and diplomatic sides of his mission. He writes, rather, in the mode of Sparrman and Paterson, as naturalist, geographer, and ethnographer. These discourses appear in highly institutionalized form in Barrow's text, and are linked with imperial expansion more explicitly than in the writings of Sparrman or Paterson, perhaps because Barrow was writing as an official (a secretary, in fact), or perhaps on account of his own temperament.

As with his predecessors, Barrow's account by and large separates Africans from Africa (and Europeans from Africans) by relegating the latter to objectified ethnographic portraits set off from the narrative of the journey. Barrow's narrative consists overwhelmingly of landscape and nature description, a thrill-free cataloguing of what Barrow, too, likes to refer to as "the face of the country." The following passage is illustrative:

> The following day we passed the Great Fish River, though not without some difficulty, the banks being high and steep, the stream strong, the bottom rocky, and the water deep. Some fine trees of the willow of Babylon, or a variety of that species, skirted the river at this place. The opposite side presented a very beautiful country, well wooded and watered, and plentifully covered with grass, among which grew in great abundance, a species of indigo, apparently the same as that described by Mr. Masson as the *candicans*.
>
> The first night that we encamped in the Kaffir country was near a stream called Kowsha, which falls into the Great Fish River. On the following day we passed the villages of Malloo and Tooley, the two chiefs and brothers we had seen in Zuure Veldt, delightfully situated on two eminences rising from the said streamlet. We also passed several villages placed along the banks of the Guengka and its branches, and the next day we came to a river of very considerable magnitude called the Keiskamma.[36]

So it goes for the better part of 400 pages, a strange, highly attenuated kind of narrative that seems to do everything possible to minimize the human presence. In the main what is narrated is a sequence of sights or settings. Visual details are interspersed with technical and classificatory information. The tendency is toward a panoramic scope with a sprinkling of esthetic terms mitigating an otherwise concertedly impassive vocabulary. The travelers are chiefly present as a kind of collective moving eye on which the sights/sites register; as agents their presence is very reduced. In the passage quoted, for example, the party's struggle to cross the river is not narrated or dramatized in human terms, but expressed in highly mediated fashion as an enumeration of the traits of the river that produced the difficulty. Heroic priorities are refused; the European protagonists absent themselves from their own story.[37] There is not even a sign of any specimen-collecting.

The residents of the country, whether indigenous Africans or Boer settlers, likewise turn up in the narration mainly as traces on the landscape. The Nguni villages mentioned above, for instance, are less important in the discourse than the rivers and streams, and there is no sign of their inhabitants. The history that motivates Barrow's presence and determines his itinerary has no constitutive role in the text. The crossing of the Fish River is narrated with no mention of the river's political significance as the frontier of Afrikaner penetration – though its status as a boundary is the very reason Barrow is there crossing it. The Snowy Mountains are traversed with no mention of their significance as the main base for anti-European guerrilla activity – a source of considerable anxiety for all travelers there. On another occasion, only after narrating one stretch of "wild, uninhabited country," does Barrow mention that the region had formerly been "one of the best-peopled divisions in the district," now depopulated by "the scandalous rupture between the peasantry and the Kaffers."[38] Later, Barrow was to say that he had "studiously avoided" political discussion in his account, partly out of discretion and partly because "I then conceived there was but one opinion with regard to the real value of the Cape of Good Hope."[39]

Drama in Barrow's travel account, then, is produced not by history, nor by the agency of the travelers themselves, but by the changing face of the country as it *presents itself* to the invisible European seers. Barrow's own language suggests the fantasy of dominance and appropriation that is built into this otherwise passive, open stance. The eye "commands" what falls within its gaze; mountains and valleys "show themselves," "present a picture"; the country "opens up" before the visitors. The European presence is absolutely uncontested. At the same time, the landscanning European eye seems powerless to act upon or interact with this landscape that offers itself. Unheroic, unparticularized, egoless, the eye seems able to do little but gaze from a periphery of its own creation: again we are in the realm of the anti-conquest.

Barrow's landscape descriptions are accompanied at times by an explanatory discourse whose appearance reflects late eighteenth-century developments in natural history. In this explanatory mode, causality – not classification – defines the task at hand; the observer's role is not only to collect the visible, but to interpret it in terms of the invisible. The description of a lovely campsite by a salt lake is followed by two pages of speculation on the origins of the salt.[40] Chemical, thermal, and geophysical hypotheses are offered to explain the presence of minerals, the composition of bogs, the directions of mountain ranges and river flows. Experiments are conducted to reveal hidden properties – the world is not simply given to the eyes, as it is to the Linnaean collector. As a discourse, explanation adds a dimension of depth to the surface blanket of Linnaean terminology. It also generates new planetary powers for the natural historian, now endowed with a kind of inner eye charged with deciphering what Alexander von Humboldt (the grand master of the explanatory mode) would call nature's "occult forces." What relation do these new powers of explanation bear to the occult forces of industrial technology and the hungry entrepreneurism newly emanating from Europe during these turn-of-the-century decades?

Leaving aside the occult depths, it is hardly surprising to find an emissary of a European imperial power concerning himself above all with defining territory and scanning perimeters, especially here in southern Africa, where territorial possession had become part of the expansionist strategy. In Barrow's account, more so than in those of his predecessors, the eye scanning prospects in the spatial sense knows itself to be looking at prospects in the temporal sense – possibilities of a Eurocolonial future coded as resources to be developed, surpluses to be traded, towns to be built. Such prospects are what make information relevant in a description. They make a plain "fine" or make it noteworthy that a peak is "granitic" or a valley "well-wooded." The visual descriptions presuppose – naturalize – a transformative project embodied in the Europeans. Often the project surfaces explicitly in Barrow's text, in visions of "improvement" whose value is often expressed as esthetic. A place at Algoa Bay is described as "the prettiest situation for a small fishing village that could possibly be imagined"; not far away lies a large swamp "that by one single drain might be converted into a very beautiful meadow";[41] a discovery of lead-bearing ore suggests "a valuable acquisition to the colony," especially because it is in a place where a mining town could readily be founded.[42] At his most pragmatic, Barrow is not averse to discussing price levels for commodities or the value of a British military presence as a market for local produce. Apart from these explicit enactments, the British "spirit of improvement" permeates Barrow's text, its prescriptions emanating from a seat of power behind the invisible, innocent speaking "I."

It is the task of the advance scouts for capitalist "improvement" to encode what they encounter as "unimproved" and, in keeping with the terms of the anti-conquest, as *disponible*, available for improvement. European aspirations must be represented as uncontested. Here the textual apartheid that separates landscape from people, accounts of inhabitants from accounts of their habitats, fulfills its logic. The European improving eye produces subsistence habitats as "empty" landscapes, meaningful only in terms of a capitalist future and of their potential for producing a marketable surplus. From the point of view of their inhabitants, of course, these same spaces are lived as intensely humanized, saturated with local history and meaning, where plants, creatures, and geographical formations have names, uses, symbolic functions, histories, places in indigenous knowledge formations.

It is not only habitats that must be produced as empty and unimproved, but inhabitants as well. To the improving eye, the potentials of the Eurocolonial future are predicated on absences and lacks of African life in the present. For Barrow, the unimproved African present includes not just the Khoikhoi (Hottentots), the !Kung (Bushmen) and the Nguni (Kaffirs), but their Afrikaner exploiters and competitors, too. Euroafricans as well as Africans must be codified specifically in relation to British aspirations; prior Dutch claims and 150 years of Dutch colonialism must be discredited. When Afrikaner settler society appears in Barrow's text, it is the object of blanket critique, defined disparagingly by its lack of taste, comfort, and the spirit of improvement. The older narrative of hospitality has outlived its usefulness:

A true Dutch peasant, or boor as he styles himself, has not the smallest idea of what an English farmer means by the word comfort. Placed in a country where not only the necessaries, but almost every luxury of life might by industry be procured, he has the enjoyment of none of them. Though he has cattle in abundance he makes very little use of milk or of butter. In the midst of a soil and climate most favourable for the cultivation of the vine, he drinks no wine. Three times a-day his table is loaded with masses of mutton, swimming in the grease of the sheep's tail. His house is either open to the roof, or covered only with rough poles and turf. . . . The bottoms of his chairs consist of thongs cut from a bullock's hide. The windows are without glass.

And so on for two pages. With the opposite value sign, of course, this portrait could be a praise song to noble savagery and the simple life. Too judgemental to be read as ethnographic, the portrait ends with a telling change of terminology (my italics):

with a mind disengaged from every sort of care and reflexion, indulging to excess in the gratification of every sensual appetite, the *African peasant* grows to an unwieldy size, and is carried off the stage by the first inflammatory disease that attacks him.[43]

As Coetzee notes, European travelers often condemned the Boers in much the same terms they used to condemn the Hottentots, with "indolence" and "idleness" being key words. Both groups, he argues, were subjected to Europeans' wilful misunderstanding of traditional lifeways in southern Africa, whether those of the colonized Africans or the Euroafrican colonists. The Boers (Afrikaners), Coetzee suggests, presented a particular challenge to European bourgeois values, precisely because as a colonial ruling class with access to virtually unlimited land and free labor, they had the means to realize European values of accumulation, consumption, and enrichment through work, yet chose not to. In his view, they raised the possibility for European observers that "beneath the dirty skins, the clouds of flies, and the rude clothing," the Afrikaner settlers might "stand for a rejection of the curse of discipline and labour in favour of an African way of life in which the fruits of the earth are enjoyed as they drop into the hand, work is avoided as an evil, and leisure and idleness become the same thing."[44] Barrow's point of comparison for the (slaveholding) "African peasants" is, not surprisingly in 1801, "the laboring poor of England," whose superiority to the Euroafricans lies somehow in the fact that "for six days in the week [they] are doomed to toil for twelve hours in every day, in order to gain a morsel of bread for their family."[45] Forgotten already, or never recognized at all, are the intense processes of indoctrination and coercion required to create the English working class and compel it to embrace upward mobility and the work ethic.[46]

The same textual strategies were at work on the other side of the Atlantic as well. Barrow's disparaging portrait of the Dutch in South Africa was matched by his counterparts writing about Dutch colonial society in the Caribbean, such as John Stedman, whose work is discussed in chapter 5, and whom Barrow had likely read. In Spanish America, a flood of English business travelers in the early nineteenth century would deride Spanish American creole society in the same terms Barrow used against the Afrikaners (see chapter 7). The parallels are not coincidental. Britain was as intensely interested in South America in 1800 as it was in southern Africa. Barrow himself drew strong parallels between the two, calling them "opposite continents" and comparing the Cape Colony with the British foothold on the island of Staaten off Cape Horn.[47] History would bear him out. Some of the same British generals who regained the Cape for Britain in 1806 moved on to Argentina to participate in the British attack on La Plata a few months later.

The chief ethnographic interest of Barrow's *Travels* is not the Khoikhoi, but the !Kung, better known by their colonial appellation, the Bosjesmans or Bushmen. A people who have remained objects of intense ethnographic interest and western ideological fantasy right down to the present, the !Kung are ancient inhabitants of southern Africa who, by the time the Europeans came to settle, were already in stiff competition with arriving Khoikhoi and Nguni pastoralists. A highly mobile population who lived in small groups, they kept neither animals nor crops. In the seventeenth and eighteenth centuries they were known and feared above all for their nocturnal raids on Khoikhoi, and later, European livestock.

Repeating the usual textual division of labor, Barrow represents the !Kung in a sixteen-page ethnographic portrait separate from the narrative proper. Let me use it as an occasion to reflect on how these standard apparatuses of travel writing produce non-European subjects for the domestic audience of imperialism. Here is an excerpt:

> In his disposition he [the Bushman] is lively and chearful; in his person active. His talents are far above mediocrity; and, averse to idleness, they are seldom without employment. Confined generally to their hovels by day, for fear of being surprised by the farmers, they sometimes dance on moonlight nights from setting to the rising of the sun. . . . The small circular trodden places around their huts indicated their fondness for this amusement. His chearfulness is the more extraordinary as the morsel he procures to support existence is earned with danger and fatigue. He neither cultivates the ground nor breeds cattle; and his country yields few natural productions that serve for food. The bulbs of the iris, and a few graminaeous roots of a bitter and pungent taste, are all that the vegetable kingdom affords him. By the search of these the whole surface of the plains near the horde was scratched.[48]

The initial ethnographic gesture is the one that homogenizes the people to be subjected, that is, produced as subjects, into a collective *they*, which distills down even further into an iconic *he* (= the standard adult male specimen). This abstracted *he/they* is the subject of verbs in a timeless present tense. These characterize anything "he" is or does not as a particular event in time, but as an instance of a pregiven custom or trait (as a particular plant is an instance of its genus and species). Particular encounters between people get textualized, then, as enumerations of such traits. The fact that late eighteenth-century !Kung communities live in constant fear and danger, for instance, is coded as a custom of hiding all day and dancing at night.

Critical anthropology has recognized the extent to which these descriptive practices work to normalize another society, to codify its difference from one's own, to fix its members in a timeless present where all "his" actions and reactions are repetitions of "his" normal habits. Like the system of nature, it makes an order where, for the outsider, there exists chaos. The textual production of the other society is not explicitly anchored either in the observing self or in the particular situation of contact in which the observing is taking place. "He" is a *sui generis* configuration, often only a list of features, situated in a different temporal order from that of the perceiving and speaking subject. Johannes Fabian has used the phrase "denial of coevalness" to refer specifically to the temporal distancing.[49] It is an old textual practice that readily complements the processes of deculturation and deterritorialization discussed earlier.

Grammatically speaking, in the passage just quoted there are two points at which the timeless "ethnographic" present of the normative description is interrupted by a narrative past tense. The trodden places around the Bushmen's huts *indicated* their fondness for dancing, and by their search for roots, the surface of the surrounding plains *was scratched*. In a ghostly way, these two past tenses refer back to a specific occasion or occasions of contact between Barrow and the Bushmen. What they historicize, however, is his encounter not with *them*, but with the traces they have left on the landscape – their scratches on "the face of the country."

The normalizing, generalizing voice of the ethnographic manners-and-customs portraits is distinct from, but complementary to, the landscape narrator. Both are authorized by the global project of natural history: one produces land as landscape and territory, scanning for prospects; the other produces the indigenous inhabitants as bodyscapes, scanned also for prospects. Together they dismantle the socioecological web that preceded them and install a Eurocolonial discursive order whose territorial and visual forms of authority are those of the modern state. Abstracted away from the landscape that is under contention, indigenous peoples are abstracted away from the history that is being made – a history into which Europeans intend to reinsert them as an exploited labor pool.

In this context one cannot help but notice that in contrast with the idleness of Afrikaners and Khoikhoi, Barrow finds in the !Kung the same qualities he values in the English working class. They dislike idleness and willingly work very hard for little recompense (bread for the British, bitter roots for the Bushmen). Neither group are agro-pastoralists, a way of life seemingly inimical to the spirit of improvement. Such observations, despite their seeming timelessness, connect Barrow's portrait to the particular historical juncture motivating the revindication of the !Kung.

Whatever !Kung lifeways were before the seventeenth century, by the time the Europeans arrived, they seem already to have been a beleaguered and mobilized population, hated by the Khoikhoi as wild and vicious. This was a myth European colonists readily took up, allying with the Khoikhoi in brutal campaigns of repression against these "savage" people who "abhor the pastoral life," as was so often said. Faced with constant complaints about "Bushman depredations," East India Company administrators periodically authorized colonists to mount their own campaigns of reprisal, which turned into genocidal hunting parties. Both Sparrman and Paterson describe the practices that had evolved for locating and attacking !Kung encampments at night.

The !Kung responded to the invaders by becoming ever more elusive and by retreating to ever remoter regions. (They have not lived eternally in their supposed "natural" habitat, the Kalahari desert.) Even by Sparrman and Paterson's time, it appears, independent !Kung communities had become difficult to locate, so well hidden were the survivors. Some !Kung, however, had been forced into the European pastoral economy, in ways which travelers often condemned. While Company law prohibited enslaving the Khoikhoi, the !Kung could be enslaved, and were, though they escaped constantly. Sparrman deplores one practice Europeans used, which was to kidnap !Kung babies, thus ensuring that the grieving mother would remain nearby and accept enslavement to the Europeans in exchange for proximity to her child. The practice was adapted from techniques for capturing animals.[50]

By the end of the eighteenth century, the !Kung had ceased to be a serious threat and had acquired the status of a conquered people. In European writings, they began to appear not as vicious savages, but in a new sentimental stereotype, as benign, ingenuous, childlike victims. Barrow is one of the writers who inaugurates this stereotype, as in the passage quoted above. In one narrative episode he encounters at the home of an Afrikaner commandant a !Kung family who have just been taken prisoner by Afrikaner raiders. Barrow's summary of an apparent conversation with the male captive is striking in contrast with the prevailing rhetoric of his book. Rather than converting the other into information, Barrow attempts to represent his perspective and to valorize his experience of colonial persecution:

> He represented to us the condition of his countrymen as truly deplorable. That for several months in the year, when the frost and snow prevented them from making their excursions against the farmers, their sufferings from cold and want of food were indescribable: that they frequently beheld their wives and children perishing with hunger, without being able to give them any relief. The good season brought little alleviation to their misery. They knew themselves to be hated by all mankind, and that every nation around them was an enemy planning their destruction. Not a breath of wind rustled through the leaves, not a bird screamed, that were not supposed to announce danger.[51]

Yet there is no question about whether the speaker will be absorbed into the Eurocolonial power structure. He already has been, in Barrow's eyes: "This little man," the episode ends, "*was intended* to have accompanied us; but as he seemed more inclined to abide by his wives, he *was permitted* to follow his uxurious inclinations" (my italics).

In the end, Barrow's humanitarian engagement with the !Kung takes him across to the other side of the scientific anti-conquest, where his visual and objectivist rhetoric breaks down. The repressed does return in his text, in an episode with which I will bring this lengthy chapter to a close. Fascinated by the !Kung, Barrow wants nothing more than to see them in their uncolonized "natural" state. Such had been the persecution of the !Kung that the only way to make contact with their communities was literally to invade them. Only through a guilty act of conquest (invasion) can the innocent act of the anti-conquest (seeing) be carried out. In the name of seeing, Barrow reluctantly hires some Afrikaner farmers to do just that. Taking up the tools of conquest – guns and horses – they descend in the night, on Barrow's condition that no one fire unless fired upon. The venture seems to have been a traumatic one for him, a veritable descent into hell, whose narration contrasts dramatically with the rest of the book. The nocturnal attack on the "horde" brings both the language of conquest and the language of remorse bursting to the surface of the text:

> Our ears were stunned with a horrid scream like the war-hoop of savages; the shrieking of women and the cries of children proceeded from every side. I rode up with the commandant and another farmer, both of whom fired upon the kraal. I immediately expressed to the former my very great surprise that he, of all others, should have been the first to break a condition which he had solemnly promised to observe, and that I had expected from him a very different kind of conduct. "Good God!" he exclaimed, "have you not seen a shower of arrows falling among us?" I

certainly had seen neither arrows nor people, but had heard enough to pierce the hardest heart.[52]

It would be difficult to exaggerate how starkly this episode stands out in Barrow's text. It is the only nocturnal scene in the work, the only instance of direct dialogue, the only occasion Barrow dramatizes himself as a participant, the only outburst of emotion, the only outbreak of violence, one of the few scenes where people and place coincide, and the only time Barrow questions his apprehension of his surroundings. One of few dramatic episodes in Barrow's book, it is the only one in which the speaking subject splits and turns up as both seer and seen. What provokes the crisis here, it seems, is the fact that Barrow chooses to exercise his state-constituted "right" to "legitimate" violence, not, however, in order to defend himself or fellow citizens, or to expel an invader, but simply in order to *get a look*, to satisfy his curiosity. The ideology that construes seeing as inherently passive and curiosity as innocent cannot be sustained, and Barrow's discursive order breaks down along with his humanitarian moral one. Into that break a sentimental counterdiscourse inserts itself. Barrow winds up in a confessional mode: "Nothing," he later says, "could be more unwarrantable, because cruel and unjust, than the attack made by our party upon the kraal."[53]

A confessional mode, but certainly not a transformative one, for Barrow's loss of innocence produces no new self, no new relations of speech. His descent into colonial hell would be repeated many times by writers to follow. A century later, by the time Northern Europe had created its own black legend in the vicious genocidal scramble for Africa, that descent would become the canonical story about Europe in Africa: the fall from the sun-drenched prospect into the heart of darkness.

HISTORICAL POSTSCRIPT

In 1803 Britain returned the Cape Colony to the Dutch, a loss which so distressed Barrow that he dropped everything for three months to compose a second volume to his *Travels*, arguing the value of the Cape to Britain's global commercial and military interests. His arguments may have worked, for in 1806 Britain indeed retook the Cape by force. Barrow's journey marked the beginning of changes brought by British rule, which was definitively confirmed in 1815. The British fortified the Fish River boundary, thereby committing themselves to joining the Afrikaners against the Nguni. Nguni resistance continued throughout the nineteenth century; wars were fought in 1819, 1834–5, 1846, 1850–3, and 1877–8.

Meanwhile, new laws attempted to legislate indigenous subjugation. "In 1809," according to Curtin et al.'s standard history, "the legal status of Khoikhoi and other dark-skinned people who were not slaves was defined in such a way that most of them were obliged to work for Europeans, though they enjoyed some protection in having written contracts of service and access to the courts." The trick the Boers invented for enslaving the Bushmen was legalized: "In 1812, European landowners became entitled to apprentice children whom they had raised on their farms . . . a ruling that immobilized their parents also."[54] In 1820, 5,000 British settlers arrived, and with them a new force from Europe: the London Missionary Society, which mounted a humanitarian challenge to some of the most brutal abuses. Humanitarianism, alongside science, is its own form of anti-conquest; its dynamics as played out in travel writing are the subject of the next chapter.

Chapter 4

Anti-conquest II: The mystique of reciprocity

It seems that for our sins, or for some inscrutable judgement of God, in all the entrances of this great Ethiopia [i.e. Africa] that we sail along, he has placed a striking angel with a flaming sword of deadly fevers, who prevents us from penetrating into the interior to the springs of this garden, whence proceed rivers of gold that flow to the sea in so many parts of our conquest.

(João de Barros (Portugal, 1552))[1]

In June of 1797, a 25-year-old Scotsman surfaced unexpectedly at Pisania on the coast of West Africa, alone, destitute, and rather the worse for wear. His name was Mungo Park, and he had just spent a year and a half in the interior exploring the Niger basin. He was about to go back to England and write one of the most popular travel books of his time. Park had traveled in the employ of the London-based Association for Promoting the Discovery of the Interior Parts of Africa, known as the African Association for short. This alliance of aristocrats and wealthy businessmen, "including peers, baronets, members of Parliament, a retired general, and a bishop,"[2] was formed in 1788 under the leadership of Joseph Banks, and directed British exploration in West Africa for the next four decades. (Banks would be succeeded in 1815 by none other than John Barrow, whose youthful travels were discussed in the previous chapter.) At the Association's inaugural meeting "twelve well-to-do gentlemen" convened to lament that, in the words of their own manifesto,

Notwithstanding the progress of discovery on the coasts and borders of that base continent [i.e. Africa] the map of its interior is still but a wide extended blank, on which the geographer, on the authority of Leo Africanus and of the Xeriff of Edrissi the Nubian author, has traced with hesitating hand a few names of unexplored rivers and of uncertain nations. . . . Sensible of this stigma, and desirous of rescuing the age from a charge of ignorance, which, on other respects, belongs so little to its character, a few individuals, strongly impressed with a conviction of the practicability and utility of thus enlarging the fund of human knowledge, have formed the plan of an Association for Promoting the discovery of the interior parts of Africa.[3]

The emphasis on practicality, the absence of any mention of science, the image of human knowledge as a "fund" reflect the predominantly commercial aims of the African Association. The members were economic expansionists, interested in "legitimate commerce," that is, not colonization or settlement, and above all not the slave trade. Within two years, the Association had ninety-five members.

The project which the group initially assigned themselves proved so difficult that it was the only one they ever undertook: to ascertain the course, direction, source, and terminus of the Niger River, and to make commercial and diplomatic contact with those who peopled its vicinity. The founders had high hopes of the prospects that might await them. The Niger, Herodotus had proposed, might well flow east all the way across Africa to the Nile, providing a transcontinental trade route to the Mediterranean; especially since Leo Africanus, the Spanish Muslim whose *History and Description of Africa* appeared in 1550, Timbuktu had existed in European mental maps as a city of gold at the center of a wealthy and cultured kingdom.[4] Early reports had led Europeans to speculate that "the knowledge and language of ancient Egypt may still imperfectly survive" in the interior and that in some hidden region even the Carthaginians might be found, retaining "some portion of those arts and sciences, and of that commercial knowledge, for which the inhabitants of Carthage were once so eminently famed." The Association's emissaries were instructed, as Mungo Park was, not only to locate the Niger, but, to quote Park's orders, to "visit the principal towns or cities in its neighbourhood, particularly Tombuctoo and Haussa."[5]

The idea of a heavily populated African interior with established cities and states, commercial networks, and markets for British goods, contrasts with views of a few decades earlier when stereotypes determined by the slave trade governed European ideologies. In 1759, for example, the English translator of Adanson's *Voyage to Senegal* (France, 1756) introduced Africa as "a country overspread with misery" whose landscape consisted of "burning deserts, rivers and torrents" populated by "tigers, wildboars, crocodiles, serpents, and other savage beasts." The inhabitants, Negroes and Moors alike, are described as "poor and indolent," though "friendly and docile."[6] Thirty years later, such views were under challenge. The Danish physician Paul Isert, in his *Travels in Guinea and the Caribbean Islands of America* (1793), argued that proponents of slavery who saw Africans as "naturally lazy, obstinate, given to theft, drunkenness, all the vices" should travel in the African interior "if they sincerely want to be cured of their prejudices."[7] In 1782 the British editor of the celebrated letters of ex-slave Ignatius Sancho explained the literary talents of her subject in similar terms. "He who could penetrate the interior of Africa," she writes, "might not improbably discover negro arts and polity, which could bear little analogy to the ignorance and grossness of slaves in the sugar-islands, expatriated in infancy, and brutalized under the whip and the task-master."[8] As such speculations suggest, the reimagining of the African interior in the late eighteenth century coincided with the extraordinary acceleration of the anti-slavery movement after 1770 and the reconception of Africans as a market rather than a commodity. Indeed, the formation of the African Association followed by only a few months the founding of an equally historic entity, the Society for the Abolition of the Slave Trade. The famed member of parliament William Wilberforce held memberships in both.

It is hard to say which is more remarkable, the fact that Mungo Park embarked on his mission to the Niger or the fact that he survived it. His effort had been preceded by a series of dismal failures.[9] The Association's first emissary, Simon Lucas, had turned back 100 miles outside Tripoli; the second, an American named John Ledyard, died before he got out of Cairo; the third, Daniel Houghton, disguised as an Arab, joined a caravan into the desert, sent out a few thrilling messages, and disappeared at Bambouk in the Sahara. Yet domestic enthusiasm for the Niger venture never waned. By the time Park offered his services in 1794, the African Association still had close to 100 members from all over the continent (including a young German named Alexander von Humboldt, whose travels were yet to come), and had succeeded in persuading the British government to post a consul and fifty troops in Senegambia to assist trade development on the Niger and Gambia Rivers, wherever they proved to flow.

In December of 1795, Park headed inland from Pisania, the highest European outpost on the Gambia River, accompanied initially by a party of six that steadily dwindled to a single boy slave who had been promised his freedom on completing the journey, and finally disappeared altogether. Traveling east, Park moved through territory populated by the Mandingos (Muslim Africans, many of whose numbers fell victim to the slave trade), then into territory of the Fulani, whose empire stretched inland to include Timbuktu. Here among the dreaded Moors, as he tells it, Park's troubles began. He began to encounter bandits, warring nations, greedy kings; he was imprisoned and tormented for a month by a Fulani ruler named Ali, depicted in orientalist fashion as a model of corrupt absolutism. His release secured, Park headed south into the rival kingdom of Bambara, which straddled the Niger. At its capital, Segu, he at last sighted "the long sought for majestic Niger, glittering to the morning sun, as broad as the Thames at Westminster, and flowing slowly *to the eastward*."[10] Abandoning an attempt to press on to Timbuktu, Park, destitute and often starving, headed back for the coast, appending himself for much of the way to a slave coffle on whose charity he depended. He returned to Pisania a year and a half after leaving it – long after he had been given up for dead.

Park never did reach Timbuktu and did not find the Egyptians, the Carthaginians, or the remains of ancient Christian kingdoms. But he did reach the Niger and make the crucial observation that it flowed eastward, leaving open the invigorating possibility that it joined the Nile. (It does not.) Equally important, Park made firsthand contact with the large and prosperous Fulani and Bambara kingdoms of West Central Africa, confirming what an English commentator described as "the higher state of improvement and superior civilization of the inhabitants of the interior on a comparison with the inhabitants of the countries adjoining to the coast."[11] A humbling discovery for Europeans, perhaps, raising the question of what part they and their slave trade had in "lowering" the "state of improvement" of African society on the coast. Humbling in another way, too, for while Europe's state of improvement was such that it remained ignorant of the West and Central African societies, they, it turned out, had long since had contact with goods and knowledge from Europe.

Most important of all, Park lived to complete the return journey to England and convey his findings to his European sponsors. The Association's market fantasies took on a new intensity. "By Mr. Park's discoveries," they exulted,

> a gate is opened to every commercial nation to enter and trade from the west to the eastern extremity of Africa. . . . On due directions and exertions of British credit and enterprise, it is difficult to imagine the possible extent to which the demand for our country's manufactures might arrive, from such vast and populous countries.[12]

Park himself took credit for both geographical and commercial feats: "rendering the geography of Africa more familiar to my countrymen and . . . opening to their ambition and industry new sources of wealth and new channels of commerce."[13]

Heaven knows the new channels were needed, not to mention the boost in morale. The last decades of the eighteenth century had been a difficult time for European imperialism. Interior exploration was stymied by disease in much of the tropical world, and by indigenous resistance in others. The murder of Cook had shaken the idyllic Polynesian fantasy. In the Caribbean, it had taken several thousand British troops to finally expel the Carib Indians from their lands on St. Vincent – lands they had been granted by treaty.[14] The United States, of course, had won their independence, and other established colonial footholds were threatened as seldom before. In Spanish America independence movements were gathering momentum, some seeking British and French support. In the Andes, indigenous resistance to colonial rule intensified steadily. In 1781, a fullscale uprising of Andean indigenous populations had shaken Spain's colonial elites to the core. Since the 1770s maroon slave communities in Surinam had threatened the stability and viability of the plantation economy. In 1790, the slave revolt in Santo Domingo had overthrown French colonial rule and produced an independent, non-white government, with the entire Caribbean threatening to follow suit.[15] The shock of Santo Domingo was

I saw with infinite pleasure the great object of my mission,—the long sought for majestic Niger, glittering to the morning sun.—P. 176.

12 Frontispiece depicting Mungo Park's sighting of the Niger. From the 1860 edition of Park's *Travels in the Interior of Africa*.

so great as to stop the British abolition movement dead in its tracks – but only temporarily. The unrelenting momentum of abolitionism remained central to the sense of crisis, not only in Britain. Experiments in alternative imperial strategies produced depressing failures, such as the British attempts to colonize Sierra Leone with ex-slaves. The quest for the northwest passage was getting nowhere, and it was difficult to see what else was of value in the polar regions. As ever, European colonial powers found their treasuries sapped by conflicts with each other, as Eurocolonial footholds passed back and forth from the hands of one to another, footholds whose value (except for the slave trade) in many cases remained unclear, as interiors remained unknown.

But above all Euroimperialism faced a legitimation crisis. The histories of broken treaties, genocides, mass displacements and enslavements became less and less acceptable as rationalist and humanitarian ideologies took hold. Particularly after the French Revolution, contradictions between egalitarian, democratic ideologies at home and ruthless structures of domination and extermination abroad became more acute. Yet the demands of capital remained. Competition among Euroimperial nations would only intensify as capital expanded. And, as always, it was their own competition with each other that bound European powers together in finding new forms for Euroimperial interventions, and new legitimating ideologies: the civilizing mission, scientific racism, and technology-based paradigms of progress and development.

Not surprisingly, the imperial exultations of the African Association in response to Mungo Park's return were expressed in a language of racism and an image of remapping: "As the great continent of Africa, amidst its seas of sand, occasionally shews its Oasis . . . so in analogy to the face of the country, does the blank and torpid mind of its people, display occasionally notes of intelligence and philanthropy, rich spots of genius, and partial scenes of improved social establishment."[16] Those insulting words do not begin to suggest the impact of Park's travels/*Travels*. Even before his book appeared, the African Association knew it had a hit on its hands. "Park goes on triumphantly," declared the officer assigned to supervise his writing. "Some parts, which he has lately sent to me, are equal to anything in the English language."[17] The first edition of *Travels in the Interior Districts of Africa* appeared in April 1799, and its 1,500 copies sold out in a month. Two more editions appeared the same year; French and German translations, and an American edition, were out by 1800. Park was paid a thousand guineas – an index of the growing health of the travel literature industry. The book has been anthologized, excerpted, and re-edited constantly since then. Its dramatic scenes and unassuming style became touchstones for European traveler-writers for decades to follow.

Though invariably read as the "plain unvarnished tale" Park claimed it to be, Park's *Travels* richly exemplifies the eruption of the sentimental mode into European narrative of the contact zone at the end of the eighteenth century. Put the other way around, his book shows some of the ways the contact zone was recuperated by European sentimentality at a time when, as Peter Hulme so aptly puts it, "sentimental sympathy began to flow along the arteries of European commerce, in search of its victims."[18] In the next few pages, I propose to consider Park's text in more detail as an instance of sentimental travel writing on the imperial frontier. My reading will underscore points of contrast with scientific travel writing, as it was discussed in the last chapter. The aim is to suggest how sentimentality both challenges and complements the emergent authority of objectivist science. I then move on to other examples of the sentimental mode in an attempt to place sentimental travel writing in the context of late eighteenth-century crises in Euroimperialism, especially debates over slavery.

THE EXPERIENTIAL UNHERO

Though he certainly could have done so, Mungo Park did not write up a narrative of geographical discovery, observation, or collection, but one of personal experience and adventure. He wrote, and wrote himself, not as a man of science, but as a sentimental hero. He made himself the protagonist and central figure of his own account, which takes the form of an epic series of trials, challenges, and encounters with the unpredictable. Park makes his way across the West African interior from town to town and village to village, negotiating safe passage with one chieftain after another, trading trinkets for subsistence and protection. He moves vertically as well, down and up (mostly down) a social scale, from courtly encounters with princes to scenes of indigence where he begs for food from slaves. He traverses desert wildernesses, suffering the trials of thirst, beasts, and banditry. The following passage exemplifies the day-to-day narrative of Park's book:

> Next morning (March 10th) we set out for Samamingkoos. On the road we overtook a woman and two boys, with an ass; she informed us that she was going for Bambarra, but had been stopped on the road by a party of Moors, who had taken most of her clothes, and some gold from her; and that she would be under the necessity of returning to Deena till the fast moon was over. The same evening the new moon was seen, which ushered in the month Rhamadan. Large fires were made in different parts of the town, and a greater quantity of victuals than usual dressed upon the occasion.
>
> March 11. – By daylight, the Moors were in readiness; but as I had suffered much from thirst upon the road, I made my boy fill a soofroo of water for my own use; for the Moors assured me that they should not taste either meat or drink till sunset. However, I found that the excessive heat of the sun, and the dust we raised in travelling overcame their scruples, and made my soofroo a very useful part of our baggage.[19]

The textual space/time that corresponds to the space/time of traveling is filled with (made out of) human activity, interactions among the travelers themselves or with people they encounter. The pause to talk to the woman and two boys is recreated textually by a pause to reproduce her story, itself consisting of a human drama. Stops for the night are characterized not by where they are made, but by what people do there. There is no landscape description at all. Nature is present in so far as it impinges on the social world: the full moon starts Rhamadan; the dust and sun make everyone thirsty. Grammatically speaking, in Park's text, human agents abound, and there is a predominance of active verbal constructions, though passives do occur. The natural world relates actively with people: the moon *ushered in* Ramadan; the dust *overcame* people's scruples and *made* the soofroo useful.

The contrast with the scientific, informational travel writing discussed in the last chapter could hardly be more schematic. Park's book appeared, for example, within two years of John Barrow's *Travels*. As discussed above, the space/time of travel in Barrow's writing is textualized primarily by the linguistic rendering of the "face of the country" as seen by agents whose presence is effaced by the language of the text. Social interactions within Barrow's own party and between them and the local inhabitants are not dramatized, and at most are mentioned tangentially. For purposes of comparison, reconsider the passage from Barrow quoted on p. 59, condensed here for convenience:

> The following day we passed the Great Fish River, though not without some difficulty, the banks being high and steep, the stream strong, the bottom rocky, and the water deep. Some fine trees of the willow of Babylon, or a variety of that species, skirted the river at this place. The opposite side presented a very beautiful country, well wooded and watered. . . . The first night that we encamped in the Kaffir country was near a stream called Kowsha, which falls into the Great Fish River. On the following day we passed the villages of Malloo and Tooley, the two chiefs and brothers we had seen in Zuure Veldt, delightfully situated on two eminences rising from the said streamlet.

In Barrow's text, not unexpectedly, stative verbs and intransitive constructions abound: banks *are* high, villages *are situated*, things *are near* other things, banks *are wooded* and watered, eminences *rise* and streams *fall*. Active constructions render not actions but motionless spectacles: trees *skirt* the river, the bank *presents* a beautiful country. In keeping with bureaucratic/scientific practices of objectivism, the authority of Barrow's discourse resides in the detachment of what is said from the subjectivity of both the speaker and the experiencer. In Park it is the opposite. Sentimental writing explicitly anchors what is being expressed in the sensory experience, judgement, agency, or desires of the human subjects. Authority lies in the authenticity of somebody's felt experience. Predicates tend to be attached to situated observers, often by verbs of experience or mental process: the Moors *assured* Park of their *intent* to fast, but he *found* by experience that they did not.

With respect to the deictic anchoring of speech, the pronoun "I" is of course the element that most clearly marks the line of complementarity between science and sentiment. Consider, for instance, Park's account of a day of severe thirst. It may be compared with Barrow's account of the grassfire quoted in note 37 of the previous chapter (my italics):

[Two boys] showed *me* their empty water-skins and told *me* that they had seen no water in the woods. This account afforded *me* but little consolation; however it was in vain to repine, and *I* pushed on as fast as possible in hopes of reaching some watering-place in the course of the night. *My thirst* was by this time become insufferable, *my mouth* was parched and inflamed; a sudden dimness would frequently come over *my eyes*, with other symptoms of fainting; and *my horse* being very much fatigued, *I* began seriously to apprehend that *I* should perish of thirst. To relieve the burning pain in *my mouth and throat*, I chewed the leaves of different shrubs, but found them all bitter and of no service.[20]

It is hard to imagine a more responsive and self-dramatizing speaker. Park's own hopes and fears, and his own bodily experience, constitute the events and register their significance. The language of the emotions – *consolation, repine, hopes, insufferable* – assigns value to events. Information is textually relevant (has value) in so far as it bears upon the speaker-traveler and his quest. In scientific narrative, by contrast, information is relevant (has value) in so far as it attaches to goals and systems of knowledge institutionalized outside the text. In Park's *Travels*, the scene that generations of readers found by far the most memorable is one that absorbs the discourse of science into the narcissism of the sentimental. The scene, which graced the title page of the 1860 edition of Park's *Travels* (see plate 13), depicts his deepest moment of crisis, when, pillaged by bandits in hostile territory, he is left for dead in the desert. Finding himself "naked and alone, surrounded by savage animals, and men still more savage," Park confesses, "my spirits began to fail me." He is saved by a naturalist's epiphany:

At this moment, painful as my reflections were, the extraordinary beauty of a small moss, in fructification, irresistibly caught my eye. I mention this to show from what trifling circumstances the mind will sometimes derive consolation; for though the whole plant was not larger than the top of one of my fingers, I could not contemplate the delicate conformation of its roots, leaves, and capsula, without admiration. *Can that Being (thought I) who planted, watered, and brought to perfection, in this obscure part of the world, a thing which appears of so small importance, look with unconcern upon the situation and sufferings of creatures formed after his own image? – surely not!*[21]

The man of sensibility, in the hour of his need, looks *through* the language of science and finds the alternative spiritual understanding of nature as image of the divine. If John Barrow's invasion of the Bushman camp provoked a breakdown in the language of science, Park's emotional bootstrapping here is a triumph of the language of sentiment and its protagonist, the individual.

If, as I suggested earlier, the landscanning, self-effacing producer of information is associated with the panoptic apparatuses of the bureaucratic state, then this sentimental, experiential subject inhabits that self-defined "other" sector of the bourgeois world, the private sphere – home of desire, sex, spirituality, and the Individual. On the imperial frontier, if the former encodes state-based territorial ambitions, the latter, as I hope to suggest, embodies ideals not of domesticity, but of commerce and private enterprise. In many ways the two discourses could not be more different – but of course that is just the point. The two could not be more different because they are so much defined in terms of each other; they are complementary, and in their complementarity they stake out the parameters of emergent bourgeois hegemony. On the imperial frontier, the sentimental subject shares certain crucial characteristics with his scientific counterpart: Europeanness, maleness, and middle classness, of course, but also innocence and passivity. He, too, is the non-hero of an anti-conquest. As I hope to show through a reading of Park's book, European expansionism is as sanitized and mystified in the literature of sentiment as in the informational/scientific mode. Though he is positioned at the center of a discursive field rather than on the periphery, and though he is composed of a whole body rather than a disembodied eye, the sentimental protagonist, too, is constructed as a non-interventionist European presence. Things happen to him and he endures and survives. As a textual construct, his innocence lies less in self-effacement than in submissiveness and vulnerability, or the *display* of self-effacement. Mungo Park writes himself as a receptor, not an initiator, as devoid of desire as his scientific counterpart.

THE MYSTIQUE OF RECIPROCITY

Some of the most dramatic moments in Mungo Park's very dramatic travel account are the arrival scenes that punctuate his narrative at particularly frequent intervals. As I have discussed elsewhere,[22] arrival scenes are a convention of almost every variety of travel writing and serve as particularly potent sites for framing relations of contact and setting the terms of its

TRAVELS

IN

THE INTERIOR OF AFRICA

BY MUNGO PARK.

EDINBURGH:

ADAM AND CHARLES BLACK, NORTH BRIDGE.

MDCCCLX.

13 Title page, 1860 edition of Park's *Travels*, adorned by the famous scene in which Park despairs after losing everything to robbers.

representation. In the following example, Park recounts his arrival at a town one evening in search of food and lodging:

> This happened to be a feast day at Dalli, and the people were dancing before the Dooty's house. But when they were informed that a white man was come into town, they left off dancing, and came to the place where I lodged, walking in regular order, two and two, with the music before them. . . . They continued to dance and sing until midnight, during which time I was surrounded by so great a crowd as made it necessary for me to satisfy their curiosity by sitting still.[23]

The structure of this episode could be described as a mutual appropriation. Park's arrival interrupts the local ritual, which then reconstitutes itself around him. He appropriates and is simultaneously appropriated by the ritual, required to play a role to satisfy people's curiosity, in exchange for satisfying his own. His role is a passive one, however, in which his own agency and desire play little part. He does not predict eclipses, cure the sick, do card tricks, or become the man who would be king. This is not conquest, but anti-conquest. Nevertheless, there exists a "necessary" relationship between him and the villagers, not a vacuum or an abyss. Again the comparison with Barrow's *Travels* is instructive. Barrow recounts an analogous arrival scene:

> A great crowd of people of all descriptions flocked down on every side and followed us along the road. The weather being warm, the men had thrown aside their cloaks and were entirely naked. But the women reserved their cloaks of calf-skin, and their exertion to gratify their curiosity by the sight of the strangers, seemed to incommode them not a little.[24]

While the trope is the same, in Barrow's version Europeans and Africans (and men and women) remain in separate non-interacting spheres, each responsible for their own desires, intentions, and actions. The villagers incommode, exert, and gratify *themselves*. The European travelers, we assume, pass and see; nothing calls upon them to sit still and be seen. In Park's version, on the other hand, the two sides determine each other's actions and desires. Park sits still of "necessity" to satisfy the curiosity of the villagers, and in exchange they shelter and feed him. As a representation, the scene is governed by reciprocity.

Reciprocity, I propose to argue, is the dynamic that above all organizes Park's human-centered, interactive narrative. It is present sometimes as a reality achieved, but always as a goal of desire, a value. In the human encounters whose sequence makes up Park's narrative, what sets up drama and tension is almost invariably the desire to achieve reciprocity, to establish equilibrium through exchange. The encounters with local rulers, which are basic building blocks of the narrative, are above all negotiations in which Park tries to secure survival and safe passage in return for gifts of European goods. They are a struggle to find an equilibrium between the finiteness of Park's goods and the degree of greed exercised by his hosts. Even when pillaging and thievery have reduced Park to indigence and beggary, we always find him striving to reciprocate. When he is taken in by a slave as a charity case, he presents his "compassionate landlady" with "two of the four brass buttons which remained on my waistcoat, the only recompense I could give her."[25] On another revealing occasion a slave who asks him for food is told by the indigent Park that he has none to give. The man replies, "I gave you victuals when you was hungry. Have you forgot the man who brought you milk at Karankalla?" "I immediately recollected him," writes Park, "and begged some ground nuts from Karfa to give him as a return for his former kindness."[26] In the end, with no buttons left, Park enters his own body into exchange in order to complete his journey. Desperate, he meets a slave trader who is en route to the coast and promises him "the value of one prime slave" to be paid on turning Park over to his British contacts there.

Park's everyday struggles, then, consist mainly of attempts to achieve reciprocity between himself and others, or to endure its absence. It is here, I would suggest, that his account figures the commercial expansion in whose name he traveled and wrote. While in Barrow's narrative the territorial, colonizing aspirations of Euroimperialism are idealized into the depopulated face of the country, in Park's, expansionist commercial aspirations idealize themselves into a drama of reciprocity. Negotiating his way across Africa, Park is the picture of the entrepreneur. Yet the decidedly non-reciprocal momentum of European capitalism can scarcely be discerned in his lone and long-suffering figure, no matter how long you (the reader or the Africans) stare at him. Trade he does, but *never for profit*. Over and over the reader sees European commodities produce symbolic exchange and subsistence. At best, Park will emerge with nothing but his life – and his innocence.

More important, perhaps, he proves himself greater than all of it in the end. The epiphany brought on by the fructifying moss is a transcendent moment not because Park has survived, but because he has at last lost *everything*. He is no longer defined by European commodities. He has become that creature in whose viability and authenticity his readers may have longed to believe: the naked, essential, inherently powerful white man.

RECIPROCAL VISION

Commodities are not the only sites of exchange in Park's subject-centered account. In contrast with scientific travel writing, seeing itself operates along lines of reciprocity in his text. As the arrival scene quoted above suggests, in exchange for seeing Africa and Africans, Park repeatedly portrays himself as subjected to the scrutiny of the Africans. In a parodic reversal Park's portmanteau becomes a cabinet of curiosities for his African "travelees," while his body is surveyed simultaneously as a landscape and a zoological specimen:

> The surrounding attendants and especially the ladies were abundantly more inquisitive; they asked a thousand questions, inspected every part of my apparel, searched my pockets and obliged me to unbutton my waistcoat, and display the whiteness of my skin; they even counted my toes and fingers, as if they doubted whether I was in truth a human being.[27]

As the passage suggests, the reciprocal seeing is organized along lines of gender, and determined by that great sentimental obsession, transracial erotics. While African men are the chief objects of Park's own seeing, African women are special agents for the viewing of Park. The scene quoted above begins with Park's approach to the despot Ali, who is looking at himself in a mirror held by a female attendant. Ali loses interest in Park when he finds he knows no Arabic; Park then becomes the object of the female gaze, whose aggressive voyeurism feminizes him in the process – another anti-conquest.

Often, such female scrutiny is the price Park pays for food. At a Mandingo court, he is turned over to the King's entire seraglio for inspection, where the imperative for reciprocity asserts itself in a comic-erotic fashion. The women tease Park, insisting that the whiteness of his skin and "the prominency of [his] nose" are artificial. "On my part," says Park, "without disputing my own deformity, I paid them many compliments on African beauty."[28] On another occasion, a crisis arises when a party of women pay Park a visit whose object is to "ascertain, by actual inspection, whether the rite of circumcision extended to the Nazarenes." Park extricates himself by insisting on a kind of reciprocity:

> I observed to them that it was not customary in my country to give ocular demonstration in such cases, before so many beautiful women; but that if all of them would retire, except the young lady to whom I pointed (selecting the youngest and handsomest), I would satisfy her curiosity. The ladies enjoyed the jest, and went away laughing heartily; and the young damsel herself . . . sent me some meal and milk for my supper.[29]

Seraglio scenes such as these owe a great deal to the conventions of the orientalist writing that flourished in Europe in the eighteenth century. As in Montesquieu's famed *Persian Letters*, much of the comedy lies in parodic reversals of Eurocentered power relations and cultural norms, especially norms about seeing and being seen. My interest here, however, is first in the particularly interactive character of Park's use of these tropes, and second, in how they are used to confirm his position as anti-conqueror.

The imperative of reciprocity extends to knowledge and culture as well. Park often takes pains to report the Africans' reactions to him as well as his to them, and to affirm the commensurability of European and African lifeways, different though they may be. His account includes many instances in which the two are very deliberately juxtaposed with what one might call "reciprocal vision."[30] On one occasion, for example, Park's medical skills are called on, and he proposes an amputation to save a young man shot in the leg. The Africans respond in horror. "They evidently considered me as a sort of cannibal for proposing so cruel and unheard of an operation, which in their opinion would be attended with more pain and danger than the wound itself."[31] Indigenous healing practices are followed, and the patient is prepared for death. Park voices no criticism of the decision to reject the European cure, nor does he attempt to counter it with commentary of his own. Rather, the reader is enabled to accept that the Africans' view of amputation is as plausible as Park's view that the patient will die without it.

It is no accident that this ideological exchange occurs around what had proven to be (and remains) one of the most effective tools of Euro-expansionism, western medicine. At a time when medicine was proving to be one of Europe's points of leverage – with the Islamic world in particular, whose rulers often summoned European physicians to tend them – Park suggests an agnostic stance on the issue. His failure to assert the superiority of European medicine over African "superstition" has blatantly equalitarian implications here, calling into question a commonplace of imperial ideology. Other instances of reciprocal vision do the same. On one occasion, for example, a group of slaves en route to the coast tell Park they believe they will be sold to be eaten. They reject Park's explanation that they are being sent off to do agricultural labor. Rather than ridiculing or rejecting their view, Park respects its plausibility, commenting only that such a belief "naturally makes the slave contemplate a journey towards the coast with great terror."[32] The question of whether slavery is the equivalent of cannibalism remains open. Sometimes Park constructs analogies to make sense of African practices in terms of English ones. To explain the Mandingoes' penchant for robbing him of his goods, for example, he reverses the racial and geographical polarities: "Let us suppose a black merchant of Hindostan to have found his way into the centre of England, with a box of jewels at his back, and that the laws of the kingdom afforded him no security . . ."[33]

One incongruity Park repeatedly addresses through reciprocal vision is that of his own presence in Africa, a matter on which he portrays Africans repeatedly challenging him. One king, "when he was told that I had come from a great distance, and through many dangers, to behold the Joliba River, naturally inquired if there were no rivers in my own country, and whether one river was not like another."[34] Another, on hearing Park's account of himself, seems "but half satisfied." "The notion of traveling for curiosity, was new to him," says Park. "He thought it impossible, he said, that any man in his senses would undertake so dangerous a journey merely to look at the country and its inhabitants." On one reading, these puzzled African interlocutors open to question the very structuring principle of the anti-conquest: the claim to the innocent pursuit of knowledge. On another reading, they reinforce Park's anti-conquest – the Africans in the end do not find him threatening, just daft. In the episode just quoted, Park re-establishes the innocence of his sightseeing by offering the "half-satisfied" King a sight in return, or rather a non-sight. To prove he does not aim to encroach on local commerce, Park shows the King the scanty contents of his portmanteau. "He was convinced; and it was evident that his suspicion had arisen from a belief that every white man must of necessity be a trader."[35] Park and his reader know, of course, that the King is not far wrong. Park recovers his innocence at the cost of displaying, through the African King's "mis"-perception, the imperialists' inevitable bad faith.

Park's reciprocal vision, and his manner of calling forth contradictions of Euroexpansionist ideology, have surely contributed to the effect of verisimilitude and reliability his book has produced in its many generations of readers. Throughout the nineteenth century, reviewers of each new edition praised Park's humility and truthfulness.[36] The spell has lasted. The eminent contemporary Africanist Philip Curtin expresses himself in the same terms: "He [Park] simply told what he had seen, without arrogance, without special pleading and (since he was not a scholar) without interpretation."[37] Though the naiveté may be misplaced, the admiration is not. In comparison with a great many other travelers, especially some of the Victorians who followed him, Park affirms plausible worlds of African agency and experience. His relational approach to culture raises genuine possibilities of critical self-questioning. At the same time, though they are relativized, or even parodied, European ideologies are never questioned directly. Park's book owes much of its power to this combination of humanism, egalitarianism, and critical relativism anchored securely in a sense of European authenticity, power, and legitimacy.

Reciprocity has always been capitalism's ideology of itself. In his compelling study of sentimental literature on the colonial frontier, Peter Hulme makes this point, recalling Marcel Mauss's classic analysis of reciprocity in *The Gift*. Mauss argues that in stateless, non-capitalist societies reciprocity functions as the basis for social interaction, even in radically hierarchical social formations such as feudalism. In Hulme's words, "only under the fetishized social relations of capitalism does reciprocity disappear altogether, however loudly its presence is trumpeted."[38] While doing away with reciprocity as the basis for social interaction, capitalism retains it as one of the stories it tells itself about itself. The difference between equal and unequal exchange is suppressed. Marx makes the point somewhat more broadly in a famous passage from *Capital*:

The sphere of circulation or commodity exchange, within whose boundaries the sale and purchase of labour-power goes on, is in fact a very Eden of the innate rights of man. It is the exclusive realm of Freedom, equality, Property and Bentham. Freedom, because both buyer and seller of a commodity, let us say of labour-power, are determined only by their own free will. They contract as free persons, who are equal before the law. Their contract is the final result in which their joint will finds a common legal expression. Equality because each enters into relation with the other, as with a simple owner of commodities, and they exchange equivalent for equivalent. Property, because each disposes only of what is his own. And Bentham, because each looks only to his own advantage. The only force bringing them together, and putting them into relation with each other, is the selfishness, the gain and the private interest of each. Each pays heed to himself only, and no one worries about the others. And precisely for that reason, either in accordance with the pre-established harmony of things, or under the auspices of an omniscient providence, they all work together to their mutual advantage, for the common weal, and in the common interest.[39]

These are the concepts, says Marx, which provide the "free-trader *vulgaris*" with "his views, his concepts and the standards by which he judges the society of capital and wage-labour." In a number of respects, this is the utopia we watch Park try to bring into being wherever he goes in Africa. The obstacles to the utopia are, of course, not European but African. African greed, African banditry, African slave trading threaten the mystique of reciprocity at every turn – and they are the only points on which Park does not reciprocate. He would rather die than steal. Can the Africans become that good too? Through his anti-conquest, Park acts out the values that underwrote the greatest non-reciprocal non-exchange of all time: the Civilizing Mission.

Thanks to malaria, yellow fever, and dysentery, the exploration of the Niger River sputtered for the next five decades until Dr. William Baikie decided to test the effectiveness of quinine against the deadly fevers that had cut short all dreams of expansion in the region. As a literary phenomenon the Niger effort was quite a success, however. It produced a lively, well-read exploration literature, much of it written along the colorful lines laid down by Park's *Travels*. Sentimental plot lines of hard luck and victimization proved very suitable for rendering the sufferings and failures of one Niger expedition after another; and the lone European protagonist indeed proved to be the only one who could stay alive in the region.[40] Failing to follow his own precedent, Mungo Park lost his life in 1806 when he returned to the Niger at the head of a large, highly militarized expedition that came out shooting, and disappeared down to the last man. The African Association, its membership reduced to fourteen, was absorbed into the Royal Geographical Society in 1831.

Chapter 5

Eros and abolition

Sentimentality and *sensibilité* began asserting themselves in travel writing about the same time science did, from the 1760s on. By the time Mungo Park's *Travels* appeared in 1799, it found readerships already primed on sentimental dramatizations of the contact zone, many of them generated by the abolitionist movement. Sex and slavery are great themes of this literature. Or a single great theme, perhaps, for the two invariably appear together in allegorical narratives that invoke conjugal love as an alternative to enslavement and colonial domination, or as newly legitimated versions of them.

Sentimental travel writing drew, as Park's account did, on older traditions of what I have been calling survival literature – first-person stories of shipwrecks, castaways, mutinies, abandonments, and (the special inland version) captivities. Popular since Europe's first wave of expansion in the late fifteenth century, this literature continued to flourish in its own right in the eighteenth century, as it does today. Though its lowbrow sensationalism was challenged by the bourgeois forms of authority I have been discussing in this book, popular survival literature benefited from the growth of mass print culture. Survivors returning from shipwrecks or captivities could finance their fresh start by writing up their stories for sale in inexpensive pamphlets or collections. In 1759, for example, the *Monthly Review* announced the availability of a fourth edition "with considerable improvements" of *French and Indian Cruelty: Exemplified in the Life, and Various Vicissitudes of Fortune, of Peter Williamson*, in which the reader is promised accounts of Williamson's kidnapping as a child, and his life as a slave, planter, Indian captive, and volunteer soldier, as well as of "Scalping, Burning, and other Barbarities," all at one shilling. Adds the *Monthly Review*: "We imagine the story of Peter Williamson to be, in general, matter of fact with a few pardonable embellishments by the hand of some literary friend. It is printed for the benefit of the unfortunate Author."[1]

Survival literature had already developed the themes of sex and slavery that would engage sentimental writers so intensely at the end of the eighteenth century. Many were the captives and castaways who lived only by becoming slaves of heathens and infidels. (In the eighteenth century European governments still had – and needed – a system for ransoming enslaved captives from the Arabs in North Africa. Contemporary hostage-taking in Arab countries reflects this tradition.) Many were the captives (and runaways) who became husbands, wives, or concubines of their captors. Throughout the history of early Eurocolonialism and the slave trade, survival literature furnished a "safe" context for staging alternate, relativizing, and taboo configurations of intercultural contact: Europeans enslaved by non-Europeans, Europeans assimilating to non-European societies, and Europeans cofounding new transracial social orders. The context of survival literature was "safe" for transgressive plots, since the very existence of a text presupposed the imperially correct outcome: the survivor survived, and sought reintegration into the home society. The tale was always told from the viewpoint of the European who returned.

In part through the rise of the abolitionist movement, and in part through the rise of travel literature as a profitable print industry, sentimentality consolidated itself quite suddenly in the 1780s and 1790s as a powerful mode for representing colonial relations and the imperial frontier. In both travel writing and imaginative literature, the domestic subject of empire found itself enjoined to share new passions, to identify with expansion in a new way, through empathy with individual victim-heroes and heroines.[2] Not surprisingly, such empathetic, subjectivist rhetorics were seen as at odds with the authority of science. Review literature teemed with discussions of how travel books ought to be written in an enlightened age, the two main tensions being between "naive" (popular) and lettered writing, and between informational and experiential writing. Stylistic debates as to relative values of "embellishment" and "naked truth" often reflected tensions between the man of science and the man of sensibility, or between the lettered and popular writer. An eroticized vocabulary of nakedness, embellishment, dress, and undress introduced the desires of readers into the discussion. In 1766, before the sentimental onrush, a book of travels on the Middle East by Linnaeus' disciple Hasselquist inspired the *Monthly Review* to celebrate the superiority of "men of science" over "men of fortune," who merely "transport themselves from country to country and town to town without speculation or improvement."[3] At the same time one finds ambivalence about the language that made books like Hasselquist's believable but often tedious to read. The reviewer goes on to regret Hasselquist's apparent lack of "talent for literary composition":

His remarks are cursorily set down, without great regard to order or system; and have the appearance of a mere journal, published in the same negligent undress in which it was originally written, in the very course of the travels to which they relate. – But a naked beauty is not perhaps the less engaging for the want of ornaments, which sometimes only serve to obscure those charms they were intended to embellish.[4]

Naked beauty or negligent undress? The reader–text relation is encoded in the same masculinist and eroticized terms that encoded the European traveler's relation to the exotic countries he visited.

Thirty years later the same periodical, reviewing John Owen's *Travels into Different Parts of Europe*, was pleased to report that "the method of writing books of voyages and travels has, of late years, received considerable improvement. Formerly, most publications of this kind were mere journals of occurrences, loaded with tedious minuteness of detail, and seldom enlivened by ingenious remarks, or embellished with the graces of style." Now, however, one finds "many productions that, on account of the manner in which they are written, independently of the information they contain, may be perused with pleasure by the scholar and the man of taste." The change has been in the direction of pleasure. For this 1790s reviewer, the potential for weakness in Mr. Owen's account lies not in lack of embellishment, but in lack of sex and sentiment, for Owen is a Protestant minister. In a statement perhaps meant as much to warn as to reassure, the reviewer found that "though the writer has both in sentiment and language uniformly preserved the decorum of the clerical character, his work contains so much interesting matter, that there is no danger of its incurring censure for insipidity or dullness."[5]

Embellishment had not always been so welcome, nor sentiment either. John Hawkesworth caused loud controversy in England in the 1770s when, assigned to edit accounts of the first Cook expedition, he took it on himself to meld them together into a single first-person account, full of his own embellishments. If required to write simply "in the name of the several commanders," he argued, "I could exhibit only a naked narrative, without any opinion or sentiment of my own."[6] The debate surrounding Hawkesworth's intervention was not only about embellishment, but about editors and ghostwriters. Travel literature did not remain immune to the professionalization of writing in the eighteenth century. Now that it had become a profitable business, traveler-writers and their publishers relied more and more on professional writers and editors to ensure a competitive product, often transforming manuscripts completely, usually in the direction of the novel. Debates about embellishment, seductiveness, naked truth, and the like are often debates about the role of these figures, and the compromises involved in writing for money. The *Monthly Review* found a 1771 survival tale, *The Shipwreck and Adventures of Mons. Pierre Viaud*, "considerably injured by embellishment," as evidenced by such implausible episodes as the author's "meeting with tygers and lions in the woods of North America." M. Viaud's account is redeemed to some degree, however, "by the certificate assessed to it . . . signed by Lieut Swettenham."[7]

No embellisher irritated the scientific establishment more than François Le Vaillant, one of the wave of naturalists who, as discussed in the last chapter, began exploring the interior of southern Africa at the end of the eighteenth century. As mentioned above, the literature on the Cape Colony was an influential one in forming European paradigms for scientific travel and travel writing. Le Vaillant was and remains today a thorn in its objectivist side. An expert naturalist, he joined the South African effort, and spent the years 1781–5 following the footsteps of Anders Sparrman and others. He built up an immense collection of specimens which he later struggled, in the midst of the French Revolution, to sell to various European governments. But in his two-volume *Voyages dans l'intérieur de l'Afrique*, which appeared in 1790 (three more volumes followed in 1796), he proved an ambiguous friend to the cause of science and information. Though generous in botanical, zoological and ethnographic information, Le Vaillant's travel book is saturated with Rousseauian *sensibilité*. Like Mungo Park, whom he surely influenced, Le Vaillant produced an explicitly experiential, narcissistic narrative structured around human dramas of which he is the protagonist. The mode is easily recognized in the following excerpt describing a wet night in camp (my translation):

> We left the woods immediately to try to settle ourselves higher, on open ground. I say with the most bitter distress that it was not possible to leave the place in which we were trapped. The little streams which earlier had seemed so merry and delightful, had become furious torrents that carried off the sand, the trees, the croppings of rock; I felt that it was impossible to cross them except at the greatest risk. In another spot, my oxen, cold and harassed, had deserted my camp. I knew not where or how to send someone to recover them. My situation was certainly not at all amusing; I experienced great distress. Already my poor Hottentots, tired and sick, had begun to murmur.[8]

From start to finish Le Vaillant, like Park, is very much the hero of his own story. Here, too, reciprocity and exchange are central axes of an overwhelmingly human drama, played out in a non-capitalist world ruled by hospitality and warfare. A relativist, egalitarian spirit is asserted; Rousseauian noble savagery and *sensibilité* abound, at least some of it added in by Le Vaillant's editorial assistant, a young man named, romantically enough, Casimir Varon.[9]

Le Vaillant's narrative was irrevocably sensationalized by one drama particularly unprecedented in the South Africa corpus: a love affair between himself and a young Gonacqua (Khoikhoi) woman named Narina. The relationship is the focus of several chapters during which Le Vaillant visits among the Gonacqua people. While Mungo Park portrays himself as the involuntary erotic object of the African women, Le Vaillant becomes a smitten suitor pursuing the object of his desire. The discoverer turns voyeur as he hides in the bushes to watch Narina and her companions bathe in the river, then steals their clothes.[10] The erotic drama is represented as simple and good-humored on all sides, and no hearts get broken. The episode contributed greatly to the sensation Le Vaillant's book caused among European readerships, at a time when transracial love stories were becoming a theme in fiction as well.[11]

Le Vaillant's account was both widely read and "vivement attaqué," as his 1932 prefacer puts it. Following the French edition of his *Travels* in 1789, there came three English editions in 1790, and one in German; a Dutch edition followed in 1791, while the Italian edition of all five volumes appeared in 1816–17, attesting to the enduring interest in the work, despite unrelenting criticism of its style and unreliability. For his objectivist contemporaries, like John Barrow, Le Vaillant's dramatism, narcissism and eroticism offended as much as his inaccuracies. Present-day commentators tend to agree.[12]

Le Vaillant is universally read as a French writer, but it is surely pertinent to note that he was actually a white creole from the Caribbean, a product of the contact zone. He was born on a plantation in Surinam, the son of a French consul from Metz and his French wife. The family moved to France when Le Vaillant was around 10 years old. It was during his plantation boyhood that Le Vaillant developed his strong vocation and precocious expertise as a naturalist. Indeed, his experience of colonial life and his knowledge of Dutch helped authorize him for South African travel. The story of Narina draws on interracial social and sexual institutions (such as "Suriname marriage" – see below) that Le Vaillant would certainly have witnessed in the Caribbean, as well as a kind of erotic drama that had long been present in European imaginings of the Americas. Le Vaillant's experience of multiracial colonial society must certainly have shaped both his relationships with people in southern Africa and his portrayal of them in the *Travels*, though there is no systematic way to assess the extent to which this is so. Much remains to be learned about the extent to which creoles, from the Americas, Africa, or Asia, participated in the dialogues that gave rise to both colonialist and anti-colonialist doctrines, not just in the eighteenth century, but from the beginnings of the European colonialisms that produced them. On the whole, an imperial tendency to see European culture emanating out to the colonial periphery from a self-generating center has obscured the constant movement of people and ideas in the other direction, particularly during the periods of the Enlightenment and Romanticism (see chapters 6 and 8 below).[13]

FROM NARINA TO JOANNA

Not coincidentally, Le Vaillant's native Surinam was the setting for a travel book that a few years later dramatically intensified the eroticization of the contact zone. Few travel accounts have received more enthusiastic international reception (and promotion) than John Stedman's *Narrative of a Five Years' Expedition against the Revolted Negroes of Surinam*, which captured imaginations all across Europe for thirty years after its appearance in 1796.[14]

Published lavishly in two volumes with 80 engravings, including 16 by William Blake, Stedman's *Narrative* is a vivid discursive compendium interweaving the whole repertoire of eighteenth-century European encodings of the imperial frontier: ethnography, natural history, military reminiscence, hunting stories, social description, survival tales, anti-slavery critique, and interracial love. The combination makes his book "one of the most detailed 'outsider's' descriptions ever written of life in an eighteenth century plantation society."[15] The polyphony seems to have been intentional. Referring to his book as "perhaps one of the most singular productions ever offered to the Public," Stedman describes it in his preface as arranged "somewhat like a large garden, where one meets with the sweet-smelling flower and the thorn, the gold-bespangled fly and loathsome reptile," in hopes that the whole will be "so variegated as to afford . . . both information and amusement."[16] In the forty years following its first appearance, the book was translated into German (1797), French (1798), Dutch (1799), Swedish (1800), and Italian (1818); its love plot was played and replayed as drama, poetry, story, and novel.

John Stedman was a Scotsman who inherited his father's commission as an officer in the Scots Brigade of the Dutch Army.[17] Born in 1744, he seems to have taken emerging modern individualism very seriously. He worked hard at fashioning himself as a kind of gentleman *picaro*; in his diary he wrote of modeling himself on Roderick Random, Tom Jones, and Bamfylde Moore Carew, an English boy who ran away and joined the gypsies. As a writer his idol was Laurence Sterne. (Much to his chagrin, and over his vigorous objections, much of the Sternian character was edited out of his manuscript, while some of its sentimentality was edited in.)

Stedman went to Surinam in 1773 as a volunteer in a military expedition that was responding to a crisis in the colonial exploitation system. For a number of reasons, including the geography of the region, slaves in Surinam had found it possible to escape in large numbers into the dense forests, where their recapture was very difficult. By the mid-eighteenth century, two full-fledged maroon societies, the Saramakas and the Djukas, had established themselves in the interior and become engaged in an ongoing war of terror with plantation owners. Unable to defeat the maroon communities, in the 1760s the plantation owners were forced to sign peace treaties with them, which included guarantees of their independence in exchange for commitments that they would not assist any further runaways. The results were disastrous to plantation owners. News of the pact accelerated slave defections astronomically, and within a few years the entire plantation economy of Surinam was in jeopardy because of the impossibility of retaining slave labor forces. In 1773 the Dutch government came to their aid, sending the mission of which Stedman was a part to rout the new maroon groups and restore them to slavery. The campaign ended in 1778, when the rebel maroons abandoned the area for French Guiana. It was a pyrrhic victory in which few slaves were recovered, while European forces demonstrated their incompetence at jungle warfare. European loss of life in the campaign ran above 80 per cent, most of it due to sickness. The descendants of the maroon communities, still called the Saramakas, still live in the region today and retain the distinctive Afro-American culture they developed in the eighteenth century.

Much of Stedman's account of his years in Surinam is devoted to vivid narration of the disorganized, dismally equipped jungle warfare, which turned out to be utterly ineffective against the maroons, while most effective at exposing the European soldiers to tropical diseases. Stedman narrates their miseries in woeful detail, interspersing the sufferings with detailed but resolutely non-technical descriptions of flora and fauna, often occasioned by hunting forays or food preparation. It is thus through the military campaign that Stedman ties himself to the new age of interior travel. While Surinam, he says in his introduction, has long been known "so far as it is inhabited and cultivated by Europeans near the sea-coast," natural obstacles have made interior exploration impossible. Only the necessity of a military campaign has "forced [it] upon my observation."[18]

Between expeditions against the maroons, Stedman lived in the heart of Dutch colonial society, whose workings he describes in dramatic and often unflattering detail. In fact, his disparaging descriptions of Dutch plantation owners, idle, sadistic, and overfed, coincide point for point with Barrow's worst depictions of the Afrikaners. It would be difficult to say which aspect of his book caused greater sensation in Europe: the lurid, and luridly illustrated, denunciations of Dutch cruelty to their slaves, or his idealized romance *and marriage* with the mulatta slave Joanna. The abolitionist movement made ample use of the dramatic engravings (especially Blake's) depicting the horrors of slavery; the love story generated a romantic literary progeny that includes a German play by Franz Kratter titled *Die Sklavin in Surinam* (1804), an 1824 story "Joanna or the Female Slave" published in London, Eugène Sue's novel *Adventures d'Hercule Hardi* (Paris, 1840), and the Dutch novels *Een levensteeken op een dodenveld* by Herman J. de Ridder (1857), and *Boni* by Johan Edwin Hokstam (1983).[19] I propose to examine Stedman's love plot here, as a re-vision of colonial relations at a moment of acute crisis in plantation society.

As Stedman tells it, he met the 15-year-old Joanna shortly after his arrival in Surinam, at the home of a colonist where she was a house slave and a family favorite. He was instantly smitten by her beauty and charm, both embellished by a state of relative undress. The explanation of her origins is as good a parable as one might find of the intricacies of colonial sex and race relations. Joanna is the daughter of a "respectable gentleman" and a woman slave who bore five children with him. The gentleman, who was not the

14 "A rebel negro armed and on his guard." From John Stedman's *Narrative of a Five Years' Expedition against the Revolted Negroes of Surinam* (1796).

March thro' a swamp or Marsh in Terra firma

15 "March thro' a swamp or, Marsh in Terra firma." From Stedman's *Narrative* (1796).

owner of his concubine, had attempted to buy his children's manumission, but was refused by their owner and died of heartbreak. The ungenerous (and ungentlemanly) slave owner himself then went bankrupt, "having driven all his best carpenter negroes to the woods by his injustice and severity." Fleeing to Holland, he left his wife behind to be arrested for his debts. This lady now lived, attended by Joanna, in the home where Stedman met her. Joanna's own fate remained uncertain, for she was one of the assets which would eventually be liquidated to pay off the slave owner's debts. On hearing one day that this hideous event might indeed be about to happen, Stedman runs to Joanna's side, frantic with anxiety: "I found her bathed in tears. – She gave me such a look – ah! such a look! – From that moment I determined to be her protector against every insult."[20]

On the spot Stedman makes the "strange determination" to buy and educate Joanna, and return with her to England. Joanna refuses his proposal, on the grounds, persuasively expressed, that in her enslaved state, "should I [Stedman] soon return to Europe she must either be parted from me for ever, or accompany me to a part of the world where the inferiority of her condition must prove greatly to the disadvantage of both herself and her benefactor, and thus in either case be miserable."[21] Stedman falls sick, and when Joanna comes to see him with her sister, her reservations have been mysteriously overcome. She does not agree to go to England and be educated, but does "throw herself at his feet" for the time being, "till fate shall part us" or her conduct displease him. Stedman recovers, and they are married at "a decent wedding . . . at which I was as happy as any bridegroom ever was."[22]

The couple's life together includes an edenic interlude in a rural cottage (built for them by slaves), and the birth of a son who is baptized Johnny. Periods together alternate with separations as Stedman returns to the jungle or Joanna to her plantation. When Stedman's regiment is recalled to Europe, he again importunes Joanna to come with him, and she again refuses. Stedman leaves without her, promising to send money. Five years later, married in England to someone else, he receives news of Joanna's death, apparently by poisoning at the hands of people envious of her prosperity and distinction. Their son arrives in England with two hundred pounds accumulated by his mother, and later dies at sea as a young sailor. Stedman closes his book with an elegy to the lost son, and a tearful farewell to the reader, who, it is hoped, has been able to "peruse this narrative with sympathetic sensibility."[23]

Stedman's marriage to Joanna, like many transracial love affairs in the fiction of this time, is a romantic transformation of a particular form of colonial sexual exploitation, whereby European men on assignment to the colonies bought local women from their families to serve as sexual and domestic partners for the duration of their stay. In Africa and the Caribbean, and probably elsewhere, such arrangements could be officially sanctioned by formal ceremonies of pseudo-marriage, for which consular permission (from people like Le Vaillant's father) was sometimes required. In 1782, for example, the Danish traveler Paul Isert described the system in detail for the Guinea Coast, noting that such concubinage was considered essential to the Europeans' survival, since the women knew how to prepare local food and medicine, and could tend Europeans when they were sick.[24] Sentimental travel writing converts this function into the beneficent female figure of the "nurturing native," who tends to the suffering European out of pity, spontaneous kindness, or erotic passion. She is a key figure in this sentimental version of the anti-conquest.

In his diary, discussed by Richard Price and Sally Price, Stedman in fact reports his partnership with Joanna as just such an arrangement of formal concubinage. She was acquired from her family, after some negotiating about the price, and became one of many sexual partners Stedman disposed of in Surinam. Traces of this arrangement remain in the romanticized version of the book, most of them expressed by or through Joanna rather than Stedman. Her unexpected appearance at his lodgings "in the company of her sister," for example, corresponds to a real-life negotiating session, recorded in Stedman's diary.[25] In the published travel account, the concubinage system seems to be articulated above all through Joanna's awareness of it, and systematic resistance to it. From the beginning Joanna objects to the match, for instance, making clear she knows the arrangement is provisional, regardless of what Stedman says. While he does not mention buying Joanna's services, Stedman recounts buying her gifts in the amount of twenty guineas – but the day after their betrothal she returns them and presents him with the money, insisting on the reality of her status as slave and wife. His love and good treatment are all she wants, she tells him. When offered the alternative of going to England as Stedman's wife, Joanna refuses in terms that pinpoint the dehumanizing side of his egalitarian and humanitarian proposal. Here is Stedman's rendering of her (supposed) exact words (my italics):

> That, dreadful as appeared the fatal separation, perhaps never more to meet, yet she could not but prefer remaining in Surinam: first from a consciousness that, with propriety, she had not the disposal of herself [she is still a slave]; and secondly, from pride, wishing in her present condition rather to be *one of the first of her own class in America, than a reflection or burthen on me in Europe* as she was convinced must be the case, *unless our circumstances became one day more independent.*[26]

As Peter Hulme has so perceptively discussed, the transracial love stories that proliferated in late eighteenth-century narrative were shaped in many ways by antecedents in classical expansionist literature, notably the *Odyssey* and the *Aeneid*. The story of Dido and Aeneas, for example, is an antecedent for the couple of the nurturing native and beleaguered traveler, and the pattern of loving and leaving.[27] At the same time, these plots respond to late eighteenth-century crises in European imperialism as it found itself stymied on new fronts by tropical disease and local resistance, and challenged on old fronts by independence movements, abolitionism, declines in the profitability of slavery, and indigenous and slave rebellions of unprecedented scale and effectiveness. Stedman's account was read, for example, in the immediate context of the Santo Domingo slave revolt of 1791, a bloody and terrifying event whose success seems singlehandedly to have paralyzed the abolitionist movement for several years. The legitimation crisis provoked by abolitionism and American wars of independence called for imagining worlds beyond slavery and military conquest. It is easy to see transracial love plots as imaginings in which European supremacy is guaranteed by affective and social bonding; in which sex replaces slavery as the way others are seen to belong to the white man; in which romantic love rather than filial servitude or force guarantee the willful submission of the colonized. Joanna and Stedman are imaginary substitutes for Friday and Crusoe. In the transformation a fundamental dimension of colonialism disappears, namely, the exploitation of labor. The Joannas, like the Fridays, are property, yet they are not possessed for their labor power. The allegory of romantic love mystifies exploitation out of the picture.

If the transracial love plots articulate "the ideal of cultural harmony through romance," to use Hulme's well-chosen words,[28] what makes the ideal an ideal is once again the mystique of reciprocity. As an ideology, romantic love, like capitalist commerce, understands itself as reciprocal. Reciprocity, love requited between individuals worthy of each other, is its ideal state. The failure of reciprocity, or of equivalence between parties, is its central tragedy and scandal. Just as Mungo Park's journey is acted out in dramas of exchange, so is Stedman's romance with Joanna. The lovers' dialogues frequently consist of heartfelt exchanges as to what counts in return for what. Joanna sends Stedman a basket of fruit to help him recover from the "depression of spirits" into which he falls on learning of her situation. That gesture, he later argues, indebts him to her for life, making his *debt* to her the basis for his *claim* upon her. Just as Mungo Park's gift exchanges are an ideological recapitulation of the aspirations of commerce, in whose name he travels, so Stedman's reciprocal romance with Joanna recapitulates white aspirations in the Americas in an era of egalitarian values. While the lovers challenge colonial hierarchies, in the end they acquiesce to them. Reciprocity is irrelevant.

Such is the lesson to be learned from the colonial love stories, in whose dénouements the "cultural harmony through romance" always breaks down. Whether love turns out to be requited or not, whether the colonized lover is female or male, outcomes seem to be roughly the same: the lovers are separated, the European is reabsorbed by Europe, and the non-European dies an early death. The fate of Joanna and Stedman, for example, differs only slightly from the fate of another famous couple whose story achieved

Joanna.

16 "Joanna." From Stedman's *Narrative* (1796).

A Negro hung alive by the Ribs to a Gallows.

17 "A negro hung alive by the ribs to a gallows." From Stedman's *Narrative* (1796).

mythic status in the late eighteenth century, Inkle and Yarico. In this popular and apocryphal story, the Amerindian woman Yarico falls in love with the shipwrecked English sailor Inkle, whom she finds on a beach and nurses back to life. They live together peacefully until, recovering his health, Inkle recovers his greed for profit as well, and sells her into slavery. In the more lurid versions Yarico tries to change her lover's mind by telling him she is pregnant with his child. Inkle responds by raising the price for which he is selling her.[29]

Stedman alludes directly to the Inkle and Yarico story in his book, citing its (all too) schematic contrast with his own. The Inkle and Yarico story thematizes the breakdown of reciprocity by capitalist greed and highlights contradictions of the ideology of romantic love. No wonder it was unforgettable. Though absorbed, as all these stories were, into abolitionist propaganda, it articulates about as clearly as one might wish the business-is-business values underwriting slavery. And yet, though Stedman is the opposite of Inkle (he returns Joanna's love and does not wish to abandon her), and Joanna is the opposite of Yarico (she refuses to follow her lover's footsteps), the bottom line is the same in both stories. Joanna and Yarico end up husbandless and enslaved in the colonies while Inkle and Stedman end up back in England. Either way, the vision of "cultural harmony through romance" is not fulfilled; the allegory of an integrated postslavery society never completes itself. It served neither the pro- nor the anti-slavery cause for it to do so. Joanna gets poisoned not by her envious neighbors, but by the genre.

As critics have noted, the colonized heroes and heroines of European sentimental literature are rarely "pure" non-whites or "real" slaves. Like Joanna, they are typically mulattoes or mestizos who already have European affiliations or, renewing an older motif, are "really" princes or princesses.[30] The conventional facial sketch of the non-European love object distinguishes her or him from the stereotypic portraits of slaves and savages. Joanna, for instance, has "the most elegant shape that nature can exhibit . . . with cheeks through which glowed, in spite of the darkness of her skin, a beautiful tinge of vermillion. . . . Her nose was perfectly well formed, rather small; her lips a little prominent," and so on.[31] While universally read as abolitionist, the transracial love stories typically neutralize concrete dimensions of slavery. The love relationships unfold in some marginal or privileged space where relations of labor and property are suspended. Shipwrecks often provide such spaces. In Joanna's case, the bankruptcy of her master has removed her from her place in plantation social structure. Living in the midst of slavery, Joanna is seen apart from it; readers are allowed to think of her as property, but not as forced labor. Such features are marks of what Hulme calls the "concessionary narrative," meaning one that "goes some way towards recognizing a native point of view and offering a critique of European behavior, but can only do this by not addressing the central issue."[32]

In their very unreality, however, these idealized half-European subalterns do embody another thoroughly real dimension of late eighteenth-century Caribbean society. By that time, in both the Caribbean and much of Spanish America, populations of non-enslaved people of mixed ancestry had everywhere come to equal or outnumber whites in both the Caribbean and much of Spanish America. Mixed-race groups (mestizos, mulattoes, "free coloreds") acquired dramatic new political importance during the anti-colonial uprisings of the late eighteenth and early nineteenth centuries in the Americas. Would they provide leadership to the revolted underclasses, or would they follow their own class interests and side with the white elites? In independence struggles, would they side with creole-led independence movements, or with the European colonial powers? From the viewpoint of European hegemony, romantic love was as good a device as any for "embracing" such groups into the political and social imaginary – as subalterns. Stedman's habit of referring to Joanna as "my mulatta" has a political valence. It is, of course, characteristic of sentimental fiction to cast the political as erotic and to seek to resolve political uncertainties in the sphere of family and reproduction. In Stedman's book such allegorizing plays off against a more literal political drama: harmonious interludes with "his mulatta" alternate with military forays into the interior to fight the black rebels; the former produces a son, the latter dead European soldiers. Despite abolitionist readings, social harmony remains aligned with slavery in Stedman's narrative, and emancipation with deadly warfare.

The new element in Stedman's account is Joanna's rejection of European culture and the invitation to assimilate. Unlike her famous predecessor Pocahontas, or even her contemporary Phyllis Wheatley, Joanna does not want to be schooled, wear shoes, meet the King of England. In the dramatic words Stedman attributes to her in his account, she would rather remain first among her own class in America than be a "reflection or burthen" on Stedman in Europe. Read as political allegory, these words allude to another prospect Europeans were increasingly called on to imagine in the 1790s, the independence of the Americas. Joanna introduces that very term in her farewell to Stedman: had she and he been more independent of each other, she says, their relationship might have worked. So it is that Joanna and her quadroon son, equipped with an income and a black slave of their own, stay behind to whiten the race, and inaugurate a new postcolonial elite. But the picture is of neocolonialism, not autonomy: the American household remains Stedman's dependency, a family incomplete without him, loyal and without means or motive to revolt. Joanna's death by poisoning is an extraordinary way of disposing of this fantasy. Poisoning, often connected with Afro-Caribbean religion, was one of the most dramatic tools used by slaves in the Caribbean to destroy their masters. Afro-America, it seems, gets the last word in the love plot, as in the military one.

*

The rebel slave communities of Surinam had their own accounts of the resistance struggle Stedman describes. In the book *First-Time: The Historical Vision of an Afro-American People*, Richard Price has collected oral tales and histories provided him by the contemporary descendants of the maroon communities of the Surinamese interior.[33] Many of these hark back to the dramatic events of the 1770s and 1780s. This testimony of the Saramakas, transposed by an anthropologist into print, enters a discursive space that also began to take shape in Stedman's lifetime. The last decades of the eighteenth century marked the beginning of African American literature, as the first ex-slaves entered the circuits of European print culture, through a door opened up by the abolitionist movement. The point of entry, in the main, was autobiography. The first slave autobiographies, their publication often facilitated by dissident western intellectuals, were self-descriptions structured to a degree in line with western literary institutions and western conceptions of culture and of self, yet in direct opposition to official ideologies of colonialism and slavery (which, among other things, excluded Africans from western conceptions of culture and of self). Stedman was highly aware of this emergent literature. He mentions the letters of Ignatius Sancho and the poetry of Phyllis Wheatley. While he was writing his book, Europeans in large numbers were reading *The Interesting Narrative of the Life of Olaudah Equiano* (1789), which was in its eighth English edition by 1794. In very elaborate ways, these early texts undertook not to reproduce but to *engage* western discourses of identity, community selfhood, and otherness. Their dynamics are transcultural, and presuppose relations of subordination and resistance. Those dynamics continue, I would suggest, in contemporary autobiography and related forms such as oral history, testimony, vernacular art. That is what I mean when I say that the Saramaka tales collected by Price enter a print circuit begun in Stedman's time. As I suggested above, when such "autoethnographic" texts are read simply as "authentic" self-expression or "inauthentic" assimilation, their transcultural character is obliterated and their dialogic engagement with western modes of representation lost.

SENTIMENT AND THE WOMAN TRAVELER

In discussing the story of Mme. Godin (see chapter 2) I suggested that women protagonists tend to produce ironic reversals when they turn up in the contact zone. While Mme. Godin's story was circulating around Europe, a British woman, Anna Maria Falconbridge, was writing a travel book about Africa that would stand the sentimental tradition, with its abolitionist ties, on its head. The book, titled *Narrative of Two Voyages to the River Sierra Leone* (1802), is one of the very few European travel books about Africa written by a woman before 1850, and one of the most unusual in any period. Gender, marriage, and male domination are conspicuous themes in a narrative that sets out to decry the hypocrisy and ignorance of abolitionist do-gooders. Sentimentality and humanitarianism are marshaled in the cause of anti-anti-slavery.

Falconbridge went to West Africa in 1791 as the young wife of Lord Alexander Falconbridge, a physician who, after years of working on slave ships, had become a noted abolitionist. He had contributed an *Account of the Slave Trade on the Coast of Africa* (1788) to the abolitionist literary arsenal, vividly documenting the horrors of the slave trade for both enslaved Africans and European sailors employed on the ships. Resigning from "the African trade," Falconbridge joined the Sierra Leone Company, the abolitionist venture to found colonies in Sierra Leone for ex-slaves (the "black poor") transported from North America. In company with his new wife, Anna Maria, he was sent by the Company in 1791 to assist a coastal settlement heard to be in severe distress. On a second voyage, Falconbridge's husband undertook a commercial mission which failed. He died in Africa of drink and despondency, as Falconbridge tells it, leaving her there to begin a new life for herself.

As with Park, Stedman, and other sentimentalist contemporaries, Falconbridge's epistolary account of her two trips to Africa often takes the form of a narrative of trials and tribulations, drawing on older traditions of survival narrative. Apart from the distresses of the Sierra Leone colonists, Falconbridge dwells on hardships of her own. Immediately on arriving in Africa, for example, she finds herself a captive and a slave. Her captor, however, is none other than her own husband, who, to prevent her from socializing with the affluent European slave traders on shore, keeps her cruelly confined on the cramped and filthy ship on which they arrived. In describing her quarters, Falconbridge certainly intended to evoke abolitionist descriptions of slave ships (such as those written by her own husband):

> Conceive yourself pent up in a floating cage, without room either to walk about, stand erect, or even to lay at length; exposed to the inclemency of the weather, having your eyes and ears momently offended by acts of indecency, and language too horrible to relate – add to this a complication of filth, the stench from which was continually assailing your nose, and then you will have a faint notion of the Lapwing Cutter.[34]

When Falconbridge does manage to free herself and get ashore, she begins, like any European traveler, to see and make discoveries. In contrast with the rhetorics of anti-conquest, however, the sights she sees are neither welcome nor innocent. She goes to dinner in the house of the local slave traders, for example, and "involuntarily strolls" to a window, "without the smallest suspicion of what I was to see." She surveys the slave-yard:

> Judge then what my astonishment and feelings were, at the sight of between two and three hundred wretched victims, chained and parcelled

out in circles, just satisfying the cravings of nature from a trough of rice placed in the center of each circle.

The guilt of the sight transfers to herself:

Offended modesty rebuked me with a blush for not hurrying my eyes from such disgusting scenes; but whether fascinated by female curiosity, or whatever else, I could not withdraw myself for several minutes . . . be assured I avoided the prospects from this side of the house ever after.[35]

The term "prospects" ironically recalls the hegemonic European subject who scans landscapes and dreams of their transformation. And as that persona is male, its desire possessive, so Falconbridge identifies her seeing and desire with her gender ("modesty," "female curiosity"). As a woman she is not to see but be seen, or at least she is not to be seen seeing.

In contrast with objectivist discovery rhetoric, whose authority is mono-logic and self-contained, Falconbridge is resolutely dialogic, seeking out rather than defying local knowledge. Her subsequent discoveries, far from accruing to the glory of European designs, give rise to a vehement critique of her husband, abolitionists, the Sierra Leone Company, and the British government. Her gaze reveals not the utopias of the anti-conquest but dystopias of exploitation and neglect, the more disturbing because they are the results of humanitarianism. The settlement whose distress they are to relieve is a biracial community of freed slaves from Nova Scotia and women transports from England. Arriving among them, Falconbridge again reports on what she wishes she were never called upon to know: "I never did, and God grant I never may again witness so much misery as I was forced to be a spectator of here."[36] In contrast with male discovery rhetoric, seeing violates norms of conduct for her gender. The division of labor is quite stark: male travelers are to be driven by curiosity, which legitimates their every move; in Falconbridge, a curiosity (desire) marked as female is in need of control. Her professed reluctance to know seems the antithesis of possession, a refusal of mastery. It is another kind of anti-conquest.

Utterly destitute, the disillusioned colonists report that they emigrated on the basis of a thousand promises on which the Company has not delivered. Disputes with local inhabitants have made it impossible to settle the colonists on lands where they can support themselves. "I am surprised," reports Falconbridge, "our boasted Philanthropists, the Directors of the Company should have subjected themselves to the censure they must meet, for sporting with the lives of such numbers of their fellow creatures, I mean by sending so many here at once, before houses, materials for building or other conveniences, were prepared to receive them."[37] She is particularly distressed by the physical and spiritual condition of seven British women in the group. On conversing with them, she reports, they tell her they are not voluntary colonists at all, but London prostitutes who had been rounded up, drugged, "inveigled on board of ship, and married to Black men, whom they had never seen before," then packed off to Africa for a new life. Again, Falconbridge's response is a protest framed by a rhetoric of innocent disbelief. "Good heaven!" she says,

> the relation of this tale made me shudder; . . . I cannot altogether reconcile myself to believe it; for it is scarcely possible that the British Government, at this advanced and enlightened age, envied and admired as it is by the universe, could be capable of exercising or countenancing such a Gothic infringement on human Liberty.[38]

Liberty, enlightenment, advancement, the universe – the official vocabulary of bourgeois humanitarianism is called sarcastically to account. Falconbridge's rhetoric of disbelief, like her professed desire not to see, mocks the authority of Europe's mastering discourses which claim to wish to see and wish to know, but which only see what they wish to see and know what they wish to know.

At the same time, in terms of the gender system, Falconbridge's rhetoric is less an antithesis to male rhetoric of discovery and possession than its exact *complement*, an exact realization of the other (Other) side of male values whose underpinnings it shares. Like the male rhetoric of discovery, Falconbridge's womanly refusal of knowledge is anchored in assumptions of European privilege and unaccountability, in anti-conquest. Her language shares the same imperative for innocence as Park, Barrow, or Stedman, though the imperative is fulfilled in a different way: Falconbridge claims an innocence already given by her gender. What is unusual about her account is that she uses that givenness as a launching pad for a very focused attack on another version of the anti-conquest.

In keeping with sentimental tradition, the political in Falconbridge's narrative plays itself out in the spheres of the erotic and the domestic. While in the Stedman–Joanna story marriage is at odds with slavery, in Falconbridge's narrative the two are one, both for the British prostitutes and for herself. She describes her husband's premature death as perfectly welcome, allowing that by his abuse she had long since been weaned "from every spark of affection or regard I ever had for him."[39] She quickly finds herself a new mate in the colony. So echoes of late eighteenth-century feminism make their way to the contact zone, paradoxically in the context of a pro-slavery tract! In her closing pages Falconbridge declares that having "acquired information enough to form independent thoughts upon the subject," she now views slavery "in no shape objectionable either to morality or religion."[40]

Anna Maria Falconbridge stands more alone in the annals of African travel writing than one might expect. As a traveler and travel writer, she has points of contact with the "social exploratresses" of the 1820s–1840s whose writings I discuss in chapter 7. Yet while Park, Stedman, and other sentimentalists had many admirers and disciples, no one seems to have followed in Falconbridge's footsteps. While women writers were "authorized" to produce novels, their access to travel writing seems to have remained even more limited than their access to travel itself, at least when it came to leaving Europe. As readers, of course, they were significant and active participants in the genre. Sometimes they came at the writing through the back door. In 1819, an Englishwoman named Catherine Hutton published a book titled *The Tour of Africa*, a fictional journey through Africa compiled out of existing travel literature on the region. The book is narrated in the first person by a fictional male persona who presents himself in loving detail:

> I am the son of an English country gentleman of good family and large fortune. The first thing impressed upon my mind by my mother was, that I was born to be a great traveller. Whether the hearing of this predestination constantly repeated, during my infancy, had any influence in forming my character . . . I must leave to philosophers to determine; but certain it is that, when I could escape from my nurse, I was found in some field, or on some path where I had not been before. . . . At twenty-one, I found myself rich, independent, bound to my native country by no tie of consanguinity, and I resolved to fulfil my destiny, or gratify my inclination, whichever were the ruling principle, by seeing the world.[41]

One cannot help wondering whether this conventional opening was Hutton's fantasy for herself as well.

No text could display more clearly the gendered division of labor around travel and writing than a book called *Stories of Strange Lands and Fragments from the Notes of a Traveller* (1835) by Sarah Lee (or Mrs. R. Lee, as she signed herself). Lee was the widow of a well-known naturalist and trader T. Edward Bowdich, who had traveled in West Africa trying to negotiate trade agreements with the Ashanti. As she tells it, Lee was dutifully engaged in editing her husband's posthumous writings when a magazine editor urged her to write some stories based on her own African experiences. The stories narrate dramas of local West African life, mainly with African protagonists.[42] All, claims Lee in her preface, are "founded on truth; every description of scenes, manners and customs, has been taken from the life."[43] Though she admits a great penchant for "matter-of-fact studies and reflections," Lee raises no possibility of writing her own account of her years in West Africa.

As it turns out, however, Lee ingeniously makes her stories an occasion rather than a substitute for her own account of Africa. Each comes accompanied by an enormous string of footnotes, some of them pages long and complete with illustrations. It is here in the notes that we find the makings of the travel book Lee never wrote: explanatory commentary, ethnographic descriptions, observations on flora and fauna, personal anecdotes.[44] The notes seem to be Lee's main source of pride in the book. In her introduction she complains of the need to contain herself in writing them, "to repress

an exuberance of observation and circumstances" and to "avoid egotism":
"The number of I's that I have scratched out, the sentences that have been
turned and twisted, to avoid this provoking monosyllable, almost surpass
belief."[45]

Scratched out, turned and twisted: Lee herself names the constraints on her
writing, while only partially defying them. Not coincidentally, Lee dedicates
her book to a new female authority figure on the European stage, Queen
Victoria. In the dedication Lee pointedly reminds her that "the protection
of literature and of female writers is an object worthy of a British Queen."
As far as travel writing goes, Victoria was certainly to meet that demand,
for she did preside over a profusion of women's travel writing as global and
imperial as her own territorial ambitions.[46]

POSTSCRIPT

July 23, 1989:

> A guerrilla war in Suriname has ended in a truce that will allow the rebels
> to keep their weapons and eventually join the South American nation's
> police force, Dutch newspapers reported Sunday.
>
> (*San Jose Mercury News*)

December 20, 1989:

> Despite new peace talks held last week between Army Commander Desi
> Bouterse and rebel leader Ronny Brunswijk, fighting continues to increase
> in the nation's three year-old civil war, which until recently was relatively
> dormant. At dawn on Dec. 4, according to the government, mercenaries
> hired by Brunswijk attacked the military outpost at Kraka in eastern
> Suriname, killing six government troops. The attack came on the heels of
> talks with the rebels, which Bouterse had characterized as both "positive
> and optimistic."
>
> (*Washington Report on the Hemisphere*)

Part II

The reinvention of América, 1800–50

Chapter 6

Alexander von Humboldt and the reinvention of América

In the Old World, nations and the distinctions of their civilization form the principal points in the picture; in the New World, man and his productions almost disappear amidst the stupendous display of wild and gigantic nature. The human race in the New World presents only a few remnants of indigenous hordes, slightly advanced in civilization; or it exhibits merely the uniformity of manners and institutions transplanted by European colonists to foreign shores.

> (Alexander von Humboldt, *Personal Narrative of Travels to the Equinoctial Regions of the New Continent* (1814))

You are interested in botany? So is my wife.

> (Napoleon's (only) words to Alexander von Humboldt (1805))

It was an intricate social fabric and a critical historical juncture into which Alexander von Humboldt and Aimé Bonpland set foot when they arrived in South America in 1799. For the five eventful years that followed, they participated in that moment as they made their way around what they liked to call the New Continent. Their historic journey, and the monument of print it produced, laid down the lines for the ideological reinvention of South America that took place on both sides of the Atlantic during the momentous first decades of the nineteenth century. For thirty years, while popular uprisings, foreign invasions, and wars of independence convulsed Spanish America, Alexander von Humboldt's vast writings on his equinoctial travels flowed in a steady stream from Paris, reaching thirty volumes in as many years. At a time when loosening travel restrictions began sending European travelers to South America by the dozen, Humboldt remained the single most influential interlocutor in the process of reimagining and redefinition that coincided with Spanish America's independence from Spain. Humboldt was, and still is, considered "the most creative explorer of his time"; his American travels were regarded as "a model journey of exploration and a supreme geographical achievement."[1] He was as celebrated in Euroamerica as in Europe, and his writings were the source of new founding visions of America on both sides of the Atlantic. Charles Darwin wrote from on board the *Beagle* that his "whole course of life is due to having read and re-read" Humboldt's *Personal Narrative* as a youth.[2] Simón Bolívar, chief architect of Spanish American independence, paid homage to "Baron Humboldt" as "a great man who with his eyes pulled America out of her ignorance and with his pen painted her as beautiful as her own nature."[3]

This chapter and the two that follow are about the ideological reinvention of South America in the first decades of the last century. They adopt a range of perspectives. Here I examine Alexander von Humboldt's South American writings in their relation to prior paradigms of travel literature and to European ambitions in the region. Chapter 7 takes up the wave of traveler-writers who followed in the 1810s, 1820s, and 1830s when Spanish America opened fully to North European visitors and above all North European capital. There, I foreground a comparison between women and men writers. Chapter 8 considers how South American intellectuals, facing the new republican era and a European investment boom, selected and adapted European perspectives as they sought to create decolonized values and hegemonies. As throughout this book, a chief concern remains the relations between travel writing and processes of European economic expansion. The end of Spanish colonial rule entailed a full-scale renegotiation of relations between Spanish America and Northern Europe – relations of politics and economics, and with equal necessity, relations of representation and imagination. Europe had to reimagine América, and América, Europe. The reinvention of América, then, was a transatlantic process that engaged the energies and imaginations of intellectuals and broad reading publics in both hemispheres, but not necessarily in the same ways. For the elites of Northern Europe, the reinvention is bound up with prospects of vast expansionist possibilities for European capital, technology, commodities, and systems of knowledge. The newly independent elites of Spanish America, on the other hand, faced the necessity for *self*-invention in relation both to Europe and the non-European masses they sought to govern. One can only be fascinated, then, that the writings of Alexander von Humboldt provided founding visions to both groups.

"A MOST EXTRAORDINARY AND COMPLICATED SITUATION"

By the time Humboldt and Bonpland set sail from La Coruña, Spanish America's colonial structure had been in open crisis for at least two decades. In another ten years full-fledged revolutionary transformations would take hold, ending in the independence of all continental Spanish America by 1825. Spanish colonial society was culturally complex, intensely hierarchical, and saturated with conflict. European-born Spaniards occupied the top of the social scale and held a monopoly on the greatest political and economic privilege. Below them stood the *criollos* (creoles), that is, persons born in

America and claiming European (or white) ancestry. Below them stood the vast majority of the American populations, grouped according to various non-European ancestries: *indios*, *negros* (free and slave), *mestizos*, *mulatos*, *zambos*, and others[4] – the categories multiplied, signaling degrees of Indian, European, and African ancestry. (Thus did Spain's obsession with *pureza de sangre*, the legacy of its contact with northern Africa, play itself out in the Americas.) The labor of these subordinated majorities, especially enslaved Amerindians and Africans, had produced the wealth of Spain, and indeed of Europe, in the two and a half centuries since the Spanish conquest. When the indigenous peoples of the Andes rose in revolt in the 1780s, their demands included release from an awesome list of burdens imposed by colonial, religious, and creole elites.[5]

Despite their own subordination to the Spaniards, by the end of three centuries Euroamerican creoles had solidly established themselves as land-owning, merchant, mining, and bureaucratic elites with control over enormous resources, including vast amounts of land, the forced labor of thousands of African slaves and indentured Indians, and the power to extract taxes and tribute from everyone below them in the hierarchy. In 1800, for example, in the province of Caracas, where Humboldt and Bonpland began their South American journey, the population comprised nearly half a million people, of whom 25.5 per cent were classified as whites (mainly creoles), 15 per cent enslaved blacks, 8 per cent free blacks, 38.2 per cent *pardos*, who in contemporary parlance would be "coloreds," and 14 per cent Amerindians.[6] Some 4,000 people, around 0.5 per cent of the population, held *all* the usable land, which was worked by a labor pool made up of African slaves, free blacks, mixed-race peons, and poor whites. Home of revolutionary leaders Francisco Miranda, Simón Bolívar, and Andres Bello, Venezuela was to be the crucible of the creole-led independence movement in South America, and it was there that Humboldt and Bonpland spent their first year.

As they easily learned, creole landholders and merchants had long since grown impatient with Spanish political privilege and economic restrictions. On the other hand, many saw Spain as the only power able to keep the subaltern majorities in check. Their fears were well founded. The unexpected power of maroon rebels in Surinam, the tenacity of the Carib Indians in St. Vincent, the huge but unsuccessful Andean Indian uprising in 1781, and the successful slave revolt in Santo Domingo in 1790 had rightly terrified feudal and slaveholding castes everywhere. All these violent dramas were still unfolding when Humboldt and Bonpland turned up (still are unfolding, for that matter). Such precedents, along with revolutionary ideologies from France, the Caribbean, and the United States, were galvanizing the already rebellious subordinated populations, often around educated leaders prepared to press their demands along institutional lines. In 1795 in Venezuela a group of revolted slaves demanded the formation of a republic under "French law," emancipation of slaves, and abolition of some particularly offensive taxes. Two years later, an even more threatening multiracial alliance of workers and small proprietors produced a radical conspiracy with the same program, plus "abolition of Indian tribute, and distribution of land to the Indians." It also called for "harmony between whites, Indians and Coloreds, 'brothers in Christ and equal before God.'"[7]

Such upheavals coincided with a late eighteenth-century effort on Spain's part to reaffirm its grip on its American colonies. Indeed, Spain's sponsorship of Humboldt and Bonpland's travels was part of this effort. As their local internal economies had expanded, the American colonies had become less dependent and less profitable to Spain. Contrary to what stereotypes might suggest, the Spanish crown sought to reassert control by means of a liberal reform movement. Sparked in part by the reports of Antonio de Ulloa and Jorge Juan, who accompanied the La Condamine expedition, Spain began pushing to modernize what it saw as unenlightened colonial social and political structures built on religious dogmatism, local despotism, slavery, and brutal exploitation of indigenous peoples. To many members of the creole elites, Spain began to look less and less like their protector against the rebellious masses; to members of the subordinated majorities, it began to look less and less like the enemy oppressor. Conservative creoles were infuriated by legislation to guarantee the rights of the subordinated majorities in the colonies, to open schools to the "free colored" population, to correct abuses of slaves, indentured labor, tribute systems, and so on. The mission system was challenged, too, as Spain sought to bring missions into the normal church hierarchy and replace the independent missionaries with priests and a centralized governance. As the colonial conflicts heated up, around the time Humboldt and Bonpland arrived, it was not uncommon to find the exploited majorities siding with the "enlightened" Spanish crown against the creole "liberators." Likewise, some creoles supported independence mainly as a way to secure their class privilege against the liberal challenge from the mother country. Venezuelan planters in 1794 succeeded in forcing the repeal of a new slave law Spain had imposed five years earlier which had clarified the rights of slaves and responsibilities of slave owners. It was, as Simón Bolívar put it in his famous Jamaica letter of 1815, "a most extraordinary and complicated situation."[8]

Beginning in the 1780s, independence-minded creoles of all persuasions had been trekking to London and Paris seeking support against Spain. The governments of Britain and France had refused official alliances with the independence movements, though they made no attempt to conceal their designs on the region. In the commercial sector, on the other hand, contact between North European and Spanish American commercial interests flourished. Spanish protectionism had been legendary, keeping Spanish American ports officially closed to foreign goods, and nearly all foreign people. Contraband had always been common, but by the 1780s the demand for broader commercial relations had made the whole system unenforceable. Many scholars doubt the Spanish American independence movements would have crystallized at all had it not been for the relentless pressure of North European capital. Many also regard expansionist European interests as one of the reasons the movements did so little to change basic socioeconomic structures.

THE THIRTY-VOLUME VOYAGE

In part we have Romantic ideology to thank for the towering scale to which the figure of Alexander von Humboldt is drawn in nineteenth-century historiography. More than any other writer discussed in this book, Humboldt existed and exists not as a traveler or a travel writer, but as a Man and a Life, in a way that became possible only in the era of the Individual. Humboldt produced himself as such. Unlike the disciples of Linnaeus or the employees of the African Association, he did not write or travel as a humble instrument of European knowledge-making apparatuses, but as their creator. He was not sent on missions in the name of a paternal schema embodied in an authority figure back home. A person of extraordinary energy, ability, and education, he produced his own journeys and subject matters and spent a lifetime of energy promoting them. Both his travels and his writings have an epic scale which he devoted his life and his fortune to creating. For Humboldt did have a Life in the way only a Fortune can provide. Unlike the Anders Sparrmans or the Mungo Parks, Humboldt was a member of a national elite possessed of independent wealth with which he mounted and promoted his geographical and literary endeavors. The epic scale of his achievements is due to both his fortune and the tenor of his times, as well as to his own audacious genius and passionate self-realization. In writing about Humboldt, then, one encounters an imperative to refer everything back to the Life and the Man. What follows both acknowledges and resists that imperative.

In a paradigm most often associated with Victorian women travelers, what set Alexander von Humboldt in motion was inheritance and a long-awaited orphanhood.[9] He was born in 1769, the same year as Napoleon, and was only 8 when his father died in 1777, after serving for many years in the Prussian court as chamberlain to Frederick II. Alexander and his brother Wilhelm, then 10, were left with their mother, a French Huguenot and a stern Calvinist. Their childhoods were spent in an austere environment devoted entirely to booklearning. They benefited a great deal from the curious but fruitful privilege of growing up at court without belonging to the nobility. Bold intellects, they made a strong impression as young men in Berlin, where they frequented the liberal Jewish salons rather than those of the German aristocracy. Wilhelm became fascinated with language and philosophy, Alexander with the natural sciences, which he studied at the University of Göttingen and at Freiburg's School of Mines. As a student, Alexander became a close friend of Georg Förster, the naturalist who had accompanied Cook on his second voyage, and whose writings had made him famous. The two traveled together in 1790 to England and revolutionary Paris.

His studies completed, Alexander secured himself economically by working as a mining consultant and inspector for the Prussian government, a position that failed to exhaust either his talents or his ambitions, but which did permit him to pursue his scientific interests, begin publishing, and travel within Prussia. He had long since developed the habits that would characterize his life, according to a present-day admirer: "He slept only four hours a day, spent little time in female company, and read a vast number of good books."[10] When his mother died in 1797, Humboldt found himself free at 30 to leave the career of which he had tired and act on his passionate desire to leave Europe – for nearly anywhere at all.

It took a while to get going. Plans for the West Indies fell through; then an invitation to join an English party heading up the Nile was thwarted by Napoleon's invasion of Egypt. A chance to join a French expedition round the world arose, then evaporated. Partnered with Bonpland, whom he had met in Paris, Humboldt again made plans for Egypt, hoping to join Napoleon's expedition; again war and Franco-Prussian politics intervened. Stranded in Marseilles with no place to go, the two set out for Spain with the ambitious hope of arranging an American journey. In Madrid, with months of lobbying they won the support of Spanish Prime Minister Mariano de Urquijo, who helped them persuade Charles IV to award them an unprecedented *carte blanche* to travel in Spain's American territories, entirely at Humboldt's expense. It was a diplomatic coup of perhaps even greater moment than La Condamine's in 1735, due in large part to Humboldt's combination of courtly experience, scientific expertise, and sheer tenacity. Undoubtedly he reminded the King how useful the reports of Antonio de Ulloa and Jorge Juan had proven (especially their confidential findings) in reforming Spanish colonial policy. Perhaps Charles IV hoped Humboldt and Bonpland would help him regain control of his restless colonies. Certainly he was eager to make use of Humboldt's mining expertise, and asked him to report back in particular on mineralogical findings.

The two partners sailed (in a vessel called the *Pizarro*, no less) to Venezuela in 1799. They spent over a year there traveling up and down the Orinoco, across the great plains (the *llanos*), up mountains, down rivers, through jungles, from village to village, hacienda to hacienda, mission to mission, measuring, collecting, experimenting, sketching, writing it all down. On the Orinoco they were able to witness and report in detail on the preparation of curare poison, a subject on which there was great curiosity in Europe. By personally traveling the interior waterway that joins the Orinoco and the Amazon, Humboldt and Bonpland definitively confirmed its existence for European doubters. (Non-doubters had been using it for decades as a mail route.) It was here too that local inhabitants demonstrated to them the wonders of the electric eel. Laden with immense collections of specimens and plants, they moved on to Havana early in 1802, but almost immediately heard that a French expedition round the world was expected to stop in Peru. Hoping to join it, they returned to South America. The *System of Nature* continued to unify the planet: Humboldt and Bonpland decided to travel to Peru by land rather than by sea, in order to pass through Bogotá and share notes with the Linnaean naturalist José Celestino Mutis. They spent two months with him and his collections.[11] Crossing the Cordillera, they arrived in Quito, where they spent another six months. Their stay was marked by the feat which more than any other captured the public imagination in Europe when word of it reached the papers a few months later: the attempt to scale the Andean peak Chimborazo, then believed to be the highest mountain in the world. Dressed in a frock coat and button boots and accompanied by a small party, Humboldt came within 400 meters of the 6,300-meter summit before turning back because of cold and want of oxygen. In late 1802 his expedition reached Lima, already aware that the French rendezvous would not materialize. Instead they sailed for Mexico, where they spent another year, mainly researching in a wealth of Mexican archives, libraries, and botanical gardens never before open to non-Spaniards. They made a brief visit to the United States, where Humboldt was befriended by Thomas Jefferson. In August of 1804 they returned to Paris to a hero's welcome from a public which, off and on, had followed their feats through their letters, and in between, had imagined them both dead.

Like La Condamine, and perhaps following his example, Humboldt set out immediately to capitalize on his travels in the interlocking Parisian worlds of high society, science, and officialdom. Within weeks of his return, he set up a botanical exhibition at the Jardin des Plantes. While Bonpland faded into the background, and eventually disappeared back into the contact zone,[12] Humboldt became a continental celebrity. The hunger for firsthand information on South America was widespread and intense, and Humboldt had made himself a walking encyclopedia. He gave lectures, organized meetings, wrote letters by the hundred, visited dignitaries, held forth tirelessly (and, for some, tiresomely) in salons. Meanwhile, he set teams of annotators and illustrators to work converting his collections and his notes into books.

Books! Humboldt's authorial ambitions were on the same epic scale as his travels. During the course of his American journey, he had often busied himself sketching out plans for the vast monument of print his voyage would produce. Spanish America, in Northern Europe, was a virtual *carte blanche* which Humboldt seemed determined to fill completely with his

18 Alexander von Humboldt and Aimé Bonpland in the Orinoco. Engraving by O. Roth (Staatsbibliothek, Berlin).

writings, drawings, and maps. He took to unprecedented lengths the encyclopedic impulse which in the case of the French expedition to Egypt would produce the twenty-four-volume *Description de l'Egypte*. For one present-day admirer, Humboldt's textual ambitions amounted to "an incredible, almost maniacal addiction to papers, registers and annotations . . . a cultural hypochondria."[13] Nothing could be more distant from the mansized aspirations of the sentimental storytellers than the thirty-volume *Travels to the Equinoctial Regions of the New Continent in 1799, 1800, 1801, 1802, 1803, and 1804*, all published in Paris and in French, and much of it attributed jointly to Humboldt and Bonpland.[14] The print epic began a few months after their return to France, with the *Essay on the Geography of Plants* (1805), and ended in 1834 with the final volumes of the *Survey of Grasses*, the *Geographical and Physical Atlas*, and the *History and Geography of the New Continent*. In all the *Travels* includes sixteen volumes of botany and plant geography, two of zoology, two of astronomical and barometric measurements, seven of geographical and geopolitical description (including the famed *Political Essay on the Kingdom of New Spain*), and three of travel narrative per se. An experimenter with form, Humboldt specialized not only in print but graphics as well, at great expense to himself. His visual innovations set new standards for the use of charts, graphs, and tables. In his non-specialized works the engravings of archeological and natural phenomena are still breathtaking (see plates 19, 22, 23, and 24).

It was through his non-specialized writings rather than his scientific treatises that Humboldt sought, and won, his broadest impact on the public imaginations of Europe and Euroamerica. Those are the works on which I will be focusing here: first, *Ansichten der Natur* (*Views of Nature*, 1808, revised and expanded in 1826 and 1849), one of Humboldt's favorite works on his American travels and the only one he wrote in German; *Vues des cordillères et monuments des peuples indigènes d'Amérique* (*Views of the Cordilleras and Monuments of the Indigenous Peoples of America*), which appeared in two luxuriously illustrated volumes in 1810, followed by an abridged popular edition in 1814; and finally the unfinished *Relation historique* or *Personal Narrative* of his travels, whose three volumes appeared in 1814, 1819, and 1825.[15] These above all were the books that continental and Spanish American reading publics were reading, reviewing, excerpting, and discussing in the 1810s and 1820s. Travel writings in the immediate sense, these non-specialized works are also bold discursive experiments in which, as I will argue, Humboldt sought to reinvent popular imaginings of América, and through América, of the planet itself. Even as he undertook to recreate South America in connection with its new opening to Northern Europe, Humboldt sought simultaneously to reframe bourgeois subjectivity, heading off its sundering of objectivist and subjectivist strategies, science and sentiment, information and experience.

Along with others of his time, he proposed to Europeans a new kind of planetary consciousness.

Commentators often read Humboldt's American writings in relation to the famous *querelle d'Amérique* – the long and arrogant dispute among European intellectuals over the relative size, value, and variety of American flora and fauna, in comparison with those of Europe and the other continents. In the second half of the century, Buffon had championed the view that nature was less developed in the Americas than in the rest of the world because the continent was younger. As Antonello Gerbi has shown in his encyclopedic *Dispute of the New World* (1955, 1983), the issue was hotly debated, and every thinker of the period seems to have found it necessary to take a position.[16] Though he does not discuss the debate itself at any length in his popular works, Humboldt's celebration of American nature is an engagement with it, largely aimed at revindicating the "New Continent." However, Humboldt by no means saw his work as grounded in the debate or subsumed by it. Gerbi sees his position in the dispute as "anomalous" and "somewhat marginal," exercising only a "belated and lateral influence."[17] In the discussion below, I have found it most useful to treat Humboldt's writings and the *querelle d'Amérique* as intersecting phenomena shaped by shared European preoccupations and anxieties with respect to the Americas.

"WILD AND GIGANTIC NATURE"

As the titles of his writings suggest, Alexander von Humboldt reinvented South America first and foremost as nature. Not the accessible, collectible, recognizable, categorizable nature of the Linnaeans, however, but a dramatic, extraordinary nature, a spectacle capable of overwhelming human knowledge and understanding. Not a nature that sits waiting to be known and possessed, but a nature in motion, powered by life forces many of which are invisible to the human eye; a nature that dwarfs humans, commands their being, arouses their passions, defies their powers of perception. No wonder portraits so often depict Humboldt engulfed and miniaturized either by nature or by his own library describing it.

So engulfed and miniaturized was the human in Humboldt's cosmic conception that narrative ceased to be a viable mode of representation for him. He deliberately avoided it. His first non-specialized writings on the Americas took the form of descriptive and analytical essays prepared as lectures. *Views of Nature*, which first appeared in 1808 in German as *Ansichten der Natur* and in French as *Tableaux de la nature*, began as a series of widely acclaimed public lectures given in Berlin in 1806. It was followed by the lavishly illustrated *Views of the Cordilleras and Monuments of the Indigenous Peoples of America* in 1810. The "view" or tableau was the form Humboldt chose for his experiments in what he called "the esthetic mode of treating subjects of natural history." His were innovative attempts to correct what he saw as the failings of travel writing in his time: on the one hand, a trivializing preoccupation with what he called "the merely personal," and, on the other, an accumulation of scientific detail that was spiritually and esthetically deadening. Humboldt's solution in his *Views* was to fuse the specificity of science with the esthetics of the sublime. The vividness of esthetic description, he was convinced, would be complemented and intensified by science's revelations of the "occult forces" that made Nature work. The result, in the words of one literary historian, "introduced into German literature an entirely new type of nature discourse."[18]

Humboldt's discursive experimentation is well illustrated by the famous opening essay in *Views of Nature*, titled "On Steppes and Deserts." It departs, as many of the Views do, from the perspective of a hypothetical traveler, the vestige of a narrative persona. In this instance, the abstract (yet thoroughly European, and male) persona turns his eyes away from the cultivated coastal zone of Venezuela toward the *llanos* or great plains of the interior. In the following excerpt, notice the interweaving of visual and emotive language with classificatory and technical language, and the deliberate orchestration of the reader's response:

At the foot of the lofty granitic range which, in the early ages of our planet, resisted the irruption of the waters on the formation of the Caribbean Gulf, extends a vast and boundless plain. When the traveller turns from the Alpine valleys of Caracas, and the island-studded lake of Tacarigua, whose waters reflect the forms of the neighboring bananas, – when he leaves the fields verdant with the light and tender green of the Tahitian sugar cane, or the somber shade of the cacao groves, – his eye rests in the south on Steppes, whose seeming elevations disappear in the distant horizon.

From the rich luxuriance of organic life the astonished traveller suddenly finds himself on the drear margin of a treeless waste.[19]

Having produced his reader's desolation, Humboldt sets about alleviating it, filling the wasteland ("stretched before us, like the naked stony crust of some desolate planet") with dense and powerful meaning. Displaying his own brand of planetary consciousness, he compares the Venezuelan *llanos* to the heaths of Northern Europe, the interior plains of Africa, the steppes of central Asia. Pages of analytical, often statistical, description ensue, but in a language that is also filled with drama, struggle, and a certain sensuality. In the following rather lengthy excerpt, for instance, Humboldt undertakes to explain why South America is less hot and dry than lands at similar latitudes elsewhere. The passage is not narrative; not a single animate being appears. Yet the prose is so action-packed as to

Pl. 3.   Vol. XIII p.55.

Natural Bridges of Icononzo.

Pub.d by Longman, Hurst, Rees, Orme & Brown, Aug.t 1.st 14.

19 Natural bridges of Icononzo. From Humboldt's *Views of the Cordilleras*
(1814).

promote exhaustion. Readers should imagine it being delivered as a lecture (my italics):

> The narrowness of this extensively indented continent in the northern part of the tropics, where the fluid basis on which the atmosphere rests, occasions the ascent of a less warm current of air; its *wide* extensions towards both the *icy* poles; a *broad* ocean *swept* by cool tropical winds; the flatness of the eastern shores; currents of cold sea-water from the antarctic region, which, at first following a direction from south-west to north-east, *strike* the coast of Chili below the parallel of 35° south lat., and *advance* as far north on the coasts of Peru as Cape Parina, where they *suddenly diverge* toward the west; the numerous mountains *abounding* in springs, whose snow-crowned summits *soar* above the strata of clouds, and cause the *descent* of currents of air down their declivities; the *abundance* of rivers of *enormous* breadth, which after many windings invariably seek the *most distant* coast; Steppes, *devoid* of sand, and therefore less readily acquiring heat; *impenetrable* forests, which, protecting the earth from the sun's rays, or radiating heat from the surface of their leaves, cover the *richly-watered* plains of the Equator and *exhale* into the interior of the country, *most remote* from mountains and the Ocean, *prodigious* quantities of moisture, partly absorbed and partly generated. . . . On these *alone* depend the *luxuriance* and *exuberant* vegetation and that *richness* of foliage which are so peculiarly characteristic of the New Continent.[20]

Here is a prose that fatigues not by flatness or tedium, as the Linnaeans sometimes did, but by a dramatic and arhythmic ebb and flow that would have been intensified by oral delivery. An "ascent" of "less warm" air flashes to "wide extensions" at "icy poles"; a "broad ocean" to a continent's "flat shores"; cold water, like an unwelcome invader of the tropics, strikes, advances, suddenly turns; mountains abound, soar; rivers are enormous, abundant, aggressively seeking coasts; forests are impenetrable, and humming with invisible activity as they protect, radiate, cover, exhale, absorb, generate. One thinks of a camera that is continually both moving and shifting focus – except that the visual actually plays almost no role in the description. Humboldt invokes here not a system of nature anchored in the visible, but an endless expansion and contraction of invisible forces. In this respect his discourse contrasts markedly with that of his Linnaean predecessors. Humboldt drew the contrast himself in a letter written the night before he left on his American journey. While he would be collecting plants and fossils and making astronomical observations, he wrote a friend in Salzburg, "none of that is the main purpose of my expedition. My eyes will always be directed to the combination of forces, to the influence of the inanimate creation on the animate world of animals and plants, to this harmony."[21] Certainly Humboldt was looking for what he found in the new continent, and found what he was looking for. His goal as a scientist became his goal as a writer. In the preface to *Views of Nature* he declares his aim is to reproduce "the enjoyment which a sensitive mind receives from the immediate contemplation of nature . . . heightened by an insight into the connection of the occult forces." Without such insight, "the wonderful luxuriance of nature" reduces simply to "an accumulation of separate images," lacking "the harmony and effect of a picture."[22]

As all his commentators have noted, Humboldt's emphasis on harmonies and occult forces aligns him with the spiritualist esthetics of Romanticism. It also aligns him with industrialism and the machine age, however, and with the developments in the sciences that were producing and being produced by that age. (Indeed, there was perhaps no clearer intersection of "inanimate creation" and "the animate world of plants and animals" than the mining industry in which Humboldt had worked for many years and which was one of Europe's main objects of interest in the Americas.) Other writers have discussed Humboldt's work in relation to European scientific debates of his time. I am approaching his writings from an entirely different angle, looking at their ideological dimensions and their relations to the literature of travel.

In contrast with the ego-centered sentimental narratives discussed in chapters 4 and 5, many of which he had certainly read, Humboldt sought to pry affect away from autobiography and narcissism and fuse it with science. His goal, he says in the preface to *Views of Nature*, is to reproduce in the reader "Nature's ancient communion with the spiritual life of man." The equatorial world is a privileged site for such an exercise: "Nowhere," says Humboldt, "does she [Nature] more deeply impress us with a sense of her greatness, nowhere does she speak to us more forcibly."[23]

Though sharing the basic structure of the scientific anti-conquest, then, Humboldt's brand of planetary consciousness makes claims for science and for "Man" considerably more grandiose than those of the plant classifiers who preceded him. Compared with the humble, discipular herborizer, Humboldt assumes a godlike, omniscient stance over both the planet and his reader. For of course it is most immediately he rather than Nature who undertakes to "impress," to "speak to us forcibly." Virtuoso-like, he plays on elaborate sensibilities he presupposed in his audience. The main sensory images above, for example, are unpredictable blasts of cold – the last thing a northerner expects or desires in the imagined torrid zone. (How fitting for that frigid current running up the Pacific to bear Humboldt's name.)

In "On Steppes and Deserts," after the long excursus on global and occult forces quoted above, the hypothetical traveler-seer finally returns to the desolate landscape of the opening paragraphs, and transforms it before his readers' eyes into a scene of movement and vitality:

> Scarcely is the surface of the earth moistened before the teeming Steppe becomes covered with Kyllingiae, with the many-panicled Paspalum, and a variety of grasses. Excited by the power of light, the herbaceous Mimosa unfolds its dormant, drooping leaves, hailing, as it were, the rising sun in chorus with the matin song of the birds and the opening flowers of aquatics. Horses and oxen, buoyant with life and enjoyment, roam over and crop the plains. The luxuriant grass hides the beautifully spotted Jaguar, who, lurking in safe concealment, and carefully measuring the extent of the leap, darts, like the Asiatic tiger, with a cat-like bound on his passing prey.[24]

In contrast with strictly scientific writing, the authority of the discourse here plainly does not lie in a totalizing descriptive project that lives outside the text. Here, the totalizing project lives *in* the text, orchestrated by the infinitely expansive mind and soul of the speaker. What is shared with scientific travel writing, however, is the erasure of the human. The description just quoted presents a landscape imbued with social fantasies – of harmony, industry, liberty, unalienated *joie de vivre* – all projected onto the non-human world. Traces of human history, unidentified, are there: the horse and oxen arrived through a force no less occult than the invading Spanish. But the human inhabitants of the *Ilanos* are absent. The only "person" mentioned in these "melancholy and sacred solitudes" is the hypothetical and invisible European traveler himself.

Views of Nature was a very popular book, and one that seems to have mattered a great deal to Humboldt. Long after he abandoned his *Personal Narrative*, he revised and expanded *Views of Nature* twice, in 1826 and again in 1849. He was right to care about it. From Humboldt's *Views of Nature* and its sequel *Views of the Cordilleras*, European and South American reading publics selected the basic repertoire of images that came to signify "South America" during the momentous transition period of 1810–50. Three images in particular, all canonized by Humboldt's *Views*, combined to form the standard metonymic representation of the "new continent": superabundant tropical forests (the Amazon and the Orinoco), snow-capped mountains (the Andean Cordillera and the volcanos of Mexico), and vast interior plains (the Venezuelan *llanos* and the Argentine pampas).[25] Humboldt singled out this canonical triad himself in the last edition of *Views of Nature*, which he introduced as "a series of papers which originated in the presence of the noblest objects of nature – on the Ocean, – in the forests of the Orinoco, – in the savannahs of Venezuela, – and in the solitudes of the Peruvian and Mexican mountains."[26]

In point of fact, it took a highly selective reception of Humboldt's writings to reduce South America to pure nature and the iconic triad of mountain, plain, and jungle. I will be referring below to some of the other ways in which Humboldt wrote and thought about South America, notably archeological and demographic ones. But it was unquestionably the image of primal nature elaborated in his scientific works and his *Views* that became codified in the European imaginary as the new ideology of the "new continent." Why? For one thing, the ideology, like the continent, was precisely not new. Nineteenth-century Europeans *re*invented America as Nature in part because that is how sixteenth- and seventeenth-century Europeans had invented America for themselves in the first place, and for many of the same reasons. Though deeply rooted in eighteenth-century constructions of Nature and Man, Humboldt's seeing-man is also a self-conscious double of the first European inventors of America, Columbus, Vespucci, Raleigh, and the others. They, too, wrote America as a primal world of nature, an unclaimed and timeless space occupied by plants and creatures (some of them human), but not organized by societies and economies; a world whose only history was the one about to begin. Their writings too portrayed America in a discourse of accumulation, abundance, and innocence. Humboldt's rhapsodic invocation of a flourishing primal world echoes such writings as Columbus' famous letter to the Spanish monarchs in 1493:

> All these islands are very beautiful, and distinguished by a diversity of scenery; they are filled with a great variety of trees of immense height, and which I believe to retain their foliage in all seasons; for when I saw them they were as verdant and luxuriant, as they usually are in Spain in the month of May. . . . There are besides in the same island of Juana seven or eight kinds of palm trees, which, like all the other trees, herbs, and fruits, considerably surpass ours in height and beauty. The pines also are very handsome, and there are very extensive fields and meadows, a variety of birds, different kinds of honey, and many sorts of metals, but no iron.[27]

In Humboldt's writings, Columbus turns up from time to time in person. In *Views of Nature*, for example, the essay on the Cataracts of the Orinoco replays Columbus' famous encounter with the Orinoco River on his third voyage to America.[28]

Ironically, the edenic edifice of the sixteenth-century chroniclers was erected on the disappointment of what Columbus failed to find: China, the Great Khan, the massive cities, and endless roadways Marco Polo had described. Humboldt always admired Columbus for responding to disillusion by assigning the place an intrinsic esthetic value. While the strategy failed to impress the King and Queen of Spain, it took deep root in the imaginations of their subjects. Three hundred years later that edenic fantasy resurges in Humboldt's renewed first contact. Even the label "New Continent" is revived, as if three centuries of European colonization had never happened or made no difference. What held for Columbus held again for Humboldt: the state of primal nature is brought into being as a state in relation to the prospect of transformative intervention from Europe. Columbus' 1493 letter to the Spanish monarchs (quoted above) was followed by a second proposing not his integration into the edenic world he had found, but a vast project of colonization and enslavement to be presided over by himself. Humboldt had no such aspirations. Yet on the eve of Spanish American independence, and the eve of a capitalist "scramble for America" not unlike the scramble for Africa still to come, Humboldt's *Views* and his viewing stake out a new beginning of history in South America, a new (Northern European) point of origin for a future that starts now, and will rework that "savage terrain." Humboldt's *Views* formulates an aboriginal starting point for a future many of his contemporaries saw as foregone, and in which they passionately believed. The formulation is a peace-loving, utopian one: none of the obstacles to occidentalist progress appear in the landscape.

The point is not to argue that Humboldt's representations were somehow implausible or lacking in verisimilitude. I do want to argue, however, that they were not inevitable, that their contours were conditioned by a particular historical and ideological juncture, and by particular relations of power and privilege. South America didn't *have* to be invented or reinvented as primal nature. Despite the emphasis on primal nature, in all their explorations, Humboldt and Bonpland never once stepped beyond the boundaries of the Spanish colonial infrastructure – they couldn't, for they relied entirely on the networks of villages, missions, outposts, haciendas, roadways, and colonial labor systems to sustain themselves and their project, for food, shelter, and the labor pool to guide them and transport their immense equipage. Even the canonical images of interior plains, snow-capped mountains, and dense jungles did not lie outside the history of humankind, or even the history of Euroimperialism. The inhabitants of the Venezuelan *llanos* and the Argentine pampas, however removed from colonial centers, were about to be recruited as soldiers in the wars of independence. The jungle had been penetrated by the colonial mission system, whose influence extended far beyond the microcosmic social orders of its outposts. The Andean Cordillera (Humboldt's "mountain solitudes") was also the living place for most of the inhabitants of Peru, among whom pre-Columbian lifeways and colonial resistance continued to be powerful everyday realities. Historically, it was also the great mother lode of colonial mineral wealth. Humboldt's ecological depiction of Mount Chimborazo (see plate 20) contrasts intriguingly with indigenous Andean representations of another famous peak, the Cerro de Potosi, where the Virgin of Copacabana presided over the biggest silver mine in the world (see plate 21).

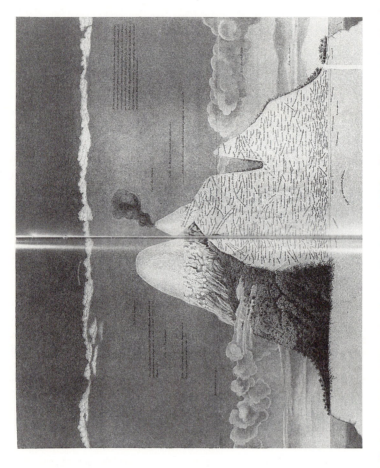

20 Pictorial representation of nature in the Andes (1805) after a drawing made by Humboldt in 1803 following his ascent of Mount Chimborazo. The written labels identify different botanical species found at the varying altitudes.

21 Drawing by an indigenous Andean artist of the Cerro de Potosí, site of
the largest Spanish mine in the Americas, dated 1588. At the foot of the
mountain lies the city of Potosí; at the summit is depicted an appearance of
the Virgin of Copacabana, long associated with the mountain. The original
artist is believed to be Francisco Titu Yupanqui.

HUMBOLDT'S *PERSONAL NARRATIVE*

In the three volumes of Humboldt's *Personal Narrative* (1814–25), narrativity itself brings European aspirations to the surface, along with the
infrastructure of Spanish American society as Humboldt encountered it.
Under public pressure to produce a narrative account of his travels,
Humboldt began this work reluctantly, a decade after his return. "Overcoming his repugnance" to personal narrative, he completed three volumes
in five years before abandoning the project and destroying the manuscript
of the fourth.[29] Initially, at least, the project was well received. "What

sympathy does the traveller excite," exults the English translator of the *Personal Narrative*, "while he imprints the first step that leads to civilization and all its boundless blessings, along the trackless desert." Euroexpansionist teleology constitutes the "charm" of the narrative.[30] The following excerpt from the account of a jungle excursion to a reputed gold mine in Venezuela illustrates how the *Personal Narrative* weaves human agency and temporality into the spectacle of nature:

> The farmers, with the aid of their slaves, opened a path across the woods to the first fall of the Rio Juagua. . . . When the cornice was so narrow, that we could find no place for our feet, we descended into the torrent, crossed it by fording or on the shoulders of a slave, and climbed to the opposite wall. . . . The farther we advanced, the thicker the vegetation became. In several places the roots of the trees had burst the calcareous rock, by inserting themselves into the clefts that separate the beds. We [*sic*] had some trouble to carry the plants we gathered at every step. The cannas, the heliconias with fine purple flowers, the costuses, and other plants of the family of the amomyms . . . form a striking contrast with the brown colour of the arborescent ferns, the foliage of which is so delicately shaped. The Indians made incisions with their large knives in the trunks of the trees, and fixed our attention on those beautiful red and golden yellow woods, which will one day be sought for by our turners and cabinet makers.[31]

The subject matter remains rapturous nature; the Americans, both masters and slaves, come alive, but only in the immediate service of the Europeans. The one action they are seen to initiate is to point out exploitable resources to the visitors. Indeed the Indians' inviting gesture seems to trigger the relatively rare allusion to a future seen securely in the hands of European ("our") capital and industry. The presence of Americans as instrumental subjects is typical of the *Personal Narrative*. Around the edges of the nature spectacle, one can learn a lot about Spanish American society from this work, but what one learns comes transmitted from within the structure of colonial relations. Americans, be they Spanish missionaries, colonial officials, creole settlers, African slaves, Amerindian servants, or *llanero* peons, appear overwhelmingly in instrumental capacities. Often, as in the passage above, they get subsumed altogether into that ambiguous "we" by which masters include themselves as agents of their servants' work. Humboldt's liberalism, his support for the French and American Revolutions, his vehement, lifelong opposition to slavery are well known. Nevertheless, the *Personal Narrative* naturalizes colonial relations and racial hierarchy, representing Americans, above all, in terms of the quintessential colonial relationship of *disponibilité*.

In the liminal space of the preface to the *Personal Narrative*, Humboldt alludes directly to the Euroexpansionist process which motivates his writing. "If some pages of my book are snatched from oblivion," we read, then

> the inhabitant of the banks of the Oroonoko will behold with extasy, that populous cities enriched by commerce, and fertile fields cultivated by the hands of freemen, adorn those very spots, where, at the time of my travels, I found only impenetrable forests, and inundated lands.[32]

Ecstasy and adornment, cities and fields: the entwined civic and esthetic fantasies are given meaning by corresponding negative visions of "impenetrable forests" and "inundated lands." But who will be this future seer? Will the future cultivators themselves behold with ecstasy (if they are allowed to stop work to behold at all)? Will the forest inhabitants, if they survive, see the fields as adornments? Between Humboldt and his ecstatic future counterpart there lies a chain of events from which Humboldt excludes himself, yet in whose name he writes.

Since I am concerned with representations of South America, I will not be discussing Humboldt's well-known *Political Essay on the Kingdom of New Spain* (i.e. Mexico) and its companion *Political Essay on the Island of Cuba*. These works approach human society through statistical and demographic description and a social analysis based on environmental determinism. Unlike the nature writings, they do not give rise to a myth, yet they share two aspects of the mythic world of primal nature: ahistoricity and the absence of culture. Scholars still value the *Political Essays* as sources, especially in the history of slavery and race relations. Humboldt's *Political Essay* on Mexico is said to have produced singlehandedly a British investment boom there in silver mining, and he was blamed for exaggeration when the boom went bust in 1830. Humboldt's exposé of Cuban slavery remained explosive: in 1856, a North American edition of his *Political Essay* on Cuba saw fit to repress the chapter arguing for abolition. Humboldt, in his eighties, protested furiously in the German press.

Geographically, the *Political Essays* dealing with Cuba and Mexico are in complementary distribution with the estheticized nature writings that depict South America. Partly this distribution has to do with the logistics of Humboldt's own travels. He stayed only a short time in Cuba, and his year in Mexico was spent mainly in and near the capital with Mexican scholars and libraries. The *Political Essays* reflect such research, following lines of reportage laid down by colonial bureaucracies. The contrast with his writings on South America is also ideological, however, for Humboldt really did regard Mexico in particular as civilized in a way South America was not. "Nothing struck me more forcibly," he wrote in the preface to his essay on Mexico, "than the contrast between the civilization of New Spain and the meagre physical and moral culture of those areas which I had

Statue of an Aztech Priestess.

22 Statue of an Aztec priestess. From Humboldt's *Views of the Cordilleras* (1814).

just passed through."[33] His project in Mexico becomes one of explaining Mexico's remarkable progress in comparison with equatorial America. Such attitudes are evident in the final work to be considered here, the popular *Views of the Cordilleras*.

ARCHEOLOGIZED AMERICA

I mentioned earlier that it took a rather selective reception of Humboldt's American writings to produce the image of América as primal nature. It is symptomatic of that reception that the popular two-volume *Views of the Cordilleras and Monuments of the Indigenous Peoples of America* (1810 and 1814) almost instantly lost the second half of its title, to be remembered only as *Views of the Cordilleras*. Originally published in 1810 as a two-volume *Picturesque Atlas* that included sixty-nine stunning plates, it was a popular companion to the *Views of Nature*. *Views and Monuments*, as I shall call it for short, combined illustrated commentaries on natural wonders – the mountain Chimborazo, natural rock bridges, cataracts, lakes – with illustrated commentaries on pre-Columbian archeological relics from Peru and (mainly) Mexico – the pyramid at Cholula, the

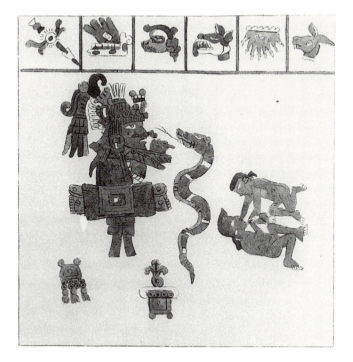

23 Aztec hieroglyphic manuscript found by Humboldt in the Vatican. From
Views of the Cordilleras (1814).

Aztec calendar stone, the statue of an Aztec priestess, hieroglyphic paintings and manuscripts. The book was not remembered for its archeological component. One modern commentator still dismisses it as "an
odd mixture of descriptions and illustrations of mountain views and
Aztec art."[34]

Humboldt himself intended more than an "odd mixture," of course. His
aim, apparently unsuccessful, was to create something that would be received
as neither odd nor a mixture, but as harmony and connection. The aim of
"presenting in the same work the rude monuments of the indigenous tribes
of America, and the picturesque views of the mountainous countries which
they inhabited" is to show that "the climate, the nature of the soil, the
physiognomy of the plants, the view of beautiful or of savage nature
have great influence on the progress of the arts."[35] The harmony results,
in this case, from assimilating culture to nature in a way that guarantees
the inferior status of indigenous America: the more savage the nature, the
more savage the culture. Nevertheless, the archeological essays in *Views
and Monuments* had at least the potential to contradict dramatically the

dehistoricized celebration of primal America and the primitivist view of the Amerindians that went with it. Even a little knowledge of Inca, Aztec, or Maya culture and history shakes up images of savages in the primeval forest, including Humboldt's own image of Amerindians as "remnants of indigenous hordes." Perhaps this is the very reason the archeological essays have never been absorbed by Humboldt's readers and commentators.

One powerful model for the archeological rediscovery of America was Egypt. There, too, Europeans were reconstructing a lost history through, and as, "rediscovered" monuments and ruins. There, too, the recovery occurred in the context of a new European expansionism and a nostalgic rethinking of earlier empires. Such Egyptian finds as the Rosetta stone no doubt inspired Humboldt's interest in American hieroglyphic manuscripts and stones, the subject of some of the longest and most erudite essays in the *Views and Monuments*. In the context of two centuries of European ignorance and indifference, Humboldt's observations on indigenous history are remarkable, sometimes even prophetic: after describing the famous "Aztec calendar" stone uncovered by water workers in Mexico City in 1790, he says the Aztecs "will become particularly interesting if a government, anxious to throw light on the remote civilization of the Americans, should make researches by digging round the cathedral in the chief square of the ancient Tenochtitlan."[36] In the 1970s the digging took place, after a team of electrical workers came across what indeed turned out to be the Great Temple (Templo Mayor) of the Aztecs.

While obviously fascinated and moved by his archeological findings, Humboldt remained relentlessly disparaging of the achievements of pre-Colombian civilizations – in comparison, of course, with those of the classical Mediterranean: "American architecture, we cannot too often repeat, can cause no astonishment, either by the magnitude of its works, or the elegance of their form," he writes, "but it is highly interesting, as it throws light on the history of the primitive civilization of the inhabitants of the mountains of the new continent."[37] While in Greece, "religions became the chief support of the fine arts"; among the Aztecs, the primitive cult of death results in monuments whose only goal is "to produce terror and dismay."[38] As with the monumentalist reinvention of Egypt in the same period, the links between the societies being archeologized and their contemporary descendants remain absolutely obscure, indeed irrecoverable. This, of course, is part of the point. The European imagination produces archeological subjects by splitting contemporary non-European peoples off from their precolonial, and even their colonial, pasts. To revive indigenous history and culture as archeology is to revive them *as dead*. The gesture simultaneously rescues them from European forgetfulness and reassigns them to a departed age.

I have spoken repeatedly in this book of how European discourse of landscape deterritorializes indigenous peoples, separating them off from territories they may once have dominated, and in which they continue to make their lives. The archeological perspective is complementary. It, too, obliterates the conquered inhabitants of the contact zone as historical agents who have living continuities with pre-European pasts and historically based aspirations and claims on the present. Those whom colonizers see as "remnants of indigenous hordes" are unlikely to see themselves as such, however. What colonizers kill off as archeology often lives among the colonized as self-knowledge and historical consciousness, two principal ingredients of anti-colonial resistance movements.[39] The Andean rebellion of 1781, for instance, involved a mass charismatic revival predicting the return of the old Incas and the restoration of their empire. It presupposed among the Andean populace an everyday knowledge of Inca history, mythology, and genealogy, preserved in quipus and oral, written, and pictorial forms. Of the couple who led the rebellion, one renamed himself Tupac Amaru after the last legitimate Inca ruler, who was burned alive in 1572 by the Spanish in the main square of Cuzco. In 1781, after the failure of the rebellion, the new Tupac Amaru was drawn and quartered in the same place.[40]

HUMBOLDT AS TRANSCULTURATOR

"The Indians," reads the passage from the *Personal Narrative* quoted above, "fixed our attention on those beautiful red and golden yellow woods." On the Orinoco a *corregidor* who "gave us three Indians to go in front and open up a path" proves in conversation to be "a likeable man, cultivated in spirit."[41] A few lines later on that very path, a missionary bores Humboldt with anxious monologues on recent slave unrest. Such traces of the everyday interaction between American inhabitants and European visitors suggest the heterogeneous and heteroglossic relationships that produced the Europeans' seeing and knowing. Brought to the surface by narrativity, the "merely personal," as Humboldt called it, raises a challenging question: What hand did Humboldt's American interlocutors have directly and otherwise, in the European reinvention of their continent? To what extent was Humboldt a transculturator, transporting to Europe knowledges American in origin; producing European knowledges infiltrated by non-European ones? To what extent, within relations of colonial subordination, did Americans inscribe themselves on him, as well as he on América?

Such questions are difficult to answer from within bourgeois, author-centered ways of knowing texts – which is why it is important to ask them, not just of Humboldt but of all travel writing. Every travel account has this heteroglossic dimension; its knowledge comes not just out of a traveler's sensibility and powers of observation, but out of interaction and experience usually directed and managed by "travelees,"[42] who are working from their own understandings of their world and of what the Europeans are and ought to be doing. For instance, Humboldt prided himself on being the first person to bring guano to Europe as a fertilizer, a "discovery" that eventually led to the guano boom which by the end of the century caused a war between Peru and Chile and brought the latter's economy into total dependence on British bankers. Of course, Humboldt's discovery consisted of coastal Peruvians telling him of the substance and its fertilizing properties. Who knows what their assumptions and expectations were? The conventions of travel and exploration writing (production and reception) constitute the European subject as a self-sufficient, monadic source of knowledge. That configuration virtually guarantees that the interactional history of the representation will turn up only as traces,[43] or through the "travelee's" own forms of representation, such as autoethnographic materials of the sort mentioned at points throughout this book.

What have been documented are Humboldt and Bonpland's encounters with Spanish American intellectuals, whom they actively sought out. In sealing off its empire from outsiders, Spain had left the rest of Europe in profound ignorance of American indigenous history, culture, and language, as well as American botany, zoology, and mineralogy. These matters had continued to be studied within the Americas, however. (Is it necessary to repeat that universities in Peru and Mexico date from the sixteenth century?) Humboldt and Bonpland, we are told, went far out of their way to meet American naturalists like Mutis in Bogota; it was Spanish American intellectuals who put them in touch with Inca and Aztec antiquity. To a great extent in his archeological essays, Humboldt was transporting to Europe an American scholarly tradition dating back to the first Spanish missionaries, and sustained by Spanish, mestizo, and indigenous intellectuals. Humboldt's year in Mexico (1803–4) was spent almost entirely in the intellectual and scientific communities of Mexico City, where he studied existing corpuses on natural history, linguistics, and archeology. On his return to Europe, he followed up assiduously on what he had learned, tracking down forgotten Amerindian manuscripts, such as Maya codicils, that since the Habsburgs had been gathering dust in libraries in Paris, Dresden, the Vatican, Vienna, and Berlin.[44]

In some sectors of creole culture, then, a glorified American nature and a glorified American antiquity already existed as ideological constructs, sources of Americanist identification and pride fueling the growing sense of separateness from Europe. In a perfect example of the mirror dance of colonial meaning-making, Humboldt transculturated to Europe knowledges produced by Americans in a process of defining themselves as separate from Europe. Following independence, Euroamerican elites would reimport that knowledge *as European knowledge* whose authority would legitimate Euroamerican rule.

ROMANTIC INTERLUDE

The perspective I have been proposing on Humboldt's writings often provokes an impatient response among literary critics. What is the point, I am asked, of all this historical-colonial-ideological explanatory apparatus, when it is perfectly obvious that Humboldt in his writings is simply *being* a Romantic, simply *doing* Romanticism? As a Romantic, the German kind, how else would he write about South America? One need read no farther than the preface to *Views of Nature*, which ends with a quotation from Schiller's *Bride of Messina* about how nature is perfect till man deforms it with care. Before he had ever set foot outside Prussia, was Humboldt not the only scientist Schiller offered to publish in his journal? Though Schiller might not have seen it this way (he apparently disliked Humboldt), might one not argue, for example, that Humboldt in his American *Views* simply carries out the program of Schiller's *Aesthetic Education of Man* (1795)? Is it not the Romantics who call for the "cultivation of the sensibilities"? Is Humboldt not, for example, trying to "culture" his reader in the way Schiller prescribes: "providing the receptive faculty with the most multifarious contacts with the world"?[45] Why does one need Columbus, Spanish colonialism, independence struggles, slave revolts, or even America to understand Humboldt's way of writing? What is already known about Romanticism provides a perfectly satisfying account without stepping beyond the borders of either Europe or Literature.

As some readers will have anticipated, it is that very satisfaction and those very borders I would call into question through Humboldt's American writings. To the extent that Humboldt "is" a Romantic, Romanticism "is" Humboldt; to the extent that something called Romanticism constitutes or "explains" Humboldt's writing on America, those writings constitute and "explain" that something. To argue that the former simply "reflects" the latter is to privilege the Literary and the European in a way which must be opened to question. The perspective of this book would call for rethinking "Romanticism" (and "Literature," and "Europe") in the light of writers like Humboldt and historical processes like changing contact with the Americas. "Romanticism," then, provides an occasion to rethink habits of imagining "Europe" and "Literature" as *sui generis* entities that invent themselves from within then project outward onto the rest of the world. One can glimpse what it is like to imagine "Europe" as also constructing itself from the outside in, out of materials infiltrated, donated, absorbed, appropriated, and imposed from contact zones all over the planet.

To the degree that "Romanticism" shapes the new discourses on America,

Egypt, southern Africa, Polynesia, or Italy, *they* shape *it*. (Romantics are certainly known for stationing themselves round Europe's peripheries – the Hellespont, the Alps, the Pyrenees, Italy, Russia, Egypt.) Romanticism *consists*, among other things, of shifts in relations between Europe and other parts of the world – notably the Americas, which are, precisely, liberating themselves from Europe. If one unhooks Humboldt from Schiller and locates him in another "Romantic" line – George Forster and Bernardin de St. Pierre (two of Humboldt's personal idols), Volney, Chateaubriand, Stedman, Buffon, Le Vaillant, Captain Cook, and the Diderot of the "Supplement to the Voyage of Bougainville" – one might be tempted to argue that Romanticism originated in the contact zones of America, North Africa, and the South Seas.

In fact, such a view was proposed in South America some fifty years ago by the Venezuelan writer Teresa de la Parra in her autobiographical novel *Memorias de Mama Blanca* (*Memoirs of Mama Blanca*, 1929). Romanticism is invoked in the figure of Napoleon's wife, the Empress Josephine, who (like the wealth that fueled the French Revolution) came from the Caribbean. "I believe," the narrator says,

> that like tobacco, pineapple, and sugar cane, Romanticism was an indigenous [American] fruit that grew up sweet, spontaneous and hidden among colonial languors and tropical indolence until the end of the eighteenth century. Around that time, Josefina Tascher, unsuspectingly, as if she were an ideal microbe, carried it off [to Europe] tangled up in the lace of one of her headdresses, gave the germ to Napoleon in that acute form which we all know, and little by little, the troops of the First Empire, assisted by Chateaubriand, spread the epidemic everywhere.[46]

It is a richly transculturated set of images. The reference to headdresses recalls the iconography of America as an Amazon with a huge feather headdress carrying the head of a Spaniard by the hair; the image of the microbe recalls the history of syphilis as the disease of empire, here imported back into Europe through its own plunder. The same microbe undoubtedly is what eventually brought the Empress Josephine together with Aimé Bonpland, who began as keeper of her gardens, and wound up her devoted friend and confidant.

Arguments about origins are notoriously pointless. It is not pointless, however, to underscore the transcultural dimensions of what is canonically called European Romanticism. Westerners are accustomed to thinking of romantic projects of liberty, individualism, and liberalism as emanating *from* Europe *to* the colonial periphery, but less accustomed to thinking about emanations *from* the contact zones *back* into Europe. Surely Europe was as much influenced *by* as an influence *on* the tensions which in the 1780s produced the Indian uprising in the Andes, revolts in South Africa,

24 Frontispiece of Humboldt's *Atlas of America*. The allegory depicts a
defeated Aztec warrior prince being consoled by Athena, goddess of
wisdom, and Hermes, god of trade. At the bottom lies a smashed statue.
In the background stands a mountain modeled on Chimborazo and the
pyramid of Cholula in Ecuador in Mexico. The caption reads "Humanity,
Knowledge, Economy."

the Tiradentes' rebellion in Brazil, the revolution that overthrew white rule in Santo Domingo, and other such events in the contact zones. Benedict Anderson has argued intriguingly that contrary to the usual diffusionist analysis, the model of the modern nation state was worked out largely in the Americas and imported to Europe during the nineteenth century.[47]

I believe one must seek a similar relational perspective on the famous *querelle d'Amérique* with which Humboldt is so often associated. For surely the debate on the supposed immaturity and inferiority of American nature was not an exclusively European, or scientific, matter. As Antonello Gerbi has documented, intellectuals from the Americas were active and highly interested participants in the debate on nature, as they were in contemporaneous debates over slavery. Indeed it is possible neither debate would have shaped up as a debate without the participation of Americans, for whom the issues had urgent significance.

Apart from specific debates on the relative ages of various continents and their ecosystems, the ideological dimensions of the *querelle d'Amérique* hinged on the attempt to bind the Americas to Europe in an essentialized relationship of negativity, the pivot of colonial semantics. The attempt came, of course, at a moment of increasing instability in Europe's colonial enterprises in the Americas. On the one hand global exploration was opening up vast new realities and possibilities. On the other, Eurocolonial control was clearly in jeopardy. Here were societies taking on a life of their own. Here, in some cases, were American intellectuals constructing positive, decolonized visions of themselves in relation to Europe. Here were non-European majorities asserting themselves against European domination. And even where white hegemony was secure, what it was producing were societies that were very different from their European forbears, and would become more different as they decolonized. They would be multiracial, many predominantly non-white, unevenly Christian at best; they would never have been monarchies; they would be built out of formations like slavery, the plantation system, the hacienda, the *mita*,[48] institutions Europeans had devised and profited from, but which had not been lived out in Europe as social and cultural formations. They would be societies Europe was unlikely even to understand, let alone control.

Occult forces indeed! Gerbi suggests that Humboldt, with his positive, totalizing vision, put to rest anxieties on both sides of the Atlantic, revindicating America *within* European-based planetary paradigms. "With Humboldt," says Gerbi, "Western thought at last achieves the peaceful conquest and intellectual annexation to its own world, the only Cosmos, of the regions which until then had been hardly more than an object of curiosity, amazement, or derision."[49] The title page of Humboldt's 1814 *Atlas géographique et physique du Nouveau Continent* carries an allegorical engraving of Hermes and Athena (see plate 24) looking sorrowfully down on a defeated Aztec prince, his head bowed, his weapons on the ground. While Hermes (patron of trade) grasps the warrior's arm, Athena offers him a piece of decidedly non-American vegetation: an olive branch. In the background rises the snow-peaked Chimborazo. But one wonders if the annexation was really so peaceful. Perhaps the subterranean events, invisible energies, and sudden cold blasts that swirl around in Humboldt's writings figured the historical upheavals so clearly underway. Certainly they did for Humboldt's admirer Simón Bolívar. "A great volcano lies at our feet," wrote Bolívar in the wake of victory over Spain. "Who shall restrain the oppressed classes? The yoke of slavery will break, each shade of complexion will seek mastery."[50]

As I hope to show in the next chapter, their very mystification of social forces is what made Humboldt's writings usable to Euroamerican leaders and intellectuals seeking to decolonize their cultures and societies while retaining European-based values and white supremacy.

POSTSCRIPT

Today, after his fame in Europe has faded or merged with that of his brother, Alexander von Humboldt is steadfastly revered and revived in South American official culture precisely for his unconditional, intrinsic valorization of the region. "Estamos sembrados de recuerdos de Humboldt," says one commentator – "We are sown with memories of Humboldt."[51] How clear a witness this bears to the legacy of the Humboldtian Euromyth of América: the speaker constitutes himself as the very ground on which Humboldt has sown his words. *Within* the Euromyth, the Spanish American is accorded scarcely any other existence, and certainly no voice: only Nature speaks.

But perhaps there are other more tangled genealogies as well. The *arpillera* or fabric picture in plate 25 is an instance of a form of export art that emerged in Peru in the 1980s, drawing on ancient traditions of Andean dollmaking and textile art. Made by proletarian women in mothers' clubs in towns and cities, the contemporary *arpilleras* often depict scenes from rural life, as this one does. Titled "La Cosecha," "The Harvest," it foregrounds the vertical organization of agricultural life in traditional Andean communities. At the top, in the high pastures, herding is going on, a little farther down grow the flowers so prized in daily life and courtship, then grains and grasses, then potatoes, and so on down to the oranges and bananas in the tropical valley below. It represents a way of life in which communities at different times of the year cultivate a great variety of crops at different altitudes, under everything from tropical through temperate to nearly frigid conditions.

Compare the *arpillera* with Humboldt's famed labeled drawing of Mount Chimborazo in plate 20 above. Humboldt used his picture to depict the same

25 *Arpillera*, Peru, 1980s. The work depicts in folkloric style the vertical organization of Andean argicultural life. Herd animals graze at high altitudes (*sierra*), where people also gather grasses and flowers; potatoes (*papas*) of various kinds are grown at mid altitudes; bananas, oranges, and other tropical fruits in lowlands. Llamas work throughout as beasts of burden.

vertical ecology of the Andean region, where multiple types of climate and vegetation coexist at a single latitude. Both representations set out a kind of atemporal mapping; both seem intended to celebrate plenitude, variety, and detail. The *arpillera* also shares with Humboldt the use of referential written labels (in a European language) identifying *papas*, Spanish "potatoes," and *sierra*, Spanish for "mountains." Differences between the two representations also stand out: the *arpillera* depicts a social space teeming with people and domestic animals whose activities contribute as much to the variety as the plant world does. The written labels signal two of the most meaningful elements of traditional Andean culture: the sierra (home of the gods) and the potato (the all-important staple food). While Humboldt's labels are referential and specific, these two signifiers in the *arpillera* are slippery in a way intrinsic to transcultural communication: they could be expected to resonate differently for Andean and metropolitan audiences. Non-Andeans, for instance, may not know of the Andean deities who reside in the mountain peaks, or of the healing powers of potatoes. And if they do "know" these things, they know them as outsiders. Know them, for instance, in Spanish, while insiders know them in Quechua or Aymara. Appropriated from Europe, labeling in the *arpillera* seems to work along lines other than European objectivism.

But is there a historical basis for relating the contemporary *arpillera* and Humboldt's 1805 drawing? Made for metropolitan consumers,[52] does the *arpillera* presuppose the western tradition of objectified, dehistoricized landscape description? Does it propose a humanized counterversion? Does it propose a miniaturized, "folkloric" counterversion the West itself has ordered up to complement the objectified tradition? And on the other hand, did Humboldt's own vertical ("fantastic," Michael Taussig calls it[53]) interpretation of Chimborazo have an Andean dimension? Did the Andean guides and interpreters who took him there convey to him some of their own knowledge of the ecosystem and their reverence for it?

In the 1960s, Andeanists became fascinated with what they labeled the "vertical archipelago" of traditional Andean agricultural production. Andean communities, they realized, comprised the most intricate agro ecological complexes known on earth. What Humboldt had marveled at in the plant world, the anthropologists and agronomists of the 1960s marveled at in the socioecological world – often as if they, too, had "discovered" it. Is the *arpillera*-maker depicting the vertical archipelago as she knows it, or as she knows the agronomists knew it, or against the way she knows the agronomists knew it? Is she reproducing a Peruvian national myth? A product of the contact zone, the *arpillera* perhaps makes what I referred to in chapter 1 as an autoethnographic gesture, transculturating elements of metropolitan discourses to create self-affirmations designed for reception in the metropolis. In such autoethnographic representations, subjugated subjects engage, and seek to engage, the metropolis's constructions of those it subjugates. In this "mirror dance," as Taussig calls it, Humboldt's América remains one of the mirrors.

Chapter 7

Reinventing América II: The capitalist vanguard and the *exploratrices sociales*

PROLEGOMENA

Andean historians recount that from the time of Sir Walter Raleigh, a prediction had persisted among Andean nobility that the English would come to South America to restore the Inca dynasty.[1] When this prophecy appeared in print in 1723, in the prologue to a new edition of Inca Garcilaso de la Vega's *Royal Commentaries of the Incas*, the book was banned by colonial authorities because of its potential insurrectional effects on the native elites. The fact that in the eighteenth century, a book written in Spanish (quoting a prophecy written in Latin) could be seen as likely to agitate the Inca nobility in Cuzco suggests both the extent to which the native elite had maintained an identity as an adversarial caste, and the extent of their interconnectedness with the cultural institutions of the conquerors. Over 250 years since the conquest, they had adapted to Spanish rule, intermarrying with Spanish colonialists and sharing the fruits of colonial exploitation, and had maintained independent identities and political aspirations.

When the English finally did arrive, a century later, the indigenous elite no longer existed as a social formation or a political force. Its power, on the increase throughout the eighteenth century, had been broken first by the wave of repression following the rebellion of 1781, and finally by the republican forces which won out in the struggle for independence. Till the very end of the wars of independence, however, the independentist general San Martín, whose mother belonged to the indigenous nobility, had fought for the restoration of the Inca monarchy as the path to independence from Spain. San Martín makes a brief appearance in what follows, as a fugitive in the home of an English traveler who had precious little understanding of the remarkable history that lay behind his peculiar aspirations. She would never have seen the Andean portraits of the thirteen heads of the Inca dynasty (see plate 26), or the newer versions in which San Martín himself appeared, in Inca dress.[2] After independence, the Inca dynasty continued to be a favored subject of the painters of Cuzco, and their serial depictions of it became

26 Inca-Spanish dynasty. From Antonio de Ulloa and Jorge Juan's *Viaje en América meridional* (Madrid, Antonio Marín, 1748). A highly stylized, and Europeanized, version of a traditional Andean depiction of the Inca dynasty. Portraits of the 14 Incas in chronological sequence from Manco Capac to Atahuallpa are followed by portraits of the 8 Spanish monarchs who followed the conquest. In certain later, independence-era versions, the final spot is occupied by Simón Bolívar or the mestizo general San Martín, in Inca dress (Gisbert, 1980).

a popular souvenir among the English travelers who finally did arrive, a century or two too late.

THE CAPITALIST VANGUARD

On the heels of Alexander von Humboldt, European travelers descended on South America by the dozen. Men, women, scientists, soldiers, speculators – they were all thrilled to be there. In 1825, W. B. Stevenson was exaggerating only slightly when he claimed, "without the least exaggeration," that although the lands of South America "were discovered in the sixteenth century, they have remained almost unknown till the beginning of the nineteenth."[3] Only twenty years before, when John Mawe was, as he put it, "induced to undertake a voyage of commercial experiment, on a limited scale, to the Rio de la Plata," he had been thrown in prison immediately on his arrival and got to know the interior only as a captive.[4]

By the 1820s, the South American revolutions, in which Britain and France were major military and monetary participants, had become a source of immense interest in Europe, making it, as Stevenson said, "an almost imperative duty" for travelers to "commit themselves to writing."[5] The revolutions were also what made travel possible, and the commercial opportunities they opened created a momentum that easily rivaled Humboldt's scientific and esthetic passions. As other commentators have observed,[6] the wave of South American travelers in the 1810s and 1820s were mainly British, and mainly traveled and wrote as advance scouts for European capital. Engineers, mineralogists, breeders, agronomists, as well as military men – these early nineteenth-century travelers were often sent to the "new continent" by companies of European investors as experts in search of exploitable resources, contacts, and contracts with local elites, information on potential ventures, labor conditions, transport, market potentials, and so forth. Except for "isolated cases," says Argentine historian Noe Jitrik,

> they were moved to visit us by a powerful mercantile curiosity, instruments, at times involuntary . . . of the relentless European economic expansion which since the end of the eighteenth century, and even earlier, combined knowledge with implantation, scientific interest with the need for concrete domination, humanism with production and markets.[7]

This chapter is about the reinvention of America that occurred in their writings, in contrast with those of Alexander von Humboldt, and with those of the American creoles themselves. It is also about gender, for this wave of traveler-writers included some European women, among the first to be taken seriously in the genre.

By the late eighteenth century the business classes of Britain and France made no secret of their designs on Spanish America. Britain unsuccessfully invaded La Plata in 1806 and again in 1807, and had a longstanding stake in the outcome of the struggles against Spain. Nor did Spanish American elites conceal their hopes of productive new relationships with Northern Europe. Creole leaders had trekked regularly to London and Paris to seek support for their efforts. That is how Simón Bolívar met Alexander von Humboldt in 1808, for example. When the Spanish American revolutions broke out in earnest after 1810, British officers, working as mercenaries, proved highly influential in the military struggle against Spain, as well as in the internal conflicts that followed. With them came thousands of British soldiers and sailors. A British Legion fought for Bolívar. Private European businessmen, like John Miers and John Robertson in Chile, provided, not always willingly, continuous financing for the republican cause. From 1817 on, Bolívar's right-hand man was an Irishman named Daniel O'Leary.

By the mid-1820s, small European expatriate communities were forming in many South American capitals, and the gates were open wide to economic adventures of all kinds. Mining was one common obsession, especially for British investment during the 1810s and 1820s. The collapse of Spanish authority had left many of América's most famous mines in ruins; reviving them called for extensive capital and technological expertise, both of which the colonies themselves lacked. Foreigners gladly stepped in; mining investment companies burgeoned overnight on the London Stock Exchange as investors prepared to get rich quick. In a letter written in 1826, Simón Bolívar reaffirmed the high hopes he had invested in Britain, "that mistress of the universe." "If we can procure alliance with her," he wrote his ally General Santander, "you may be certain that our future happiness is assured."[8]

It wasn't, and neither was that of the British investors, at least not in the short run. The logistic and technological difficulties of trade and industry proved far greater than anticipated in the new republics, shattered and impoverished by years of warfare and neglect. Several well-known travel accounts from the period, such as Francis Bond Head's *Rough Notes of some Journeys across the Pampas and in the Andes* (1826) and Joseph Andrews' *Journey from Buenos Ayres to Chile* (1827), were written by envoys of British mining associations sent to investigate the collapse of their hasty hopes. Indeed, except for the loan business and the Argentine cattle industry, the initial British investment boom in Spanish America was largely in retreat by the 1830s. European economic penetration was to regain its momentum with a vengeance in the second half of the century. From the late 1850s on, European, especially British, capital poured into South America in the form of loans to build railways and roads, modernize ports and mines, and develop new industries like nitrates in Peru and grain production in Argentina and Chile. By the late 1880s several countries, including the three just mentioned, had become complete economic dependencies of Britain, or rather of the investors in the British Stock Exchange.

This neocolonial trajectory is both presupposed and enacted by many postindependence traveler-writers in Spanish America. I call them the capitalist vanguard. Far from mystifying European expansionist designs in their writings, the capitalist vanguard tended to thematize them – indeed, consecrate them. Joseph Andrews dedicated his 1827 *Travels* to the British Chancellor of the Exchequer "for the political talent and foresight which opened to Great Britain the full commercial advantages of the newly enfranchised states of South America"[9]; W. B. Stevenson dedicated his to the British mercenary Lord Cochrane "for the important services rendered to South American Emancipation and to the commercial interests of Great Britain."[10]

One itinerary in particular became a canonical heroic paradigm for the Englishman's South American journey: landing in the port of Buenos Aires, he made his way overland across the Argentine pampas, up over the Andean Cordillera and down the other side to the capitals of Chile or Peru, from which he eventually embarked by sea for home. It was an ancient trail, much of it on Incaic and pre-Incaic roadways. The path had been worn deep during the period of Spanish colonial rule, when Spanish trade restrictions forbade direct communication between Buenos Aires and Spain. Goods and letters headed for Argentina had first to be shipped through Lima then carried overland to the southeastern parts of the continent. This grueling overland trek from Lima to Buenos Aires is the subject of the most famous travel book written within colonial Spanish America, the sardonically titled *Lazarillo de ciegos caminantes* (*Guide for the Walking Blind*, 1771). In a new, but equally imperial project, the capitalist vanguard made this same trip in reverse, relying on the same infrastructure the Spanish had used. Following independence, Buenos Aires and its environs rapidly overtook Lima as a point of entry and center of transatlantic entrepreneurial energies, which then flowed westward as they were doing in North America.

Unlike explorers and naturalists, these travelers of the 1820s did not write up realities they took for new; they did not present themselves as discoverers of a primal world; the bits of nature they collected were samples of raw materials, not pieces of Nature's cosmic design. In their writings, the contemplative, estheticizing rhetoric of discovery is often replaced by a goal-oriented rhetoric of conquest and achievement. In many accounts, the itinerary itself becomes the occasion for a narrative of success, in which travel is a triumph in its own right. What are conquered are destinations, not kingdoms; what are overcome are not military challenges, but logistical ones. The travelers struggle in unequal battle against scarcity, inefficiency, laziness, discomfort, poor horses, bad roads, bad weather, delays. Indeed, Spanish American society is mainly encoded in this literature as logistical obstacles to the forward movement of the Europeans. While such matters were seldom thematized by Humboldt (much less acquiring heroic potential), for the capitalist vanguard, they were at times almost obsessive, the journey allegorizing the lust for progress. Timetabling proliferates, as in John Miers:

We had been thirteen days, travelling 180 leagues, averaging only fourteen leagues per day, instead of the twenty-five leagues we expected to have accomplished. Now that we had fairly entered upon the high post road, I was not disposed so easily to admit the excuses for delay which the peons were ever ready to urge on all occasions.[11]

Miers, mind you, was in a particular hurry, because he was crossing the Andes accompanied by his wife, who was about to give birth. She did, on the floor of a posthouse, and became famous, like Mme. Godin, for a story she never wrote down.

As one might expect, primal nature held considerably less interest for these economic adventurers than it did for Humboldt and his disciples. Certainly it had none of the intrinsic, esthetic value Humboldt assigned it. Indeed, as Jean Franco has discussed, this wave of traveler-writers often sought out a consciously anti-esthetic stance in their writings, introducing pragmatic and economistic rhetorics that shared neither the estheticism nor the tolerance of Humboldt and his more courtly followers. In 1815 John Mawe declared himself flatly incapable of describing the "wild and romantic" landscape of La Plata, and satisfied himself by exclaiming simply: "What a scene for an enterprising agriculturalist! At present all is neglected."[12] In direct contrast with Humboldt, unexploited nature tends to be seen in this literature as troubling or ugly, its very primalness a sign of the failure of human enterprise. Neglect became the touchstone of a negative esthetic that legitimated European interventionism.[13] Probably influenced by Humboldt's esthetic descriptions, Robert Proctor in 1825 expressed disappointment at the view from the top of the Andes. He conspicuously encodes the letdown in terms of money and dominance:

Making all allowance for poetical exaggeration, I certainly thought from what I had read in the accounts of other travellers that I should be able to stretch my sight to Chili, described as the richest country of the globe, spread out at our feet like a map, and repaying our toil by the boundlessness and luxuriance of its prospects.[14]

Instead, before him, "enormous black mountains were piled together without order, and seemed much more barren and savage than those we had already passed." Charles Brand in 1828 found the Argentine pampas "barren and inhospitable," while encountering esthetic satisfaction in scenes of indigenous labor. "It was beautiful," he says when two mule trains meet on a trail, "to see the peons keeping their own troops separate from each other."[15] Charles Cochrane, in Colombia to investigate the potential of mines and pearl fisheries, wrote up the American landscape as a dormant machine waiting to be cranked into activity:

In that country there is every facility for enterprise, and every prospect of success: man alone is wanting to set the whole machine in motion, which is now inactive but which, with capital and industry, may be rendered productive of certain advantage and ultimate wealth.[16]

"Man" here evidently refers to someone other than the country's current inhabitants. For Frenchman Gaspar Mollien (*Travels in the Republic of Colombia*, 1824), primal nature was either uninteresting or indecipherable. In the following passage, the forest is textualized as a site not of density of meaning, but of absence of meaning; beauty is found in domesticated landscapes reminiscent of his native France:

> After traversing a very thick wood, we kept continually on the ascent till we arrived at a spot from which a prospect truly magnificent burst upon our view: the whole province of Maraquita lay before us, its mountains appearing from the place where we stood, but as insignificant hillocks: we could however distinguish the white houses of Maraquita. Much nearer to us lay the town of Honda, the walls of which are washed by the Magdalena, whose verdant banks impart peculiar beauty to the surrounding landscape. One would have supposed it to have been the Seine meandering through the rich meadows of Normandy. This beautiful sight however soon vanished as I again struck into the wood.[17]

Description ends rather than begins with the primeval forest; the exoticism and spectatorial estheticizing of Humboldt and his followers are completely set aside. Sometimes Humboldt's writings were specifically singled out for criticism. Stevenson finds they are "too scientific, and enter into too few details to become fit for general perusal."[18] (The details lacking in Humboldt are, it appears, logistical ones that inform potential visitors on practical matters.) The edenic and the pastoral are often replaced in the capitalist vanguard's writings by a modernizing extractive vision best exemplified by a trope one might call "industrial revery." Here is one mining engineer's view of the Andes in 1827:

> Gazing on the nearest chain and its towering summits, Don Thomas and myself erected airy castles on their huge sides. We excavated rich veins of ore, we erected furnaces for smelting, we saw in imagination a crowd of workmen moving like busy insects along the eminences, and fancied the wild and vast region peopled by the energies of Britons from a distance of nine or ten thousand miles.[19]

While Spanish American society occupied the margins of Humboldt's travel writings, it was an integral part of the capitalist vanguard's account of América. The elites are frequently praised for their hospitality, their aristocratic way of life, and their appreciation of Europeans. Spanish American society in general, however, is relentlessly indicted for backwardness, indolence, and, above all, the "failure" to exploit the resources surrounding it. The anti-esthetic of neglect is applied to the American social world as well as the landscape. "While nature has been profuse in her blessings," said John Mawe, "the inhabitants have been neglectful in improvement of them."[20] Notes Mollien, "The greater proportion of the lands lie fallow; they would, however, produce considerable crops, if the inhabitants were less indifferent. No encouragement can rouse them from their indolent habits and usual routine."[21] According to John Miers, "The people out of the villages, although living on the most fertile ground, and having nothing to do, never cultivate the smallest spot."[22] The maximizing, extractive paradigm of capitalism is presupposed, making a mystery of subsistence and non-accumulative lifeways.

The failures of Spanish American economic life are diagnosed in this literature not simply as the refusal to work, but also more specifically as the failure to rationalize, specialize, and maximize production. European visitors expressed dismay at the absence of enclosures and fences, the indifference to the separation of weeds from crops, the absence of interest in diversifying crops, the failure (particularly irksome to John Mawe) to "preserve the breed" in dogs, horses, even themselves. With equal vigor the creoles (i.e. Euroamericans), especially in the provincial interior, are criticized for failing to develop modern habits of consumption. Though enthusiasm was often expressed for the picturesqueness of provincial society, traveler after discomfited traveler complains of creole indifference to the virtues of comfort, efficiency, cleanliness, variety, and taste. Such criticisms are particularly telling in Argentina, where the "interior," the part of the country closest to the viceregal capital in Peru, was the most not the least developed part of the region. The critique of Argentine provincial society, then, was directed not just at gaucho subsistence life, but also at the traditional hacienda-based culture of the colonial elite. John Mawe declared himself scarcely able to conceive, let alone tolerate, a society whose members, even the privileged, chose to live on a diet of beef and *mate* tea. The colonial interior generates a litany of complaints. Accommodations are found disgustingly crude, horses hard to come by, delays unbearably long. Equally horrifying is the sharing of food plates, cooking pots, drinking vessels, and beds. Employees are lazy, deceitful, dishonest. As in Africa, the population's "filthy habits" are a subject of constant comment. It is most often in this unseemly context that American women make their rare appearances. Arriving in Lima, Charles Brand is only one of many travelers to declare himself repulsed by the Limeña women, who are "slovenly and dirty," "smoke cigars," and "never wear stays."[23] (See below for Flora Tristan's dramatically different account of the women of Lima.) John Miers registered a similar impression in the Argentine pampas: "Such are the filthy habits of these people, that none of them ever think of washing their faces, and very few ever wash or repair their garments: once put on, they remain in wear day and night until they rot."[24]

Such a litany of criticism is anchored, of course, in the sheerest hypocrisy,

FATHER.	MOTHER.	CHILDREN.	COLOUR.
European......	European......	Creole	White.
Creole	Creole	Creole	White.
White	Indian	Mestiso	$\frac{6}{8}$ White, $\frac{2}{8}$ Indian—Fair.
Indian	White	Mestiso	$\frac{4}{8}$ White, $\frac{4}{8}$ Indian.
White	Mestiso	Creole	White—often very Fair.
Mestiso	White	Creole	White—but rather Sallow.
Mestiso	Mestiso	Creole	Sallow—often light Hair.
White	Negro	Mulatto	$\frac{7}{8}$ White, $\frac{1}{8}$ Negro—often Fair.
Negro	White	Zambo.........	$\frac{4}{8}$ White, $\frac{4}{8}$ Negro—dark copper
White	Mulatto	Quarteron ...	$\frac{6}{8}$ White, $\frac{2}{8}$ Negro—Fair.
Mulatto	White	Mulatto	$\frac{5}{8}$ White, $\frac{3}{8}$ Negro—Tawny.
White	Quarteron ...	Quinteron......	$\frac{7}{8}$ White, $\frac{1}{8}$ Negro—very Fair.
Quarteron	White	Quarteron......	$\frac{6}{8}$ White, $\frac{2}{8}$ Negro—Tawny
White	Quinteron ...	Creole	White—light Eyes, fair Hair.
Negro	Indian	Chino	$\frac{4}{8}$ Negro, $\frac{4}{8}$ Indian.
Indian	Negro	Chino	$\frac{2}{8}$ Negro, $\frac{6}{8}$ Indian.
Negro	Mulatto	Zambo.........	$\frac{5}{8}$ Negro, $\frac{3}{8}$ White.
Mulatto	Negro	Zambo.........	$\frac{4}{8}$ Negro, $\frac{4}{8}$ White.
Negro	Zambo.........	Zambo.........	$1\frac{5}{16}$ Negro, $\frac{1}{16}$ White—Dark.
Zambo.........	Negro	Zambo.........	$\frac{7}{8}$ Negro, $\frac{1}{8}$ White.
Negro	Chino	Zambo-chino	$1\frac{5}{16}$ Negro, $\frac{1}{16}$ Indian.
Chino	Negro	Zambo-chino	$\frac{7}{8}$ Negro, $\frac{1}{8}$ Indian.
Negro	Negro	Negro	

27 Table from W. B. Stevenson's *Narrative of Twenty Years Residence in South America* (1825) depicting "the mixture of the different castes, under their common or distinguishing names." Despite its detail, Stevenson cautioned that the chart "must be considered as general, and not including particular cases." "I have classed the colours," he warned, "according to their appearance, not according to the mixture of the castes, because I have always remarked, that a child receives more of the colour of the father than of the mother" (vol. 1, p. 286).

for it is América's purported backwardness that legitimates the capitalist vanguard's interventions in the first place. Ideologically, the vanguard's task is to reinvent América as backward and neglected, to encode its non-capitalist landscapes and societies as manifestly in need of the rationalized exploitation the Europeans bring. Students of colonial discourse will recognize here the language of the civilizing mission, with which North Europeans produce other peoples (for themselves) as "natives," reductive, incomplete beings suffering from the inability to have become what Europeans already are, or to have made themselves into what Europeans intend them to be. So did the capitalist vanguard read themselves into the futures of those they sought to exploit, as a kind of moral and historical inevitability.

Readers accustomed to thinking about the civilizing mission with respect to Africa may be startled to find the same language applied to the postcolonial populaces of Spanish America – from ranchers, traders, small businessmen, and other decidedly non-tribal subjects to a range of indigenous societies with three hundred years' experience negotiating life under Eurocolonialism. Such, however, is the immense flexibility of this normalizing, homogenizing rhetoric of inequality. It asserts its power over anyone or any place whose lifeways have been organized by principles other than the maximizing, rationalizing mechanisms of industrial production and the manipulations of commodity capitalism.[25] It tolerates all manner of contradiction. In Spanish America, like everywhere else, the judgements of indolence remained quite compatible with the labor-intensive forms of servitude the travelers were concretely witnessing. The human infrastructure required by their own travels required armies of muleteers and peons, not to mention the famed Andean *silleteros* who carried Europeans across the Cordillera on their backs (see plate 28).[26] Most travelers in the Andes saw firsthand such spectacles as indigenous miners living lives of unspeakable misery toward certain death in the frigid, mercury-poisoned mines of the Cordillera. Such counterevidence posed little problem to the essentializing imperial eye. One needed only to see a person at rest to bear witness, if one chose, to the trait of idleness. One needed only to see dirt to bear witness to the trait of uncleanliness. This essentializing discursive power is impervious until those who are seen are also listened to.

Contradictions do make their way to the surface from time to time in this literature. On the pampas, John Miers was at least slightly puzzled that the people who seemed so indolent were "notwithstanding healthy, robust, muscular and athletic."[27] Charles Brand was inspired by the liberty and equality of pampa society: "Living as free and independent as the wind, they cannot and will not acknowledge the superiority of any fellow mortal." Yet he found it "strange withal" that these free agents should freely choose to be "so dirty and indolent; the women in particular . . . are disgustingly so. Comfort they have no idea of . . ."[28] Other writers, like Robert Proctor, were broader-minded. Francis Bond Head, in a dramatic, quite popular account, wrote in exception to the entire discourse. In his romantic *Rough Notes taken during Some Rapid Journeys across the Pampas and among the Andes* (1826), Head aggressively reversed the value signs of his compatriots. In his account of the canonical Buenos Aires to Chile journey, he expressed a wild, unmitigated enthusiasm for free-wheeling pampa life, idealizing it, in fact. He idealized its ecology too, arguing that left to itself, the pampa produced a natural crop rotation and had no weeds. Head vociferously denounced the neglect and abuse of the Pampas Indians. The deathly exploitation of the Andean miners inspired his profound horror: "no sentiment but that

28 Andean *silletero* carrying a European across the Cordillera on his back. But for the rain, the passenger would probably have been depicted reading a book, the recommended way to pass the time while riding this way.

of avarice could approve of establishing a number of fellow creatures" in a spot so desolate.[29] Head's conclusion reveals a wilful naiveté, however: he wonders that the miners should "voluntarily continue such a life of hardship" when they could simply move to the pampas.[30] Nevertheless, his account stands out among those of the business emissaries for its critical perspective on Euroexpansionism and its relativizing perspective on culture.

Subsistence lifeways, non-monetary exchange systems, and self-sustaining regional economies are anathema to expansive capitalism. It seeks to destroy them wherever it finds them. The bottom line in the discourse of the capitalist vanguard was clear: América must be transformed into a scene of industry and efficiency; its colonial population must be transformed from an indolent, undifferentiated, uncleanly mass lacking appetite, hierarchy, taste, and cash, into wage labor and a market for metropolitan consumer goods. These aspirations were widely shared by the liberal, urban Spanish American creoles who sought political and ideological dominance after independence. And yet, though they do not seem to have objected to the discourse of the capitalist vanguard, they did not adopt it wholesale as their own. As I will be discussing in the next chapter, precisely because these creoles were not the capitalist vanguard, but its hosts, they tended to express their modernizing, republican aspirations by other means.

THE *EXPLORATRICES SOCIALES*

Though often enough accompanied by women, the capitalist vanguardists scripted themselves into a wholly male, heroic world. The genderedness of its construction becomes clear when one examines writings by women travelers of the same period – women the vanguardists were *not* with.

Flora Tristan was burned in effigy in Lima and Arequipa when her travel book *Peregrinations of a Pariah* reached Peru from Paris in 1838. At least some members of the Peruvian upper classes were not flattered by the portrait she had painted after living among them for a year in 1833–4. Probably even fewer appreciated the sermon she offered in her prologue on how they ought to be handling their country's affairs. Radicalized and empowered by her Peruvian experience, Tristan herself went on to become one of France's most prominent pre-Marxian socialists, founder of the Workers' Union. Years later, her daughter Aline was to return to Peru as a young widow with a small son named Paul Gauguin, who, like his extraordinary grandmother, would make his name in the contact zone.

Flora Tristan is one of two women who wrote prominent accounts of South American travels in the decades following independence. Her writings and those of the English traveler Maria Callcott Graham (*Voyage to Brazil* and *Journal of a Residence in Chile*, 1824) are my subject in the second half of this chapter. These texts, fascinating in their own right, offer interesting comparisons with those of the capitalist vanguard, and suggest some of the outlines of bourgeois women's travel writing as it began to coalesce in the first half of the last century. They constitute yet another face of what I have been calling the reinvention of América.

Flora Tristan's mother was a French woman married to a Peruvian aristocrat, son of the wealthy Tristan family of Arequipa. She grew up in France, in a house frequented by elite Spanish Americans, including Simón Bolívar.[31] The early death of her father and his failure to leave a will sent

Flora and her mother abruptly into poverty. Tristan went to work in a print shop at a very early age, then married its owner as an escape from hardship. The marriage was disastrous. By her mid-twenties she had three children, of whom two survived, had separated from her husband, and was already engaged in what was to be an unspeakably vicious, lifelong battle with him over custody of their children. (In the end, in a very public scandal, Tristan's ex-husband shot her in the back. She survived and he went to prison for many years.) This brutal marital history, coupled with the gender-related loss of the property and status she should have inherited from her father, underlay Tristan's lifelong commitment to feminism and economic justice.

After eight years struggling to support herself and her children, Tristan made a desperate decision to go to Peru in hopes of claiming an inheritance from her father's family and thereby gaining financial independence. She left by ship on her thirtieth birthday. Her Peruvian relatives received her warmly, according to her account, but the family's reigning patriarch, the noted royalist Pío Tristan, took advantage of a legal technicality to deny Flora an inheritance (she was promised a small allowance).[32] Tristan made no attempt to conceal her devastation at his refusal. Nevertheless she remained with her relatives in Peru for over a year and there underwent the political awakening that plunged her into full-scale activism on her return to France in 1834.

Tristan spent the remaining ten years of her life writing and agitating in France and England for workers' rights, "the total emancipation of women, and the peaceful re-organization of society along co-operative lines."[33] In the guise of travel accounts, she wrote critiques of social conditions in England (*Promenade in London*, 1840) and France (*A Tour of France*, unpublished till 1977), in addition to a novel called *Mephis the Proletarian* (1838), and numerous essays. In 1843 she published the work for which she became best known, the *Union ouvrière* (*Workers' Union*), a social and political manifesto aimed at uniting France's workers, women and men, into a single workers' union that would achieve equality and justice for the working class, and ultimately bring about a peaceful transformation of French society. As for other socialist thinkers of the period, the total emancipation of women was the prerequisite for everything else. In the year following the publication of the *Workers' Union*, Tristan literally worked herself to death in its cause, embarking on a tour of French industrial cities, advocating the *Union* and her ideas at workers' meetings. Persecuted by public authorities, she was quite possibly on her way to starting the non-violent mass movement she hoped for when she fell ill with typhoid and died in late 1844. Tristan was quickly forgotten in Europe until her memory was revived by the feminist movement after World War I and again in the 1970s. In Peru her story was revived in the 1870s when Bolivian feminist Carolina Freyre de Jaimes called for her revindication. In the 1930s the Peruvian socialist leader Magda Portal likewise reclaimed Flora Tristan in a biography hailing her as the precursor of socialist feminism. Today, her name identifies one of Peru's most influential feminist institutions, the Centro Flora Tristan in Lima.

Maria Graham Callcott's *Journal of a Residence in Chile during the Year 1822* is easier to find these days in Spanish than in English. Since its Spanish translation appeared in 1902, Graham's account has come to be highly valued in Spanish America as a perceptive and sympathetic source on Chilean society and politics in the independence period. Born in 1785, Graham was nearing 40 when she sailed for South America with her husband, Thomas Graham, a British navy captain commissioned to assist in the war against Spain. Graham left as a wife and arrived a widow, for her husband died in her arms en route around Cape Horn. Turning down a chance to return directly to England, she remained in Chile a year (1822–3) under the protection of Lord Thomas Cochrane, a well-known British mercenary engaged in the *independentista* cause. In 1823, possibly following Cochrane's activities, Graham moved on to Rio de Janeiro, where she associated with the Portuguese court (located in Brazil since Napoleon's invasion of Portugal). She worked briefly as a tutor to the Portuguese royal family before returning to England in 1824.

By the time of her South American trip, Maria Graham was already an experienced traveler, travel writer, and political observer. Born into a naval family, she received her education under the direction of an "extremely enlightened" governess, and in her early twenties accompanied her father (who must also have been quite "enlightened") to India.[34] A second stay there with her husband in 1810–11 resulted in her first travel book, *Journal of a Residence in India* (1812), then *Letters from India* (1814), followed in 1820 by *Three Months in the Hills of Rome*. Though the book doesn't say so, it was Graham who edited and compiled diaries and journals by "officers and other gentlemen" to produce the *Voyage of HMS Blonde to the Sandwich Islands* (1826), the account of Lord Byron's South Sea expedition of 1824–5. Following her American travels, she translated some political memoirs, published a *History of Spain* (1829) and a *History of Painting* (1836), and became very well known for her children's books.[35]

Graham and Tristan died within two years of each other (1842 and 1844 respectively). Though their South American travels were separated in time by a decade and geographically by the (highly contested) border between Chile and Peru, both were spellbound and astute witnesses to the South American independence struggles and the political and military upheavals that followed. Contrary to stereotype, the political dramas of Spanish America show up far more fully in the writings of these women travelers than in those of either the capitalist vanguard or the disciples of Humboldt. That is one of a number of intriguing points of contrast between them and their male counterparts.

In structuring their travel books, I have suggested, the capitalist vanguardists often relied on the goal-directed, linear emplotment of conquest narrative. Graham's and Tristan's accounts do not, though they might have. They are emplotted in a centripetal fashion around places of residence from

29 "View of the Bay of Valparaiso from my house," Maria Graham, *Journal of a Residence in Chile* (1824). Note that the view is constructed from an indoor perspective.

which the protagonist sallies forth and to which she returns. Both women begin their accounts by taking up residence in an urban center (Graham in Valparaiso and Tristan in Arequipa). Though both do make lengthy inland journeys into the country or across it to other cities, it is this initial fixed positioning that organizes the narrative. Urban-based rather than rural, the women's accounts follow a different descriptive agenda as well. Social and political life are centers of personal engagement; each shows a strong ethnographic interest. In the accounts of the capitalist vanguard, interventionist goals often produce a reactive, judgemental energy. Though they share many of those goals, Graham and Tristan have little immediate stake in the outcomes of what goes on around them and write along more interpretive, analytical lines. They reject sentimentality and romanticism almost as vehemently as the capitalist vanguard did. For them identity in the contact zone resides in their sense of personal independence, property, and social authority, rather than in scientific erudition, survival, or adventurism. No less than the men, these women travelers occupy a world of servants and servitude where their class and race privilege is presupposed, and meals, baths, blankets, and lamps appear from nowhere.

"I took possession of my cottage at Valparaiso," begins Graham in her entry for May 9, 1822, "and feel an indescribable relief in being quiet and alone."[36] It is ten days since her arrival in Chile, a week since her husband's burial. For both Graham and Tristan, the indoor world is the seat of the self; both privilege their houses and above all their private rooms as refuges and sources of well-being. Graham describes her house in detail, including the views from the doors and windows: initially Chile will be seen from within. (One is reminded of Anna Maria Falconbridge looking out into the slave-yard from a parlor window.) It must be underscored, however, that the indoor, private world here does not mean family or domestic life, but in fact their absence: it is the site above all of solitude, the private place in which the lone subjectivity collects itself, creates itself in order to sally forth into the world. Tristan, lodged in the homes of her relatives, repeatedly depicts herself violating social convention by retiring to her room to collect herself. The rooms themselves become allegories of her subjective and relational states:

> This room, at least twenty-five feet long and twenty-five feet high, was lit by a single tiny window set high in the wall. . . . The sun never penetrated this suite, which in its shape and atmosphere was not unlike an underground cave. A profound sadness pervaded my soul as I examined the place my family had allotted me.[37]

The predictable fact that domestic settings have a much more prominent presence in the women's travel accounts than in the men's (where one is hard pressed indeed to find even an interior description of a house) is a matter not just of differing spheres of interest or expertise, then, but of modes of constituting knowledge and subjectivity. If the men's job was to collect and possess everything else, these women travelers sought first and foremost to collect and possess themselves. Their territorial claim was to private space, a personal, room-sized empire. From these private seats of selfhood, Graham and Tristan depict themselves emerging to explore the world in circular expeditions that take them out into the public and new, then back to the familiar and enclosed. One version of this paradigm was of course the rounds of visiting so prominent in urban social life, for men and women. Both women moved in elite creole and expatriate circles. Graham takes her readers to visit the governor, to have tea with her landlady, to call on educated women like the poet Mercedes Marín del Solar. Tristan, less tolerant of Peruvian society, complains repeatedly of the tedium of continual visiting. Her interest was roused rather by local spectacles like Holy Week processions, a mystery play, carnival celebration, and, we shall see below, a civil war.

Equally pertinent to these books is the more specifically exploratory activity identified with urban middle-class women in the early nineteenth century. The political work of social reformers and charity workers included the practice of visiting prisons, orphanages, hospitals, convents, factories, slums, poorhouses, and other sites of social management and control. German critic Marie-Claire Hoock-Demarle uses the term *exploratrice sociale* ("social exploratress") to discuss the work of Flora Tristan and her German contemporary Bettina von Arnim.[38] In Peru Tristan takes a great interest in the life of Arequipa's numerous convents, and visits a military encampment, a flour mill, and a sugar plantation as well as

> a hospital, a madhouse, and an orphanage, all three for the most part, very badly maintained. . . . The obligations of charity are thought to be satisfied if the children are given just enough to sustain their miserable existence; what is more, they receive no education or training, so any who survive become beggars.[39]

The label fits Maria Graham as well. Graham's social explorations in Chile include visits to a prison, an artisan village, ports, markets, and religious retreats for young girls: "There under the direction of an old priest, the young creatures who retire thus are kept praying night and day, with so little food and sleep that their bodies and minds alike become weakened."[40]

As such quotations recall, written or spoken critique is integral to social exploration as a political practice. Obviously this institutional critique differs from the taste-based denunciation of American living habits offered by the capitalist vanguard – though both are equally anchored in class values. Another branch of the civilizing mission, social reformism might be said to constitute a form of female imperial intervention in the contact zone. This is not to say, of course, that the critique of taste belonged exclusively to men. Flora Tristan indulges in it with gusto, and with more flair than many male writers. Arequipan cuisine she finds "detestable":

The valley of Arequipa is very fertile, yet the vegetables are poor. The potatoes are not floury, the cabbages, lettuce, and peas are hard and tasteless. The meat is dry, and the poultry is as tough as if it had come out of the volcano. . . . The only things I really enjoyed in Arequipa were the cakes and other dainties made by the nuns.[41]

Hoock-Demarle's study of social exploratresses focuses in particular on the language women writers used to recount their explorations and frame their critiques. The terminology of "exploratresses" and "exploration" is introduced by Hoock-Demarle to distinguish the work of these "contestatory women" from officialist "research" and "researchers" (enquêtes, enquêtrices), whose authoritative discourse was statistical and technical description. Aiming at broad audiences, she argues, the social exploratresses avoided specialized statistical languages anchored in expertise, and instead called upon novelistic practice to express their findings, producing a "subtle fusion of the literary and the social carried out at the level of style." The rejection of statistical description had everything to do, of course, with the oppositional and often specifically anti-statist momentum of their work. Their adaptation of realist novelistic language, says Hoock-Demarle, enabled the social exploratresses to

avoid the trap of bureaucratic technicity, the preserve of official masculine discourse, which they recognize has little impact on the masses. They also escape from the facile socio-sentimentality that is beginning, not without success, to exploit the genre of the pamphlet.[42]

Hoock-Demarle's stylistic observations are pertinent to both Tristan's and Graham's South American writings. Visiting the seaside resort of Chorrillos near Lima, for example, the ever inquisitive Tristan makes an excursion to a sugar refinery ("Up to then I had only seen sugar in the Botanical Gardens in Paris"). She describes the place experientially in a language that is explanatory but non-technical:

I was very interested in the four mills used to crush the canes; they are powered by a waterfall. The aqueduct which brings the water to the refinery is very fine and cost a great deal to build because of the difficulties of the terrain. I went over to the huge shed where the vats for boiling the sugar are housed, then we proceeded to the adjoining refinery where the sugar is separated from the molasses.[43]

Not surprisingly the visit provides an occasion for a verbal attack on slavery and plantation economics. Tristan presents the critique novelistically through a long dramatized dialogue with the plantation owner, in which she plays the heroine of the enlightenment. The tactics are those of the realist, not the sentimental novel, however. As the following excerpt shows, Tristan's critique shows not a trace of the sentimentality found in earlier abolitionist writing. In fact, she establishes her authority in part by appropriating a few elements of economic rhetoric:

> [Tristan:] "The slave has to work such long hours that it is impossible for him to exercise his right to purchase his freedom. If the products of his labour were to lose their value I am certain that slavery would be changed very much for the better."
>
> [Plantation owner.] "How so, mademoiselle?"
>
> "If the price of sugar bore the same relation to the cost of the labour that produces it as prices bear to labour costs in Europe, the master, having no compensation for the loss of his slave, would not make him work so hard and would take better care of him."
>
> "Mademoiselle, you speak of negroes like someone who knows them only from the fine speeches of philanthropists in parliament, but unfortunately it is only too true that you cannot make them work without the whip."
>
> "If that is so, monsieur, I can only pray for the ruin of your refineries, and I believe my prayers will soon be answered. A few years more, and the sugar beet will replace your sugar cane."[44]

Tristan concludes that talking to the old planter "was as much use as talking to the deaf," and rather smugly declares herself "overjoyed" to learn that a "band of English ladies" were boycotting sugar produced under slavery. In contrast with monovocal, totalizing forms of discursive authority, Tristan seeks out and exploits heteroglossia.

Though Graham and Tristan opt for personal narrative and dramatic discourses associated with the novel, neither relies heavily on the resources of sentiment. Graham's grief following her husband's burial is summed up in a one-line diary entry: "I have been very unwell; meanwhile my friends procured a small house for me at some distance from the port, and I am preparing to remove to it."[45] Tristan does sensationalize her inner life, but is often anti-sentimental with respect to those around her. Very early in her book, for example, she presents what appears to be a deliberate counterversion to the then-famous story of Stedman and Joanna (see chapter 5). During a dinner conversation with a French landowner on the Cape Verde Islands, her host tells her that after his slaves tried to poison him three times, he was forced to marry "one of my negresses" in order to stay alive. Now his wife does the cooking and has to taste everything before he does. They have three children together and "she loves them dearly." So, says Tristan, "You no longer think of returning to France?" "Why do you say that?" he replies. "Is it because of this woman?" As soon as his fortune is made, he says, he will prepare to return and invite her to come along, knowing she will refuse because "these women are all terrified of the sea." Abandoned, the wife will not complain: "She'll sell her children for a good price, then she'll find another husband." Tristan is left "crimson with indignation."[46]

In dramatic dialogues like the ones just quoted, Tristan constructs and idealizes herself as an aggressive, interactive seeker of knowledge. Maria Graham does the same, in deliberate contrast with objectivist ways of knowing based on a static relation between seer and seen. Early in her stay in Chile, for instance, Graham sets out one day to visit a pottery works. She arrives in a poor village where there is no sign of the factory she expected to encounter, "no division of labor, no machinery, not even a potter's wheel, none of the aids to industry which I had conceived almost indispensable to a trade so artificial as that of making earthenware." Instead she finds a family seated in front of a hut on sheepskins, with a pile of freshly prepared clay. "As the shortest way of learning craft is to mix at once with those we wish to learn from, I seated myself on the sheepskin and began to work too. . . . The old woman, who seemed the chief, looked at me very gravely, and then took my work, and showed me how to begin it anew."[47] Graham goes on to describe the pottery-making process, again in explanatory but resolutely non-technical language. In contrast with the seeing-man or the statistical observer, Graham here quite self-consciously presents herself acquiring knowledge in participatory fashion, and from an infantile rather than a patriarchal position. Yet, to recall terms used in chapter 4, the experiential occurs here without the sentimental.

Rather than treating the artisanal pottery works as a deplorable instance of backwardness in need of correction, Graham presents it in this episode almost as a utopia, and a matriarchal one at that. The family-based, non-mechanized production is presided over by a female authority figure. Yet even as she affirms non-industrial and feminocentric values, Graham also affirms European privilege. In relation to her, the potters retain the essential colonized quality of *disponibilité* – they unquestioningly accept Graham's intrusion and spontaneously take up the roles Graham wishes them to. When Graham turns a critical eye on her surroundings in the village, her judgements refer not to neglect, ignorance, or failure on the part of the inhabitants, but to the humanitarian, though also negative, category of poverty: "It is impossible to imagine a greater degree of apparent poverty than is exhibited in the potter's cottages of the Rincona. . . . Its natives, however, pointed out to me their beautiful view, which is indeed magnificent, across the ocean to the snow-capped Andes."[48]

On other occasions, Graham explicitly criticizes the objectivist knowledge of her male counterparts. She recounts a lunch at which she "had an opportunity to observe how carelessly even sensible men make their observations in foreign countries."[49] She listens while a physician and naturalist extols the medicinal qualities of a plant called *culen*, which, he proposed, could be cultivated in Chile. Graham replies that local people have shown her a plant they called *culen*, but she is told by the expert that it is not possible, for he has "never heard of such a plant here." Graham goes home and in the brush behind her house finds the rocks covered with the plant. Herself an amateur naturalist, Graham gives an account of her own herborizing which consciously mixes objectivist, elite knowledge with the lay expertise of local people. She depicts herself as a somewhat naive agent of both. Describing a flower called *cabello de angel* or "angel's hair" (*cuscuta*), she uses a decidedly non-specialized language, and soon turns to local expertise:

> The flower grows in thick clusters, and looks like white wax, with a rosy tinge in the centre. . . . Both these parasites are considered by the natives as emollients, and are applied to wounds.
>
> I soon found myself beyond my own knowledge of plants, and therefore took a large handful to a neighbour, reputed to be skilful in their properties.[50]

Culen, she finds out, has powers against evil curses.

Graham also has words for the capitalist vanguard. Riding from Valparaiso to Santiago, she marvels at never having read of the beauty of the route. Her skepticism as to Europe's industrial aspirations is summed up in a vivid allegorical picture she constructs at Viña a la Mar:

> I was grieved to see a great quantity of very fine machinery, adapted for rolling copper, lying on the shore, where Mr. Miers had thrown out a small pier. This machinery has been regarded with envy by certain members of the government because some part of it may be used for coining; and yet that jealousy will not, I fear, prompt the state to buy it, and therefore reform their own clumsy proceedings at the mint. However here lie wheels, and screws, and levers waiting till more favorable circumstances shall enable Mr. Miers to proceed with farther plans.[51]

POLITICS AND FEMINOTOPIAS

Though official histories were being made at the time on the battlefield, Tristan and Graham make their houses and themselves privileged sites of political understanding and action. The elite social circles in which both moved were heavily caught up in the intrigues and upheavals of the period. During Graham's stay, Chile was at war (with the assistance of her friend Lord Cochrane) against the royalist and monarchist stronghold of Peru. Cochrane's employer, the Argentinian general San Martín, had led the army that won independence first for Chile in 1818, then for Peru in 1821. By 1822 San Martín was struggling to consolidate his victory, resisted both by royalists and by liberal republicans who rejected his plans to found an American constitutional monarchy. Simón Bolívar, leader of the republican cause, refused to support San Martín, and in late 1822 the disappointed general left Peru for Chile. Via Maria Graham's house in Valparaiso, he headed for exile in Europe. Graham comments at length on the crisis of 1822 as it unfolds. Offering advice and judgements ("if I were a legislator . . ."),

30 Portrait by Maria Graham of "Dona Maria de Jesus, a young woman
who has lately distinguished herself in the war of the Reconcave." Adds
Graham: "Her dress is that of a soldier of one of the Emperor's battalions,
with the addition of a tartan kilt, which she told me she had adopted from a
picture representing a highlander, as the most feminine military dress. What
would the Gordons and MacDonalds say to this?" (*Journal of a Voyage to
Brazil*, 1824, p. 292.)

she depicts herself lobbying on behalf of prisoners of war, offering her own home as a meeting place and a retreat for Lord Cochrane's allies, and, in a climactic episode, receiving the fugitive San Martín after his defeat.

Flora Tristan's visit to Peru coincided with a later stage of the same crisis. In the intervening decade, Peru had twelve different heads of state. Tristan witnessed a period of civil war following a coup d'état in early 1834, heavily involving her royalist uncle Pío. She too depicts the Tristan family house as a strategic meeting place when the conflict leads to a battle in Arequipa itself. Tristan engages deeply with the crisis in her account, portraying herself offering sound advice to all sides, remaining calm in the crisis, visiting military encampments, and heroically climbing to the rooftop to survey the battlefield ("Only a person of my intrepid nature could have borne to remain there long"[52]).

Out of her political engagement in Peru and the shattering of her personal hopes, Tristan formed the ambition of becoming a political activist. Crucial to her transformation was one of the most dramatic figures in Peruvian public life, Doña Pencha, wife of Agustín Gamarra, Peru's president from 1829 to 1833. An extraordinary, ambitious woman, Doña Pencha is said to have run the country during her husband's tenure. In cape and breeches on horseback, she led the military campaign to resist a coup against the man she had chosen to replace him. Tristan dwells at length in her book on this example of female militarism and leadership. She is equally intrigued by another female battlefield phenomenon, the *rabonas*, the indigenous women who live in large numbers as camp followers to the armies, sustaining the (mainly indigenous) troops and joining in battle when they can. To Tristan, the courage, stamina, and self-reliance of the *rabonas* clearly demonstrate "the superiority of women in primitive societies." "Would not the same be true," she asks, "of peoples at a more advanced stage of civilisation if both sexes received a similar education? We must hope that some day the experiment will be tried."[53]

Tristan's admiration for the *rabonas* exemplifies the feminocentric perspective available to her and to Graham, and their debt to images of female power produced by the French Revolution and early feminism. Both writers repeatedly point up instances of female strength and heroism. Graham presents such figures as a woman rancher famous as "the best horsebreaker in these parts," a woman footsoldier she encounters in Brazil (see plate 30), a former statesman's wife imprisoned and exiled for refusing to read encoded letters from her husband, a woman who walked 500 miles to Santiago to find her husband in a military prison. In addition to Doña Pencha ("this woman of truly Napoleonic ambition"), Tristan returns repeatedly to the story of her cousin Dominga, who spent eleven years in a convent against her will and escaped by smuggling in a corpse into her bed and setting it on fire.

Both women's accounts also include elaborate constructions of what might appropriately be called "feminotopias." These are episodes that present idealized worlds of female autonomy, empowerment, and pleasure. Tristan finds such a feminotopia in Lima, where she travels alone to spend the last weeks of her stay. She becomes fascinated by the independence of the Lima women. "There is no place on earth," she exults, "where women are so *free* and exercise so much power as in Lima."[54] Like Francis Bond Head on the pampas, she idealizes: the *Limeñas* are taller than the men, mature early, have easy pregnancies, are "irresistibly attractive" without being beautiful, and are far above the men in intelligence and will-power. They come and go as they please, keep their names after marriage, wear men's jewelry, gamble, smoke, ride in breeches, swim, and play the guitar. They lack education, however, and are very ignorant.

At the core of Tristan's feminotopia is a long analysis of the *Limeñas'* unique style of street dress, the *saya y manto*, which she sees as central to their social and sexual freedom. The *saya* is a long, very tight skirt, made of tiny pleats in such a way as to "reveal the whole shape of the body and to give with every movement of the wearer";[55] the *manto* is a black, hood-like garment that completely covered the head and upper body except for one eye. The costume, unique to Lima, was very striking and a favorite for illustrators (see plate 31), even as outsiders criticized it for its form-fitting display and the horrifying absence of stays (see Charles Brand above, p. 151). Tristan offers a detailed and thoroughly feminist analysis of this dress code. Because it permits women to go about unrecognized, she argues, the *saya y manto* is the instrument of their freedom. What other writers record as the uncleanliness and unkemptness of Lima women, Tristan presents as a strategic cultural practice:

> When the women of Lima want to make their disguise even more complete, they put on an old bodice, an old *manto* and an old *saya* which is falling into rags and losing its pleats; but to show that they come from good society they wear immaculate shoes and stockings and carry one of their finest handkerchiefs. This is a recognised form of disguise and is known as *disfrazar*. A *disfrazada* is looked upon as eminently respectable, so nobody ever accosts her.[56]

Tristan's analysis of the *saya y manto* has a direct antecedent in the writings of another famous feminist traveler, the Englishwoman, Lady Mary Montagu. Montagu had traveled to Constantinople in 1714 when her husband was named ambassador to Turkey, and lived there till 1718. Though she was unable to publish her letters during her lifetime, they were widely read in Europe when they did appear in 1763. Tristan had surely read them, for her analysis of the *saya y manto* directly echoes Lady Montagu's discussion of Turkish women's dress. Likewise condemning the "extreme stupidity" of previous writers on Turkish women, Montagu observes, "'Tis easy to see they have more liberty than we have, no woman of what rank soever being permitted to go in the streets without two muslins, one that covers her face all but her eyes and another that hides the whole dress of her head." After describing the voluminous body coverings she concludes,

> You may guess how effectually this disguises them, that there is no distinguishing the great lady from her slave, and 'tis impossible for the most jealous husband to know his wife when he meets her, and no man dare either touch or follow a woman in the street. This perpetual masquerade gives them entire liberty of following their inclinations without fear of discovery.[57]

Interestingly enough, the feminotopia in Maria Graham's text also has a decidedly orientalist flavor. She recounts an outing in Valparaiso to a private garden retreat run by an elderly mother and her five middle-aged daughters. Graham takes a young woman friend there, where they spend a delightful day that ends with an elaborate meal prepared for them by the proprietors. It is an unusual episode full of allegorical overtones and seems to stand apart from the rest of Graham's narrative. Graham herself invokes the image of a Garden of Eden kept, but carelessly, by women. The family of women are represented in terms that evoke and remake Europe's traditional allegorical representations of América as a female figure, usually a bare-breasted Amazon. The mother, who greets them when they arrive, is extremely old, her gray hair in a long braid down her back. The youngest of the daughters "appeared to be at least fifty, muscular, well-made, with the remains of decided beauty, with an elastic step and agreeable voice."[58] So Graham contests the cult of youth, the valuing of women solely in terms of reproduction, and the very image of América as "new continent." In a scene with sensual, orientalist tones, the women sit on rugs and cushions eating oranges. The elaborate meal they share later in the day takes place the same way, the old woman eating and distributing food with her fingers, though plates and forks are brought for the two Europeans. The garden itself is not decorative but productive: it contains no domestic flowers, but fruit trees of all kinds, including conspicuously American fruits like the *lucuma* and the *chirimoya*. At the end of their visit, Graham abruptly turns to the subject of witchcraft: "there is something in her look when surrounded by her five tall daughters, that irresistibly put me in mind of the weird sisters and I felt half inclined to ask what they were."[59] So the episode ends, shrouded in an atmosphere of paganism, female erotics, and mysterious sisterhood.

If the discourse of the capitalist vanguard is structured by a melding of the esthetic (or anti-esthetic) and the economic, that of the social exploratresses melds politics and the personal. While the vanguardists tend to emplot their accounts as quests for achievement fueled by fantasies of transformation and dominance, the exploratresses emplot quests for self-realization and fantasies of social harmony. These features are evident in the ways Graham and Tristan end their books, with episodes that allegorize the personal quest in highly political terms. In a fashion unthinkable for either Humboldt

31 "Females of Lima," by W. B. Stevenson in *Narrative of Twenty Years Residence in South America* (1825), depicting the *saya y manto*.

or the capitalist vanguard, the reinvention of América coincides with a reinvention of self.

As she leaves Chile, Graham constructs what one might think of as a feminist anti-utopia. En route around Cape Horn her ship stops briefly at the Juan Fernández islands. Once a political prison, the islands are most famous as the place where Alexander Selkirk, the model for Robinson Crusoe, was marooned for many years. During a landing there, Graham finds herself alone in a clearing, where she experiences her own version of *Robinson Crusoe*: "Though at first I might begin with exultation to cry 'I am monarch of all I survey/My right there is none to dispute.' Yet I very soon felt that utter loneliness is as disagreeable as unnatural."[60] The possessive, territorial paradigm rejected, Graham ends up quoting Cowper's lines, "Better dwell in the midst of alarms/than reign in this horrible place."

As she heads off into the world, widowed and alone, such fears may have been all too real. (See below for another revision of *Crusoe* when Argentine traveler Domingo Faustino Sarmiento visits Juan Fernández.)

Flora Tristan, too, constructs her moment of departure as a political allegory and personal prophecy. When the ship she plans to sail on arrives in Callao, whom should she find on board but Doña Pencha Gamarra, the woman political and military leader whose career had so fascinated her? Gamarra is in desperate disarray, routed and heading into exile (sent there by the new military commander, Flora's uncle Pío). Doña Pencha, too, is described in tones that invoke the allegorical figure of América, a two-sided image, in fact. When Tristan encounters her, Señora Gamarra is wearing a bright embroidered silk gown, pink stockings, white satin slippers, a red crêpe-de-Chine shawl, "the most beautiful I ever saw in Lima," rings on every finger, diamonds and pearls. "Her fresh, elegant, distinguished toilette," remarks Tristan, "formed a strange contrast with the harshness of her voice."[61] Gamarra herself solves the enigma. These "European clothes" are not hers, she says, but forced upon her by her sister. The gown hampers her movements, the stockings "feel cold to [her] legs," and she is afraid of burning the shawl with her cigar. She describes herself to Flora in "the only clothes that suit [her]":

> For years I have been travelling all over the country in breeches of the coarse cloth they make in my native Cuzco, a greatcoat of the same material embroidered in gold, and boots with gold spurs. I love gold, it is the precious metal which gives the country its reputation, the finest ornament a Peruvian can have.[62]

Before the eyes of spellbound "Florita," Gamarra collapses in a series of violent epileptic fits that bring her near death – a death not unlike Tristan's own only six years later when she, too, had exhausted herself in political combat.

In 1828 a cranky reviewer in *Blackwood's Magazine* complained of the mediocrity of contemporary travel writing. The catalogue of offenders included "the inexperienced novice," "the superficial coxcomb," and "the romantic female, whose eyes are confined to some half dozen drawing rooms and who sees everything through the medium of poetical fiction."[63] One takes note of the fact, not the content, of the complaint: by 1828 there were enough European women travel writers in print to form a category for men to complain about. Some of them were traveling beyond the borders of Europe; a literature was emerging to create specifically female relationships to North European expansionism, a female domestic subject of empire, and forms of female imperial authority in the contact zone. Flora Tristan and Maria Graham were early instances in a series of women travelers in Spanish America whose accounts would attain high visibility in the second half of the century: Fanny Calderón de la Barca, whose classic *Life in Mexico* first appeared in 1843; the remarkable Ida Pfeiffer, whose *A Lady's Travels Round the World* appeared in 1852; and Lady Florence Dixie, author of *Across Patagonia* (1881), to name a few.

In discussing the emergence of women's travel writing on Africa (chapter 5 above), I observed that women's access to travel writing seemed even more restricted than their access to travel itself. Often women published their travels in occasional forms such as letters, used by Lady Montagu in Turkey, Mary Wollstonecraft in Scandinavia (1794), and Anna Maria Falconbridge in West Africa. Maria Graham used the diary form common to both men and women travelers. Flora Tristan, however, took up the form that had become canonical and authoritative in the bourgeois era, the autobiographical narrative. She constitutes herself as the protagonist of her travels and her life, and claims the intentionality of direct address to all posterity. Tristan's claim to authority attaches directly to European feminism of the late eighteenth and early nineteenth centuries. It is not coincidental that many of the early women travel writers also were *and wrote as* feminists, notably Lady Montagu and Mary Wollstonecraft. The first text Tristan herself wrote about Peru was a manifesto titled *La Necessité de faire un bon acceuil aux femmes étrangères* (*On the Need to Welcome Foreign Women*, 1835), in which she laid out the needs of women traveling abroad and exhorted women to educate themselves through travel. The manifesto itself suggests a new legitimacy for bourgeois women's travel. Not coincidentally, as Tristan's *Peregrinations of a Pariah* went to press in 1837, Queen Victoria ascended the throne of England ready to codify what would be the European woman's Imperial Quest *par excellence*: the Civilizing Mission. At the same time the claustrophobia of her reign would set loose another figure particularly likely to turn up in the contact zone: the Spinster Adventuress, her back to Europe, fleeing the confines of her time and returning – sometimes – to write about it.

Chapter 8

Reinventing América/Reinventing Europe: Creole self-fashioning

America is the ark that holds the mysterious
future of mankind and one day will open;
then the Eternal will raise in its hand
the inheritance promised to all men.
> (José Mármol, *Songs of the Wanderer* (Argentina, 1847))

Attentive only to the joys he imagines
Swiftly he flies across the vast distance,
Arriving hoarse, exhausted, spent,
At the happy destination of his hope,
Where at last he is given to look upon, with wonder . . .
A great desert carpeted in lava!
> (Gertrúdis Gómez de Avellaneda, "The American Traveler"
> (Cuba, 1852))

In October of 1826, as Spain resigned itself to the loss of its American empire, and John Miers to the failure of his copper enterprise in Chile; as Simón Bolívar routed the last royalist stronghold in Peru, and Alexander von Humboldt toiled in Paris on the third volume of the *Personal Narrative*, the first issue of a new periodical appeared in London. It was a Spanish-language magazine titled the *Repertorio Americano*, founded by Venezuelan intellectual Andrés Bello, who had traveled to London in 1810 with Bolívar to seek Britain's help against Spanish rule. Enmeshed in the metropolis, Bello remained in London for nineteen years before returning to South America in 1829 to become one of the foremost statesmen and intellectuals of the postindependence era.

Bello's *Repertorio Americano* was an attempt to contribute knowledge and vision to the task of founding the new American republics. Bello made himself a conduit and a filter for European writings that might be useful to the nationbuilding process there. The magazine, he promised in the prospectus, would be "rigurosamente americana." The section on Physical and Natural Sciences would include only materials "with a direct and immediate application to America"; the sections on Humanities and on

Intellectual and Moral Science would include only materials "in keeping with the current state of American culture."[1]

The first issue of the *Repertorio* contained articles on Virgil and Horace, on the use of the barometer and the improvement of cotton, on the use of time and on the revolutionary process in Colombia. It also included a long poem by Bello that has been regarded ever since as "the beginning, and conscious proclamation of Americanist literature on the [South American] continent."[2] Identified as an "American ode" ("silva americana"), the poem is titled "La agricultura de la zona tórrida" ("Agriculture in the Torrid Zone"). Originally it was to introduce a three-part epic titled *América*, which Bello never completed. For contemporary postcolonial readers, the fact that one of the founding texts of Spanish American literature should have been written and published in England by someone who had been abroad for over fifteen years, and as part of a totalizing work that remained unfinished, may all seem the ironic symptoms of a neocolonial cultural predicament. But for Bello, an *americanismo* transmitted westward from Europe suggested neither irony nor a predicament. This Euroamerican (creole) cultural logic is my subject in this chapter.

Writing in celebration of Spanish American independence, Bello opened his "silva americana" with a gesture of discovery: "Salve, fecunda zona," the poem begins – "Hail, o fertile zone," as if said by a traveler approaching a place for the first time. In an intricate poetic syntax soon to be supplanted in Spanish, the poet sings a praise song to American nature (the literal translation is my own):

Salve, fecunda zona,
que al sol enamorado circunscribes
el vago curso, y cuanto ser se anima
en cada vario clima,
acariciada de su luz, concibes!

(Hail, o fertile zone,
you who circumscribe the wandering course
of the enraptured sun, and caressed by its light
give life to every living creature
of every varied clime!)

A celebratory catalogue follows extolling America's natural riches:

Tú [fecunda zona] tejes al verano su guirnalda
de granadas espigas; tú la uva
das a la hirviente cuba;
no de purpúrea fruta, o roja o gualda,
a tus florestas bellas
falta matiz alguno; y bebe en ellas

aromas mil el viento y greyes van sin cuento
paciendo tu verdura desde el llano
que tiene por lindero el horizonte, hasta el erguido monte,
de inaccessible nieve siempre cano.

(You weave for the summer its garland
of heavy grain; you give the grape
to the bubbling cask;
not a single shade of fruit, purple, red or white
lacks in your beautiful forests, where the wind
drinks in a thousand fragrances,
where herds without number
graze your pastures, from the plains
whose boundary is the horizon
to the uplifted mountain,
eternally white with inaccessible snows.)[3]

The catalogue goes on for another forty lines in a forcefully Americanist vein, singing the praises of such uniquely American products as sugar cane, cochineal dye, the nopal, tobacco, yucca, cotton, breadfruit, and so on. The influence of Virgil's *Georgics* in this poem has been much discussed. These opening lines also bear the mark of Christopher Columbus, invoking the primal world of Europe's rhapsodic arrival discourse on América. Bello alludes to Columbus directly in an earlier companion poem called "Alocución a la poesía" ("Invocation to Poetry," 1823), where he calls upon "divina poesía" to leave "cultivated Europe, which disdains your native rusticity" and come to América, where "the world of Columbus opens its vast stage."[4] Colonial ironies again abound. The claims for rusticity are made in the least rustic, most learned poetic rhetoric Spanish afforded at the time; at the same time, this cultivated Spanish is peppered with American(ist) historical and material referents – *Aztec, yaravi, Caupolicán, yucca* – that Bello rightly felt obliged to explain in footnotes.

Quite a few of those explanatory footnotes cite a figure who, temporally and textually, towers between Christopher Columbus and Andrés Bello: Alexander von Humboldt. As a young student in Cumana, Bello had met Humboldt and Bonpland shortly after their arrival in Venezuela, and accompanied them on some local outings. He followed Humboldt's writings assiduously as they emanated from Paris in the 1810s and 1820s. Not an issue of the *Repertorio Americano* appeared without an excerpt from Humboldt, selected and translated into Spanish by Bello. The opening of Bello's American ode does not simply resemble Humboldt's estheticized invocations of América in the *Views of Nature*. It repeats and subsumes Humboldt's gesture, right down to the famed triad of "floresta" ("forest," line 9), "llano" ("plains," line 12), and "monte siempre cano" ("mountain, ever white," line 15).

"If some pages of my book are snatched from oblivion," Humboldt had declared in 1814, "the inhabitant of the banks of the Oroonoko will behold with extasy . . . populous cities enriched by commerce, and fertile fields cultivated by the hands of freemen."[5] He couldn't have been more wrong about the Orinoco, but he was right about the book. Pages were indeed snatched. Humboldt's writings – far more than those of the capitalist vanguard or the social exploratresses – became essential raw material for American and Americanist ideologies forged by creole intellectuals in the 1820s, 1830s, and 1840s. His writings were a touchstone for the civic literature that claimed Spanish America's literary independence, formulating self-understandings that were proudly *americanista* and at the same time, as cultural historian Pedro Henríquez Ureña put it, not *europeo* ("European") but *europeizante* ("Europeanizing").[6] Over and over in the founding texts of Spanish American literature, Humboldt's estheticized primal América provided a point of departure for moral and civic prescriptions for the new republics. His reinvention of América for Europe was transculturated by Euroamerican writers into a creole process of self-invention. That transculturation, and its aspects of selection and invention, is the focus of what follows.

In a way, the distinction between the "European" and the "Europeanizing" encapsulates the transatlantic appropriation through which elite liberal creoles first sought esthetic and ideological grounding as white Americans. Such grounding was hard to come by, and highly vulnerable to tremors and volcanic eruptions from below. Politically and ideologically, the liberal creole project involved founding an independent, decolonized American society and culture, while retaining European values and white supremacy.[7] In an important sense, América was to remain the "land of Columbus," as Bello said (Gran Colombia was the name Simón Bolívar chose for the great South American republic he hoped to found). At the same time, the creoles were obliged to grapple with the blatant neocolonialist greed of the Europeans they so admired, and with the claims for equality of the subordinated indigenous, mestizo, and African majorities, many of whom had fought in the wars of independence. Within creole ranks, liberals faced powerful conservative forces which, though favoring independence, opposed such changes as free trade, abolition, secular education, or even republicanism itself.[8]

One does not need to identify with the interests and prejudices of the creole elites to recognize the challenges South Americans faced at the moment of decolonization. "Independence" was not a known process, but one being improvised in the Americas even as they wrote. The words "decolonization" and "neocolonialism" did not exist. In both North and South America, this first wave of decolonization truly meant embarking on a future that was quite beyond the experience of European societies (as it remains today). It was not in Europe, after all, that "European" institutions like colonialism, slavery, the plantation system, the *mita*, colonial tribute, feudal missionism,

32 Frontispiece, first issue of the *Repertorio Americano* (1826) edited in
    London by Andrés Bello. The European figure of Liberty, carrying the
    Phrygian cap, greets America in its traditional European depiction as a
    barebreasted Amerindian woman.

and so on had been lived out as history, language, culture, and everyday life.
In this sense, Spanish America at independence was indeed a New World
on its way down a path of social experimentation for which the European
metropolis provided little precedent. The elites empowered to construct new
hegemonies in América were challenged to imagine many things that did not
exist, including themselves as citizen-subjects of republican América.

Let me point up some of the workings of those imaginings in Andrés

Bello's "Ode to Agriculture in the Torrid Zone." I suggested earlier that the poem's opening lines ("Hail, o fertile zone!") replayed Humboldt's appropriative gesture of *rediscovering* América as primal nature: replayed, that is, Humboldt's replay of Columbus. The important point, however, is that Bello repeats the discovery *only as a gesture*. After sixty lines of nature rhapsody, Bello's poem abruptly changes direction, moving from celebration to exhortation. He calls on his readers to "close the deep wounds of war," to go to work to claim the wild terrain:

Cerrad, cerrad las hondas
heridas de la guerra; el fértil suelo,
áspero ahora y bravo
al desacostumbrado yugo torne
del arte humana, y le tribute esclavo.
Del obstruido estanque del molino
recuerden ya las aguas el camino;
el intrincado bosque el hacha rompa,
consuma el fuego; abri en luengas calles
la oscuridad de su infructuosa pompa.
Abrigo den los valles
a la sediente caña;
la manzana y la pera
en la fresca montaña
el cielo olviden de su madre España;
adorne la ladera
el cafetal . . .

(Close, close the deep
wounds of war; the fertile ground
harsh now and wild, let it
turn to the unaccustomed yoke
of human art, pay it the slave's tribute.
Let the waters recall the path
of the dam and the mill pond;
let the axe fell the tangled forest
and fire consume it; open in long streets
the darkness of its unfruitful pomp.
Let the valleys shelter
the thirsty sugar cane;
let the apple and pear
in the mountain cool
forget the sky of their mother Spain;
let the coffee grove adorn the hillside.)[9]

After staging the primal fantasy of the European seeing-man, Bello calls into being the transformative future that the European seeing-man only dreams of, but which his presence presupposes. A social vision is introduced into the empty landscape of *disponibilité*. Selfconsciously foundational, the text spells out its version of the diffusionist narrative of progress, seeking to legitimate it as a collective, hegemonic project.

Certain details of the vision are of interest with respect to that project. Bello's fantasy of the new América is agrarian and non-capitalist, and pointedly neither industrial, urban, nor mercantile. In marked contrast with both Columbus and the capitalist vanguard, minerals are absent from Bello's catalogue of natural riches, for example, and his call to work does not include mining. Nor is commerce part of the prescription. Virgil aside, this is not a purely literary decision. Such absences are conspicuous given the fact that for both European and American capitalists, commerce and minerals were thought to be the primary stakes in the struggles for independence. Bello moves resolutely from the pastoral mode into the agricultural (Georgic), not the industrial or the mercantile. The capitalist vanguard's critique of taste and consumerist prescriptions are nowhere to be found. On the contrary, Bello exhorts the inhabitants of the new republics to reject the enervating evils of the cities in favor of a simple country life: "O young nations, o raise/ to the astonished west your heads/ newly crowned with laurels,/ honor the country, honor the humble life/ of the laborer and his frugal simplicity."[10] In his call for humble farmers unafraid of toil, Bello shares the European bourgeois critique of traditional provincial society which has failed to seize hold of its environment to better itself. At the same time, neither wage labor nor consumerism, neither cleanliness nor comfort has any place in Bello's call for a frugal, simple life on the land. The non-industrial, pastoral outlook of his "Silva" should probably be understood not simply as nostalgic or reactionary, but as a dialogic response to the commodifying, greed-glazed gaze of the English engineers.

As in other texts I will examine below, in Bello's poem the American wasteland becomes a fact of history *as well as* (not instead of) nature. Spain is defined as the backward force whose "barbarous conquest," we read, destroyed the fields and cities of Atahualpa and Moctezuma; the sons of América must now expiate this loss. The landscape must "forget its Spanish mother."[11] The closing lines of the poem equate the defeat of Spain with the scaling of the Andes as great feats for which posterity will immortalize the new Americans. The canonical image of the snow-capped mountain is thus appropriated into the republican civic vision.

In a curious way, though, the limits of the emancipation enterprise surface in the language Bello uses to imagine his Americanist agrarian paradise. Stylistically minded readers may have noticed that in the lines quoted above, the syntax leaves agents unspecified. Whose arms are to wield the axe that cuts down the tree? Who will plant the coffee bushes that are to adorn the hillside? As if Bello were uneasy about such matters himself (or as if he were

33 The sap of the sandi (cow-tree). Engraving by E. Riou from Paul Marcoy's *Travels in South America*, 1875.

anticipating deconstructionist criticism), he interrupts his own description to pose a surprising and crucial question. Referring to the scene he has depicted, the poet asks, "Is this the blind error of an illusory fantasy?" As if to resolve the uncertainty, for the first and only time in the poem the authoritative figure of the seeing-man makes an overt appearance. "I gaze upon them now," the text says,

> invading the thick
> opacity of the forest; I hear the voices;
> I sense the confused noise; the iron rings
> the distant echo of blows; the ancient trunk groans,
> for long hours wearies the laboring throng;
> struck by a hundred axes, it shudders at last,
> splits, and surrenders its copious crown.[12]

Uncertainty persists, however. The "they" here remains vaguely defined as a "laboring throng" – and even this nebulous presence is detected only as a "distant echo." When it comes to concrete relations of labor and property, the seeing-man's powers seem to dissolve into confused noise, distant sounds, a tree cut down by unseen hands. The question invited here is not "Where is everybody?" but "Who is doing the work?" and "For whom?" It is on this point that liberal aspirations seem to become unable to represent themselves. Creole civic consciousness often seems even less inclined than Humboldt to represent to itself the Americans in whose names, and by whose bodies, the wars with Spain were fought, whose labors would build the new republics, and whose continued subjugation formed the basis for Euroamerican privilege. In the esthetic (as in the political) realm, the unquiet American multitudes could not be dealt with.

Similar dynamics prevail in another Humboldtian page-snatching, a text by Simón Bolívar himself, written in the midst of the independence wars. By late 1821, fifteen years after meeting Humboldt in Paris, Bolívar was renowned as the Great Liberator in South America. Leaving the newly founded Republic of Gran Colombia in the hands of General Santander, he set out with his army and his Irish aide Daniel O'Leary to capture Quito and Guayaquil in Ecuador. He accomplished this mission, and spent the next year in Ecuador waiting for an opportunity to move in on the royalist stronghold of Peru. Perhaps to pass the time, Bolívar organized an expedition to climb – of course – Mount Chimborazo. Perhaps also to pass the time, he wrote a personal account of the experience which uses Humboldt as a primary point of reference. "I sought out the footsteps of La Condamine and Humboldt," he says. "I had already visited the enchanted sources of the Amazon, and I wished to climb the watch-tower of the universe."[13]

Indeed, Bolívar's ascent was apparently the first official attempt to scale Chimborazo since Humboldt's own incomplete effort in 1802. Recalling Humboldt's dramatic account of the physical effects of altitude, Bolívar describes how he "reached the glacial region" where "the ether smothered [his] breath." Nearing the place where (as he notes) Humboldt had been forced to turn back, the American is "seized by the violence of a spirit unknown to me" which enables him to continue. "I left behind the footprints of Humboldt," to reach at last "the eternal crystals that encompass Chimborazo."[14] At the summit Bolívar collapses into a delirious vision in which the ascent of Chimborazo becomes an allegory for his own epic political mission as liberator of the Américas. The "father of the centuries" appears and tells Bolívar how infinitesimally small are all human achievements in the presence of infinity: "Why do you swoon, child or elder, man or hero? . . . Do you think your actions have some value in my sight?" Identifying raw altitude with raw power, Bolívar replies, "What mortal would not faint, having risen so high? . . . I dominate the earth with my feet; I reach eternity with my hands . . . in your face I read the history of the past and thoughts of destiny." The spirit then instructs him to "Observe, learn," to "paint for the eyes of your fellows the picture of the physical universe, the moral universe," to "tell the truth to mankind." Bolívar is then called back to his senses by the "tremendous voice of Colombia."[15]

Though it follows on Humboldt's cosmic footprints, nothing could be more at odds with Humboldt's imaginative and verbal repertoire than this mystical delirium and its undisguised paternal/imperial allegory. While Humboldt sought to obliterate his status as a historical and political subject in his writings, that is the very recognition Bolívar claims for himself atop Chimborazo. Humboldt's mode of representation depends on an ideological distinction between knowledge and conquest; Bolívar's account collapses the two. It makes nature an allegory for human history, and subsumes human history into eternity. Nothing could contrast more sharply with Humboldt's estheticized scientism than the stark symbolism Bolívar invokes. For Humboldt, it is science that will reveal the "occult forces" of the cosmos, as he put it – not mysticism, delirium, revolutionism, or oxygen deprivation.

In terms of both travel and discourse, then, Bolívar leaves his European predecessor's footprints behind – but only after choosing to walk in them in the first place. Bolívar's vignette in many ways sums up Humboldt's place in early criollo letters: as a point *from which* Americanist consciousness set out, and *beyond which* it sought to go. Humboldt's "aesthetic mode of treating subjects of natural history" re-enacted an América in a primal state from which it would now rise into the glory of Eurocivilization. In the myth that followed from his writings (and for which Humboldt must not be held solely responsible) América was imagined as unoccupied and unclaimed terrain; colonial relations were offstage; the European traveler's own presence remained unquestioned. I have called this configuration an anti-conquest, expressing an incipient expansionist project in mystified fashion. As I hope to suggest, this very mystification is what made

Humboldt's writings especially usable to creole leaders and intellectuals seeking to re-envision their societies and themselves.

WAIT UNTIL DARK

When one reads the canonical literary texts of the independence period in Spanish America, one is struck by how often Humboldt is invoked as an opening gesture to inaugurate (and presumably legitimate) specifically creole imaginative and intellectual aspirations. Those aspirations in turn are often expressed in abstract allegorical terms that, as I am suggesting, maintain in abeyance some of the contradictions involved in trying to legitimate hierarchical societies through egalitarian ideologies.

In another classic text from the 1820s, Cuban poet José María Heredia repeats Humboldt's ascent of the Pyramid of Cholula in Mexico, described in *Views of the Cordilleras* (see plate 34). Heredia visited the site in 1820 while in political exile from Cuba for his *independentista* activities. His visit gave rise to his famous poem "In the Teocalli [temple] of Cholula." Like Bolívar on Chimborazo, and like the European Romantic poets Heredia admired, the "I" of the poem climbs the pyramid in search of a position of power and knowledge. The poem opens in the voice of the seeing-man, with a stanza praising canonical American nature. "How beautiful is the land where the valiant Aztecs lived!" Heredia begins. "In its breast, in a single narrow zone, one sees with awe all the climates that exist from the poles to the equator."[16] The allusion here, directly or otherwise, is to Humboldt's famous observation about the vertical ecology of the equinoctial zone (see p. 127 above). The stanza moves on through the canonical triad of American images: the *llanos*, the forest, the snow-capped peak:

> Its plains/ the golden grain and sweet cane/ blanket together. The orange tree, pineapple, sonorous banana,/ sons of the equinoctial soil, entwine/ with the leafy grape, the rustic pine/ and Minerva's majestic tree [the olive]./ Eternal snows crown the heads/ of virgin Iztaccihual, Orizaba/ and Popocatepec; yet the harmful hand/ of winter never touches/ the ever-fertile fields.[17]

When night falls on this scene, however, a new vision brings history to the stage. Pre-Columbian Aztec society parades before the poet displaying the "inhuman superstition" in whose name the pyramid was built. The pyramid, Heredia concludes, is a reminder "of human madness and furor," such as have caused his own exile. Spanish tyranny is equated with what for Heredia was Aztec barbarism.

Here again Humboldtian tropes function as pretext for an Americanist historical and political meditation that is not at all Humboldtian but *criollísimo* ("extremely criollo") as Heredia himself has been called.[18]

Humboldt, for example, compared the Teocalli extensively with Egypt and the Ancient Mediterranean, dating the Teocalli from "an epoch when Mexico was in a more advanced state of civilization than Denmark, Sweden, and Russia." This is a very different attitude to the Aztec legacy from that expressed by the *criollísimo* Heredia. As in several texts discussed below, exile rather than exploration situates the seeing-man and creates the otherness between the seer and the seen. The dynamics of discovery are transculturated into a framework of nostalgia and loss. Fifty years later, referring to Heredia as "el primer poeta de América" ("the first poet of America"), Cuban essayist José Martí described Heredia's verse in the same Humboldtian vocabulary as "volcanic like [America's] bowels and serene like her heights." Heredia, he said, shows "the difference between a forest and a garden: in the garden everything is polished, pruned, graveled. . . . Who dares to enter a jungle with an apron and a pruning knife?"[19] So two generations later the estheticized primal landscape determines an Americanist critical vocabulary.

It is the indigenous peoples of the present rather than the past that Esteban Echeverría allegorizes in his long narrative poem *The Captive* (Argentina, 1837), yet another work that launches itself from the Humboldtian landscape trope. By the 1830s, when the poem was written, the honeymoon with the English engineers had faded for the time being, and Echeverría's native Argentina was embroiled in longterm civil warfare among progressive *independentistas*, traditional centers of power, and emerging transatlantic business alliances. On the empty American landscape Echeverría stages not a utopian vision as Bello had, but a moral and civic dystopia. In conventional fashion, *The Captive* opens with the landscape of Humboldt's "On Steppes and Deserts," the sun gilding the distant peaks of the Andes while "the desert, incommensurable, open and mysterious" spreads itself out like the sea. And again this landscape is invoked only as a gesture. The curtain of darkness drops on it and rises, as in Heredia's contemplation at Cholula, on American race war. The Pampas Indians stream onto the nocturnal wasteland in a wild horde represented (as in Bello) not as a sight, but as a chaos of disembodied images and confusing sounds:

> Then, like the noise/ of thunder when it rolls in the distance/ in the peaceful plain was heard a dull and confused clamour/ it wanes . . . and then violent like the horrendous howl/ of a teeming multitude in the wind it swelled blood-red/ striking the beasts with terror.[20]

The ground trembles. A cloud of dust, horses, lances, heads, manes – and a lapse (like Bello, like John Barrow) into panicked interrogatives: "Who is it? What senseless throng/with its howls disturbs the silent solitudes of God? . . . Where is it going? Where did it come from? Why does it shout, run, fly?"[21] Except for the horses, Echeverría's representation of the Pampas Indians is scarcely distinguishable from that of their Bushmen counterparts in the literature on southern Africa discussed in chapter 3. As

34 The Pyramid of Cholula, as depicted in Humboldt's *Views of the Cordilleras* (1814).

with John Barrow's nocturnal descent upon the Bushmen, when it comes to entering the contact zone and confronting the object of extermination, the visual code and the seeing-man's imperial authority break down into sound, blindness, confusion. It is hard to imagine that just a decade or so earlier these same Pampas Indians had been sought out as potential allies in the military struggle for independence. Now they have become fearsome and unknown.

The Captive goes on to dramatize the defeat of civilization at the hands of barbarism. A symbolic settler family made up of the white creole María, her English husband Brian, and their little daughter are pursued and brutally killed by the Indians. Unlike much writing of the previous decade, Echeverría's poem actually dramatizes the indigene–European confrontation, the violence and terror of the contact zone, albeit in the rather mystified mode of romantic racial and family allegory. Mechanically speaking, the allegory seems clear: civilization, as embodied in the triad of English man, creole woman, and their female child, loses the battle – the promise of the capitalist vanguard is reduced in *The Captive* to a single English corpse. The future, one supposes, lies in creole men and their male offspring. But where are they? In Buenos Aires, perhaps (writing long poems?), or, as I will discuss shortly, en route to Paris. After witnessing three decades of civil war and chaos, Echeverría seems to have lacked positive terms in which to formulate the great American experiment. Both Europe and América seem to have failed him – or he them, for he, the American creole, has no counterpart in his own narrative. I suggested in chapter 2 that captivity narrative traditionally constituted a safe context in which to narrate the terrors of the contact zone because the story is told by a survivor who has returned, reaffirming European and colonial social orders. Echeverría's *Captive*, despite its title, does the opposite. Narrated in the third, not the first person, it tells the other story, of the ones who did not survive the encounter and did not succeed in engendering a white social order.

A few years later the American foundational allegory gets historicized to a degree in a non-fictional work often considered the single most important piece of writing of the Spanish American independence period. I refer to the political biography *Civilization and Barbarism: Life of Juan Facundo Quiroga* (1845), by Argentine Domingo Faustino Sarmiento. *Civilization and Barbarism* is another instance in which Humboldt's reinvention of América provides the point of departure for a distinctly creole discursive project that "leaves Humboldt's footprints behind." In this case the project involves confronting not the uncertainties of the future but the ambiguities of the past. Sarmiento's essay is a polemic in which the author legitimates liberal creole values by discrediting the legacy of colonial traditions, embodied in the figure of Juan Facundo Quiroga, a powerful political and military leader from the Argentine interior.[22] *Civilization and Barbarism* draws on

Humboldt's *Political Essays* as well as his esthetic writings in an attempt to confront the "dark and bastard heritage" that seemed such an obstacle to the aspirations of the "Europeanizing" creoles.[23] The "barbarism" against which they saw "civilization" pitted consisted simultaneously of indigenous societies – still the majority in many regions – slave and ex-slave populations, and traditional Spanish colonial society, autocratic, conservative and religious, and the mixing of the three. Miscegenation was seen as the result of colonial violence preying upon already inferior beings, whose own barbarism has made them susceptible to European conquest.

In a fashion so conventional it must have felt natural, Sarmiento's essay opens with the empty land – a chapter on "The Physical Aspect of the Republic of Argentina and Characters, Habits and Ideas that it Engenders," and an epigraph in French from Humboldt's "On Steppes and Deserts" – "The extent of the pampas is so prodigious that to the north they are bounded by palms and to the south by eternal snows."[24] Following the trope of *disponibilité*, Sarmiento introduces the "immense extension" of Argentina as "entirely unpopulated." He sees "immensity everywhere: immense the plains, immense the forests, immense the rivers." Sarmiento rejects the Humboldtian celebration of these empty spaces, however, resymbolizing them as "the ill from which the Argentine Republic suffers." They provoke "confusion," he says, and, when the inhabitants of the pampas are included in the picture, terror:

> The horizon is always uncertain, always confusing itself among the thin clouds and mists which at a distance prevent one from fixing the point at which the world ends and the sky begins. To the south and the north, the savages lie in ambush, waiting for moonlit nights to descend like a swarm of hyenas on the cattle grazing in the fields and on the defenseless settlers.[25]

Here they are again, the undifferentiated nocturnal indigenous horde. Wild in the night, they surge onto the vacant landscape in the disembodied image that all over the planet legitimates European campaigns of conquest and simultaneously displays white guilt by seeking cover of darkness. Always part of an expansionist narrative, this polarizing rhetoric negates indigenous claims to the land (they always come from nowhere, or some other unseen place), as well as whole histories of contact, like that between the Pampas Indians and Spanish colonialism.

Setting aside the Indians, Sarmiento goes on to initiate an official vision of the contact zone and its cultural *mestizaje*. European theories of environmental determinism are applied to the mestizo inhabitants of the pampas, the gauchos. The extended plains of the Argentine interior, argues Sarmiento, lend an "Asiatic" (alias despotic) character to human life there: "the predominance of brute force, domination by the strongest, authority without limits or responsibility, justice without procedures or debates."[26] At the same time, in a way that reflects his enthusiastic reading of Francis Bond Head, Sarmiento is fascinated and attracted by gaucho society and lifeways. The rest of his book displays with astonishing clarity Sarmiento's contradictory and unresolved recognition that the "barbarous" gaucho (contact) culture he despises supplies uniquely "Argentine" elements which exert tremendous force on the decolonizing elites. In a way unimaginable in Europe, the arbiters of culture in the emergent Argentine metropolis seized on gaucho culture as the source of a fiercely androcentric esthetic of authenticity. So do the contradictions of white decolonization play themselves out in this extraordinary textual experiment.

The body of *Civilization and Barbarism* comprises a historical biography of the provincial autocrat or *caudillo* Juan Facundo Quiroga. Through an account of Facundo's life and violent death, Sarmiento explores Argentina's difficulties in consolidating itself as a nation. In Sarmiento's analysis, Facundo's ruthlessness, his conservative authoritarianism, his reliance on violence and a private army as basic political tools exemplify the "barbarism" that infects Argentine society and obstructs the republican nation-building process. At the same time as he condemns this barbarism, Sarmiento conveys a profound fascination with Facundo as a figure and with the mestizo lifeways of the interior (where Sarmiento himself grew up). While condemned as backward, the interior provinces, centers of Argentine life under Spanish rule, are simultaneously recognized as a source of authentically American, authentically Argentine cultural material – the ingredients of a (manageable) independent cultural formation. Later, Sarmiento would reclaim the interior for the new national imagination, in an auto-biographical work called *Recuerdos de provincia* (*Provincial Memoirs*, 1850).

In sum, despite their often passionate Anglophilia, when South America's lettered elites reflected on emergent American society in the 1820s, 1830s, and 1840s, they did not simply assume the interventionist, industrializing vision of the capitalist vanguard. The English and French travelers were read in Spanish America; one finds them quoted here and there, and journalists like Bello translated selections from their writings. And yet, faced with the challenges of decolonizing their cultures, subjugating majorities, reimagining relations with Europe, forging modes of self-understanding for the new republics, legitimating themselves as ruling classes, projecting their hegemony into the future, and imagining possibilities for the unprecedented historical experiment in which they were engaged, they turned with remarkable consistency to the utopian Americanist esthetic codified by Humboldt, who had found it, in part, in them.

One would seriously misinterpret creole relations to the European metropolis (even their neocolonial dimensions) if one thought of creole esthetics as simply imitating or mechanically reproducing European dis-courses, however. Humboldt, I have suggested, was invoked mainly as a gesture and a point of departure for other, *criollisimo* imaginative and ideological projects. One can more accurately think of creole representations as *transculturating* European materials, selecting and deploying them in ways that do not simply reproduce the hegemonic visions of Europe or simply legitimate the designs of European capital. Repeatedly, for example, writers appropriated Humboldt's discourse into a problematics of nationbuilding that his own writings generally refused. In contrast with the visual appropriation of European science and esthetics, the South American writings projected moral and civic dramas onto the landscape, projections ideologically designed to legitimate creole hegemony over and against not only old Spanish domination but also French and English imperialism and, perhaps most important of all by the 1820s, the democratic claims of the subordinated mestizo, African, and indigenous peoples. Humboldt's wild scenery provides a stage for imaginings of race war, genocide, and ethnocide.

For, of course, not everyone was to be liberated, equalized, and fraternized by the South American revolutions any more than they were by those in France or the United States. There were many relations of labor, property, and hierarchy that the liberators had no intention, or hope, of decolonizing. Liberal projects like Bolívar's met with ferocious resistance from traditionalist elite sectors; radical projects got nowhere. Popular uprisings, which were frequent, were suppressed. With respect to the subjugated indigenous peoples, slaves, disenfranchised mestizo and colored sectors, and women of all groups, the independence wars and their after-math for the most part reconfirmed white male dominance, catalysed Eurocapitalist penetration, and often intensified exploitation. For the self-sufficient subsistence peoples of the jungles and the plains, independ-ence meant the incursion of commodity culture, wage labor, state con-trol, and genocide into areas which before had remained beyond these instruments of Eurocapitalist expansion. A massive conversion of interior lands to private property took place, for example, creating haciendas of all sizes that required armies of landless wage laborers. Llaneros and gauchos were required to attach themselves to particular ranches and carry passes – a tactic quite likely imported from southern Africa (see chapter 3).

While the capitalist vanguard could openly enthuse about such develop-ments, from an Americanist standpoint they constituted internal contradic-tions that could not easily be broached by those seeking to assert anti-colonial and egalitarian values. Perhaps that is why the civic literature so often projects abstract moral allegories. In a letter written in 1826, Simón Bolívar lamented what he had come to see as a curse that permanently compromised South America's future:

We are the vile offspring of the predatory Spaniard who came to America to bleed her white and to breed with his victims. Later the illegitimate offspring of these unions joined with the offspring of slaves transported from Africa. With such racial mixture and such a moral record can we afford to place laws above leaders and principles above men?[27]

Two decades later in 1847, Domingo Faustino Sarmiento expressed a somewhat more complex vision equally tinged with abstract despair. "What effort will it cost," he exclaimed,

> to disentangle this chaos of wars, and unmask the devil that is stirring them up, in the midst of the clamoring of parties, the odious pretensions of capital cities, the arrogant spirit of the province-turned-state, the . . . mask of ambition, and the wind that Europe blows toward America bringing us her artifacts, her immigrants, and forcing us to enter her balance-scale of development and wealth.[28]

Here Europe is pointedly part of the problem and not the solution.

REINVENTING EUROPE

That grim assessment was made in a text whose appearance, in retrospect, seems almost inevitable in the wake of independence: a creole travel book about Europe. The postcolonial creole subject, like all subjects, was constituted relationally, with respect (among other things) to Spaniards, to Northern Europeans, and to non-white Americans. Within American society, that subject imagined itself into being in part through the image of the indigenous horde constructed as its barbarous other. Spaniards, too, were barbarians. It was inevitable that creole culture would eventually claim and define Northern Europe for itself as well: inevitable, or so it seems, that sometime around 1850 a creole intellectual would write a travel book about Europe. Though not inevitable, it is certainly not surprising that that intellectual should be the same one who wrote *Civilization and Barbarism*. In fact, it was because of *Civilization and Barbarism* that Domingo Faustino Sarmiento was sent abroad in 1845. The furor generated by the book was sufficient to inspire Sarmiento's employer, the Chilean government, to send him abroad to study public education systems and to assess the immigration potential of other countries. He was gone two years and visited France, Spain, Italy, Switzerland, and Germany, as well as North Africa and the United States.

What is new is not the fact that Sarmiento went abroad, or even where he went. What is new is that he wrote a book about it. Spanish American creoles commonly traveled to Europe and often sent their children there to study, but they did not produce a literature on Europe. One might suggest that as colonial subjects they lacked a discursive authority or a legitimate position of speech from which to represent Europe. Within colonial strictures there perhaps existed no ideological project that could motivate a creole representation of Europe. (Certainly, Spanish Americans lacked access to printing licenses and presses.) So do colonial asymmetries play themselves out in writing apparatuses: the metropolis ongoingly, indeed perhaps obsessively, represents the colony to itself, and also ongoingly calls upon the colony to represent itself to the metropolis, in the endless recording and bureaucratic documentation that the Spanish Empire seems particularly to have specialized in. For colonies to lay claim to their mother countries, however, even a purely verbal claim, implies a reciprocity not in keeping with colonial hierarchies.

Sarmiento's *Travels*, which appeared in book form in 1849, comprise over 600 pages consisting of eleven public letters sent to friends and mentors back home, plus an essay highlighting his stay in the United States, and over a hundred pages of penny-by-penny expense accounts that remind us how Sarmiento idolized Benjamin Franklin. As with the other materials in this chapter, I will make no attempt to comment comprehensively on this work, but will merely suggest some relevant highlights.

Not surprisingly, Sarmiento opens his *Travels* pondering the question of his own discursive authority. For any writer in the present day, says Sarmiento in the preface, it is difficult to produce an interesting travel book, now that "civilized life everywhere reproduces the same characteristics. The difficulty is even greater if the traveler comes from one of the less advanced societies in order to learn about more advanced ones." Then, he says, "the inability to observe, the lack of intellectual preparation leaves the eye clouded and myopic because of the breadth of the views and the multiplicity of objects they include."[29] As an example, Sarmiento cites his own inability to see factories (a highly charged example at this point) as anything but inexplicable piles of machinery. If he thought his own text would be compared to those of great European travel writers like Chateaubriand, Lamartine, Dumas, or Jaquemont, he concludes, "[He] would be the first to abandon the pen."[30]

Despite this deferential gesture, Sarmiento goes on to write his account with no evidence of the crippling of spirit he ascribes to himself in this preface. In effect, he takes up the question before him: In the age of independence, how does the creole citizen and man of letters position himself with respect to Europe? The book begins with a fascinating digression that poses the question in allegorical fashion. Sarmiento's ship leaves Valparaiso (Chile), bound for Montevideo then Le Havre, but as if reflecting Sarmiento's difficulties in getting his text off the ground, the ship is immediately becalmed for four days just off the Chilean coast. This non-event, decidedly out of keeping with standard travel-book rhetoric, takes place at the Juan Fernández islands, where Alexander Selkirk, the model for Robinson Crusoe, had been marooned. Sarmiento and his companions are of course as mindful of the precedent as Maria Graham was, and they, like her, use the occasion to revise the Crusoe myth for themselves. Landing to spend a day on the island of Mas-a-fuera ("Farther Out"), they are astonished to find it is already inhabited by four North American castaways living, in Sarmiento's words, "without care for the morrow, free from all subjection, and beyond the reach of the vicissitudes of civilized life."[31] As this language suggests, Sarmiento's account of life on Mas-a-fuera retains some of the utopian spirit of Defoe's *Crusoe*. He depicts a masculinist paradise that in fact retains many of the features of Bello's agricultural utopia. In keeping with the times, it is also a republican paradise; there are no enslaved Fridays, and the only visible hierarchy is generational. A gentlemanly ethos prevails. The men amuse themselves by organizing a day's hunt of the wild goats that teem the island. (Crusoe, you will recall, captured and bred these goats; the original Selkirk, on the other hand, said he danced with them for want of human company.) As the account proceeds, however, Sarmiento gradually demystifies the utopian paradigm. The four men, it turns out, are unhappy and divided among themselves – leading Sarmiento to conclude that "Discord is a condition of our existence, even where there are neither governments nor women."[32]

Like *Robinson Crusoe*, Sarmiento's Mas-a-fuera episode lends itself to an allegorical reading, here suggesting Sarmiento's own complex relations to North European, North American, and traditional Argentine cultures. On his all-important scale of civilization, the inhabitants of Mas-a-fuera are "farther out" (as the name says) than himself, but not as far out as some inhabitants of the Argentine interior. Noting that the American castaways have maintained an accurate calendar, Sarmiento is reminded of the time the populace of one of Argentina's provincial capitals discovered from a passing traveler that they had somehow lost track of a day. For going on a year, so it was told, they had been "fasting on Thursday, hearing mass on Saturday, and working on Sunday."[33] Even marooned, it seems, Anglo-Americans can keep a better grip on rationalized time than the colonial provinces.

Allegorically the Mas-a-fuera episode enables Sarmiento to situate himself with respect to the multiple cultural referents that impinge upon him. With respect to Europe, he is slightly "mas afuera" – a little out of it. At the same time, his marginality has an affirmative dimension. The transculturated Crusoe episode makes the gesture that contemporary terminology now calls "magic realism." Facing the metropolis, the magic realist flashes back a message from the frontier: your fictions (*Robinson Crusoe*) are my realities (Mas-a-fuera); your past is my present; your exotic (a world outside of clock time) is my everyday (the Argentine interior). Only after so situating himself does Sarmiento take on the travel writer's role as cultural mediator. The wind picks up and they sail on.

Reaching Paris, Sarmiento enters his cultural Mecca not as a pilgrim or a conqueror, but as an infiltrator. He does not take up the position of the seeing-man looking out panoramically over a Paris that is radically different from himself. Sarmiento introduces himself in Paris in the role of the *flaneur*, who, he argues, is the privileged observer of the city:

> *Flaner* is a thing so holy and respectable in Paris, it is a function so privileged that no one dares interrupt it. The *flaneur* has the right to stick his nose everywhere. If you stop in front of a crack in the wall and look at it attentively, some enthusiast will come along and stop to see what you are looking at; a third joins you, and if eight gather, then everyone who passes stops, the street is blocked, a crowd forms.[34]

Though Sarmiento himself does not draw the analogy, the *flaneur* is in many ways an urban analogue of the interior explorer. Indeed, his joys and privileges, as Sarmiento describes them, uncannily resemble those of the naturalist. Like the explorer, "the *flaneur* pursues something he himself does not know; he searches, looks, examines, passes on, goes softly, turns around, walks, and arrives at the end . . . sometimes the banks of the Seine, others the boulevard, most often the Palais Royal."[35] To the *flaneur* Paris yields the analogue of what Humboldt found in the equinoctial regions: a bulging cornucopia, a place of endless, exotic variety and plenty, all the possibilities simultaneously present. What Humboldt saw in the jungles and pampas, Sarmiento sees in the shops of the Rue Vivienne, the collections of the Jardin des Plantes, the museums, galleries, bookstores, and restaurants. Sarmiento's catalogue-laden descriptions of Paris reproduce Humboldt's discourse of accumulation and its posture of innocent wonderment:

> "Are you a literary man? Then spend a year reading what is published here each day. . . . Are you an artist? The Louvre exposition of 1846 is still on. Two thousand four hundred art objects, paintings, statues, engravings, vases, tapestries. . . . Do you care for political systems? Oh! don't even enter the labyrinth of theories, principles and questions!"[36]

In a parodic, transculturating gesture, Sarmiento refocuses the discourse of accumulation back on its own context of origin, the capitalist metropolis. It is the metropolitan paradigm minus one dimension, however, that of acquisition. An alienated figure, the *flaneur* has no capital and accumulates nothing. He does not buy, collect samples, classify, or fancy transforming what he sees. He does react, however, and Sarmiento the arch-*flaneur* reacts to the spectacle of the *flaneurs* by asking a very American and very republican question: "Is this really the people who made the revolutions of 1789 and 1830? Impossible!"[37] A bold and arrogant statement for an ex-colonial to make. And on the eve of 1848, a prophetic one.

The world becomes simpler for Sarmiento when he goes to North Africa, where his status with respect to the civilization/barbarism dichotomy is clear. Here, and perhaps only here, does he get to be a European pure and simple, and a colonialist. In surprisingly schematic fashion, Sarmiento identifies completely with the French and their colonial project in Algeria. The Bedouins become the exact analogue of the Argentine gauchos, primitive and ignorant; the world divides off into civilization and barbarism much more clearly than in Sarmiento's own book of that title. Sarmiento himself begins to sound like the capitalist vanguard, repulsed by discomfort and uncleanliness, people eating with their hands. Only the Europeans can save the desert from neglect and "primitive sterility."[38] In what he in part identifies as a Fourierist paradise, Sarmiento envisions the future colonization of Algeria:

> Everywhere the European populace busied itself in the multiple workings of civilized life. The plains today deserted I saw covered with farmhouses, gardens, golden fields; and the lakes . . . had taken regular shapes, their waters contained in orderly canals[39]

and so forth. If Algeria is now France, América, on the other hand, remains in the grip of the Arabs; the continent suffers, declares Sarmiento, from a tendency

> to wander alone in her solitudes, fleeing contact with other peoples of the world, whom she does not wish to resemble. *Americanismo* . . . is nothing more than the reproduction of the old Castilian tradition, the pride and immobility of the Arab.[40]

Later, as President of Argentina (1868–73), Sarmiento presided over a series of genocidal campaigns against the Pampas Indians and the further break-up of independent gaucho society. All his life he advocated public education and immigration from Europe to dilute the "inheritance of bastard obscurity" that Echeverría, Bolívar, Mármol, and the others worried about. At the same time, legitimated in part by *Civilization and Barbarism*, gaucho lifeways and art forms were appropriated into lettered culture, to create what came to be thought of as an Argentine national tradition.

BARBAROUS WORDS

The primal América reinvented through Humboldt was by no means the only paradigm that grounded the emergent *americanismo literario* of the independence period, though it was an extremely prominent one. Creole women writers of the period drew quite different maps of meaning, for instance. Understandably, they did not take up the androcentered speech position of the seeing-man, even as a gesture. After all, in that paradigm the woman *is* the landscape – which is to say that the landscape paradigm is not a device through which creole women could found or legitimate themselves as subjects.[41] In the 1830s and 1840s, Cuban writer Gertrúdis Gómez de Avellaneda, for example, wrote Americanist poetry of a very different sort from her compatriot and contemporary Heredia, and a novel not about civilization versus barbarism, but about the unrequited love of a noble mulatto slave for a white creole woman.[42] Avellaneda's portrait of the American traveler, quoted in the epigraph to this chapter, elaborately invokes the conventional Americanist landscapes, then says that the traveler who seeks them finds only "a great desert carpeted with lava." The utopian myths are "optical illusions of the soul."[43] Avellaneda's use of a field of dried lava to symbolize broken dreams draws directly (and parodically) on the Humboldtian fascination with volcanos and the forces of volcanic energy.

The Argentine prose writer Juana Manuela Gorriti allegorized creole cultural and political dilemmas in ways that often inverted the conventions of her male contemporaries. One of her stories, written in the 1840s while she was in exile (like Sarmiento and Mármol) from the dictator Rosas,[44] begins with what Gorriti titled "A Glimpse of the Homeland" ("Una ojeada a la patria"). The glimpse comes through the eyes of a woman exile who, disguised as a man, returns to the hacienda of her childhood. If anything, her gaze registers a hyper-historicized rather than a dehistoricized American landscape. The protagonist finds the hacienda occupied by others – by a Spaniard, in fact, who receives her hospitably. The landscape, far from empty, is littered with history: cemeteries, ruins of missions and haciendas, old friends, stories, memories. Her own childhood paintings still adorn the walls of the house. In this tale, renegotiation of relations with the new nations is based on first-person identification with the region rather than on polarities between creole and gaucho, creole and Indian, or creole and Spaniard. The cross-dressing, it seems, is a device for imagining the woman as a republican citizen-subject (though not as a man). In another fascinating tale written from the same period, Gorriti uses an incest drama to allegorize the transcultural relationships between creoles and Europe on the one hand and between creoles and indigenous Americans on the other. In "He who does Evil should Expect no Good," a young Andean child, daughter of an indigenous woman raped by a Peruvian officer, is found and adopted by a French naturalist, who takes her to France and raises her as a Frenchwoman. Years later, a young Peruvian creole attending school in Paris falls in love with her and returns with her to Peru as his bride. The legacy of colonial rape and abduction returns to haunt them all as the narrative unravels to reveal that the young man's father was the creole officer who originally raped the young woman's mother: the Frenchwoman is not French but mestiza, and the founding couple are brother and sister. Gorriti chooses to dramatize the intertwining of racial and cultural histories, not their polarization; unbeknownst to itself, in her story, Europe is infiltrated by América, as well as the reverse.

As Gorriti's Andean tale suggests, Europe and creole America were not the only cultural formations in play in the negotiation of identity, subjectivity, and culture in postcolonial South America. Even as Andrés Bello exported European values from London, the wars of independence catalysed new internal contacts among regional, popular, and indigenous cultures. It is not in the realm of letters, however, that one most readily observes the cultural *mestizaje* that was an everyday matter in the multiethnic societies (and armies) of the Americas. Canonical literary history recognizes only a few traces left by indigenous and mestizo art forms on the official culture-building activities of the creole elites. The most conspicuous examples (as in the United States) come specifically from the multicultural contact zone of the Spanish American armies, both royalist and independentist. In the 1810s in Peru, for instance, a young mestizo poet and soldier named Mariano Melgar (who also liked to translate Ovid) transculturated an Andean Quechua song form into a written poetic form he called the *yaravi*. His work was an early instance of what became an important indigenist strand in Peruvian national literature. In Argentina, where the military brought many cultural zones into contact, an improvisational popular song form called the *cielito* entered print culture via pamphlets and newspapers and was the source of a good deal of occasional and political poetry during the independence period. The main figure remembered for this adaption, Bartolomé Hidalgo, is often celebrated in Argentine literary histories as the first national poet. Hidalgo was also an initiator of what became a widespread appropriation from gaucho oral culture into print, especially the long, improvised verse song and dialogic poetic duelling. The resultant body of Argentine gaucho literature is large and unique, including such items as a gaucho-style rewriting of the Faust myth (1866).

Materials such as these cannot readily be absorbed into ideologies of authenticity and unitary narratives of origin. Like autoethnographic expression, their expressive power is anchored in the intercultural dynamics of the contact zone, and the history of colonial subordination.

POSTSCRIPT

In one of the founding texts of modern Latin American literary criticism tellingly titled *Tientos y diferencias* (*Tints and Differences*, 1967) the Cuban writer Alejo Carpentier recounts an anecdote about Goethe. In 1831, contemplating a drawing of a landscape where he planned to build a country house, Goethe wrote with pleasure of how reasonable and peaceful the place was, and expressed the hope that like himself, nature there will have "abandoned her mad and feverish upheavals" to adopt a "circumspect and complacent beauty." Carpentier replies to Goethe, "architect of the Enlightenment," in Americanist terms: You can build me whatever kind of house you like, he says, but "our continent is a continent of hurricanes . . . cyclones, earthquakes, tidal waves, floods . . . a nature uncontained, driven still by her primal upheavals."[45]

The explicit contrast Carpentier draws here (in 1967!) is geographical, between one side of the Atlantic and the other; but equally it is the historical contrast between one side of the Humboldtian watershed and the other. The language of Humboldt rumbles as deeply through Carpentier's novels and echoes in his concept of América's *real maravilloso* ("marvelous real"). Humboldt's reinvention of América is the unspoken source that generates Carpentier's comparison with Europe, the lost step present through the adjacent figure of Humboldt's mentor Goethe. That Humboldt is missing is, of course, an essential point: Carpentier is playing Humboldt's role, occupying his discourse, as blithely as if no history separated them at all. So 150 years after *Views of Nature*, Humboldt continues to be a point of departure for creole Americanist esthetics. So Carpentier realizes himself as a transcultural Euroamerican subject, a creole crossroads who mirrors images back and forth across the Atlantic with dizzying spontaneity. For some, that transcultural subjectivity embodies a neocolonial legacy of self-alienation; for others, it constitutes the essence of culture in the Américas. Choosing one side or the other of that dichotomy determines very different readings of neo-Humboldtian texts like Carpentier's autobiographical travel novel *The Lost Steps* (Cuba, 1953). The protagonist of this novel is a Spanish American creole intellectual who, after many years in Europe, returns to South America on a research expedition up the Orinoco in search of the origins of human music. His account of the Amazonian jungle is a dystopic rewriting of Humboldt:

> As we skirted the banks, the shade cast by several ceilings of vegetation brought a breath of coolness to the canoes. But a few seconds' pause sufficed to turn this relief into an unbearable fervor of insects. There seemed to be flowers everywhere, but in nearly every case their colors were the lying effect of leaves at varying degrees of maturity or decay. There seemed to be fruit, but the roundness and ripeness of the fruits were feigned by oozing bulbs, fetid velvets, the vulvula of insect-eating plants like thoughts sprinkled with syrup, dotted cacti that bore tulips of saffron-colored sperm a handspan from the ground. And when an orchid could be discerned, high above the bamboo thickets, high above the yopos, it seemed as unreal, as inaccessible as the most dizzying Alpine edelweiss. And there were trees, too, which were not green, but dotted the banks with clumps of amaranth or glowed with the yellow of a burning bush. Even the sky lied at times when, reversing its altitude in the quicksilver of the ponds, it buried itself in heavenly abysmal depths.[46]

The place remains largely unchanged since Humboldt's "Nocturnal Life in the Primeval Forest" in *Views of Nature*, but many of the value signs are reversed. The American cornucopia here is a plenitude not of discovery but of unknowability, a world that metropolitan consciousness is unequipped to decipher or embrace. The masculine creole subject depicts himself caught in the mirror dance of postcolonial meaning-making, where even the sky lies at times. What is left of Humboldt's European certitude is the white (of course) orchid, as inaccessible from here as the Alps.

Alexander von Humboldt died in 1859 at the age of 90. In the past three decades his various centennials and bicentennials have given rise to a considerable literature about him in Spanish America. Its pages sound scarcely a critical note. "Americans should never forget Humboldt," says one commentator; "The writings of this scholar have given them to know [*les han hecho conocer*] the country [*pais*] in which they live."[47] Humboldt is thought of in official culture as *necessary*, as something that in retrospect *had* to happen. Over and over one reads that "it took" Alexander von Humboldt to "give us a beautiful vision" of South America. "Our landscape would have to await the nineteenth century to be lovingly and extensively described first by foreign travelers and then by national writers."[48] One contemporary commentator asserts that indeed it "took" Humboldt because the colonial population had somehow come to share the Amerindians' supposed lack of esthetic sense.[49] In the spring of 1985 North Americans were treated to a glossy nostalgic revival of Humboldt by the *National Geographic* magazine, whose photographs and maps undertook the most literal reconstruction possible of Humboldt's perspective and the primal world he wrote – an example of that all-American activity Jean Baudrillard calls simulation.[50] Should one conclude that the structures of reception for Humboldt's Americanist writings remain unchanged since 1820? Are the relations of authority, hierarchy, alienation, dependency, Eurocentrism that gave the essentializing aspects of Humboldt's work their appeal in 1820 still so entrenched as to be invisible? Alternatively, perhaps the post World War II era of underdevelopment, third-world industrialization, third-world debt, political interventionism, and (most recently) ecocide has revived the need for the myth of the American Eden, if only as a memory. If we started over, the metropolis longingly asks, could *they* have saved *us*?

Part III

Imperial stylistics, 1860–1980

From the Victoria Nyanza
to the Sheraton San Salvador

To land at this airport [. . .] is to plunge directly into a state in which no ground is solid, no depth of field reliable, no perception so definite that it might not dissolve into its reverse.

(Joan Didion, *Salvador* (United States, 1983))

They put me in a room and the first thing I saw when they uncovered my eyes was the United States flag and on the other side the Bolivian flag, and a framed picture with two hands that said "Alliance for Progress." [. . .] The desk was full of rubber stamps.

(Domitila Barrios de Chungara, *Let Me Speak* (Bolivia, 1978))

THE MONARCH OF ALL I SURVEY

No one was better at the monarch-of-all-I-survey scene than the string of British explorers who spent the 1860s looking for the source of the Nile. As the Linnaeans had their labeling system, and the Humboldtians their poetics of science, the Victorians opted for a brand of verbal painting whose highest calling was to produce for the home audience the peak moments at which geographical "discoveries" were "won" for England. Ironized and modernized, their vivid imperial rhetoric endures today in the writings of their postcolonial heirs, for whom there is little left on the planet to pretend to conquer.

One of my favorites in the monarch-of-all-I-survey genre comes from Richard Burton's *Lake Regions of Central Africa*, which appeared in 1860 and achieved considerable renown in that prolific and highly competitive era of travel writing. Here in a descriptive *tour de force* Burton renders the dramatic moment of his discovery of Lake Tanganyika:

Nothing, in sooth, could be more picturesque than this first view of the Tanganyika Lake, as it lay in the lap of the mountains, basking in the gorgeous tropical sunshine. Below and beyond a short foreground of rugged and precipitous hill-fold, down which the foot-path zigzags painfully, a narrow strip of emerald green, never sere and marvellously fertile, shelves towards a ribbon of glistening yellow sand, here bordered by sedgy rushes, there cleanly and clearly cut by the breaking wavelets. Further in front stretch the waters, an expanse of the lightest and softest blue, in breadth varying from thirty to thirty-five miles, and sprinkled by the crisp east-wind with tiny crescents of snowy foam. The background in front is a high and broken wall of steel-coloured mountain, here flecked and capped with pearly mist, there standing sharply pencilled against the azure air; its yawning chasms, marked by a deeper plum-colour, fall towards dwarf hills of mound-like proportions, which apparently dip their feet in the wave. To the south, and opposite the long, low point, behind which the Malagarazi River discharges the red loam suspended in its violent stream, lie the bluff headlands and capes of Uguhha, and, as the eye dilates, it falls upon a cluster of outlying islets, speckling a sea horizon. Villages, cultivated lands, the frequent canoes of the fishermen on the waters, and on a nearer approach the murmurs of the waves breaking upon the shore, give a something of variety, of movement, of life to the landscape, which, like all the fairest prospects in these regions, wants but a little of the neatness and finish of art – mosques and kiosks, palaces and villas, gardens and orchards – contrasting with the profuse lavishness and magnificence of nature, and diversifying the unbroken coup d'oeil of excessive vegetation to rival, if not to excel, the most admired scenery of the classic regions.[1]

Promontory descriptions are of course very common in Romantic and Victorian writing of all kinds. As illustrated by many examples already discussed in this book, in the context of exploration writing, the device is called upon to accomplish a particular meaning-making task that at first blush must seem quite a challenge. The verbal painter must render momentously significant what is, especially from a narrative point of view, practically a non-event. As a rule the "discovery" of sites like Lake Tanganyika involved making one's way to the region and asking the local inhabitants if they knew of any big lakes, etc. in the area, then hiring them to take you there, whereupon with their guidance and support, you proceeded to discover what they already knew.

Crudely, then, discovery in this context consisted of a gesture of converting local knowledges (discourses) into European national and continental knowledges associated with European forms and relations of power. To put the matter this way is, of course, to set aside rather aggressively what actually constituted the heroic dimension of this kind of discovery, namely the overcoming of all the geographical, material, logistical, and political barriers to the physical and official presence of Europeans in places such as Central Africa. I wish to foreground the contradictions in the heroic perspective. In the end, the act of discovery itself, for which all the untold

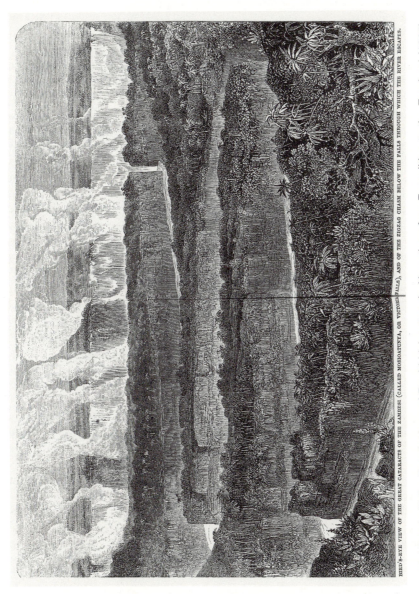

BIRD'S-EYE VIEW OF THE GREAT CATARACTS OF THE ZAMBESI (CALLED MOSIOATUNYA, OR VICTORIA FALLS,) AND OF THE ZIGZAG CHASM BELOW THE FALLS THROUGH WHICH THE RIVER ESCAPES.

35 Victoria Falls, Frontispiece of David Livingstone's *Narrative of an Expedition to the Zambesi* (1865).

lives were sacrificed and miseries endured, consisted of what in European culture counts as a purely passive experience – that of seeing. In Burton's situation at Lake Tanganyika, the heroics of discovery were particularly problematic. Burton had been so ill he had to be carried much of the way by African assistants. His companion John Speke, though able to walk, had been blinded by fever and was therefore at the crucial moment unable in a literal way to discover anything. While the ordeal required to make the discovery is unforgettably concrete, in this mid-Victorian paradigm the "discovery" itself, even within the ideology of discovery, has no existence of its own. It only gets "made" for real after the traveler (or other survivor) returns home, and brings it into being through texts: a name on a map, a report to the Royal Geographical Society, the Foreign Office, the London Mission Society, a diary, a lecture, a travel book. Here is language charged with making the world in the most singlehanded way, and with high stakes. As the explorers found out, lots of money and prestige rode on what you could convince others to give you credit for.[2]

Analyzing Victorian discovery rhetoric, I have found it useful to identify three conventional means which create qualitative and quantitative value for the explorer's achievement. The Burton text just quoted illustrates them well. First, and most obvious, the landscape is *estheticized*. The sight is seen as a painting and the description is ordered in terms of background, foreground, symmetries between foam-flecked water and mist-flecked hills, and so forth. In the Burton text there is a whole binary rhetoric at work playing off large and small, back and front. It is important to note that within the text's own terms the esthetic *pleasure* of the sight singlehandedly constitutes the value and significance of the journey. At the end of the passage quoted, Burton sums it all up: "Truly it was a revel for soul and sight! Forgetting toils, dangers, and the doubtfulness of return, I felt willing to endure double what I had endured; and all the party seemed to join with me in joy."

Second, *density of meaning* in the passage is sought. The landscape is represented as extremely rich in material and semantic substance. This density is achieved especially through a huge number of adjectival modifiers – scarcely a noun in the text is unmodified. Notice, too, that many of the modifiers are derived from nouns (like "sedgy," "capped," or "mound-like") and thus add density by introducing additional objects or materials into the discourse. Of particular interest in this respect are a series of nominal color expressions: "*emerald* green," "*snowy* foam," "*steel*-coloured mountain," "*pearly* mist," "*plum*-colour." Unlike plain color adjectives, these terms add material referents into the landscape, referents which all, from steel to snow, tie the landscape explicitly to the explorer's home culture, sprinkling it with some little bits of England. Scientific vocabulary is completely absent.

The third strategy at work here has been discussed off and on throughout this book: the relation of *mastery* predicated between the seer and the seen. The metaphor of the painting itself is suggestive. If the scene is a painting, then Burton is both the viewer there to judge and appreciate it, and the verbal painter who produces it for others. From the painting analogy it also follows that what Burton sees is all there is, and that the landscape was intended to be viewed from where he has emerged upon it. Thus the scene is deictically ordered with reference to his vantage point, and is static.

The viewer–painting relation also implies that Burton has the power if not to possess, at least to evaluate this scene. Conspicuously, what he finds lacking is more Art, where Art (mosques and kiosks, palaces, gardens) is equated with Mediterranean high culture and institutions. Evidently, the African villages and cultivations already mentioned are not enough *esthetically*. The non-Christian Mediterranean esthetics here reflect nonconformist Burton's deep ambivalences about Victorian English culture, its rigid family and class bases, its repressive morality and arrogant colonial designs. (He had sealed his fame already by making a pilgrimage to Mecca disguised as an Arab, at a time when detection would likely have cost him his life.) At the same time, depicting the civilizing mission as an esthetic project is a strategy the west has often used for defining others as available for and in need of its benign and beautifying intervention. Another Nile explorer, James Grant, in an account written a year or two after Burton's, actually supplied the missing elements in one of his discovery scenes. Reaching Lake Victoria Nyanza, he reported, he was inspired to make a sketch, "dotting it with imaginary steamers and ships riding at anchor in the bay," in addition to the African boats he has already mentioned. Often in such scenes the indigenous labor pool are called upon to verify the European's achievement. Burton asserts above that "all the party seemed to join with me in joy" at Lake Tanganyika; Grant observes that "even the listless Wanyamuezi came to have a look. . . . The Seedees were in raptures."[3] African members of "the party" doubtless did get caught up in the excitement of the quest on expeditions such as these. The writing convention that marshals their reactions to confirm the European's achievement subordinates their response, assigns them the task of carrying their masters' emotional baggage along with the rest of their stuff.

The monarch-of-all-I-survey scene, then, would seem to involve particularly explicit interaction between esthetics and ideology, in what one might call a rhetoric of presence. In Burton's rendering, if we take it literally, the esthetic qualities of the landscape constitute the social and material value of the discovery to the explorers' home culture, at the same time as its esthetic deficiencies suggest a need for social and material intervention by the home culture. Burton's partner and younger rival John Speke drew on the same equation to express his disappointment when one of his discoveries let him down. While accompanying Burton on his Nile expedition, Speke became convinced that the source of the Nile would be found in Lake Victoria N'yanza (as it was later called). In a famous dispute his mentor Burton soundly rejected the proposal, which later proved true. To confirm his hypothesis, Speke made a second expedition in the company of James Grant. The results were quite decisive, but because this second expedition was unable to map the entire circumference of the Victoria N'yanza, Speke's claim remained technically open to question. Many readers will be familiar with the vicious polemic which ensued back in England between Burton and Speke, resulting in Speke's apparent suicide. Speke's account of the expedition (*Journal of the Discovery of the Source of the Nile*, 1863) was written in the midst of this polemic. In a startlingly schematic way, Speke wrote his disappointment and filial anguish into the scene of discovery that culminates his narrative. The passage quoted below displays many elements of the monarch-of-all-I-survey trope: the value of the sight is expressed in terms of esthetic pleasure, the party spontaneously bears witness, the sketch book is mentioned, but the sight itself is expressed as a letdown (my italics):

> We were well rewarded; for the "stones" as the Waganda call the falls, was by far *the most interesting sight* I had seen in Africa. *Everybody ran to see them* at once, though the march had been long and fatiguing, and even *my sketch-book* was called into play. *Though beautiful*, the scene was *not exactly what I had expected*: for the broad surface of the lake was *shut out from view* by a spur of hill, and the falls, about 12 feet deep, and 400–500 feet broad, were *broken by rocks*. Still it was a sight that attracted one to it for hours – the roar of the waters, the thousands of passenger-fish, leaping at the falls with all their might, the Wasoga and Waganda fishermen coming out in boats and taking post on all the rocks with rod and hook, hippopotami and crocodiles lying sleepily on the water, the ferry at work above the falls, and cattle driven down to drink at the margin of the lake – made all in all, with the *pretty nature* of the country – small hills, grassy-tipped, with trees in the folds, and gardens on the lower slopes – as *interesting a picture* as one could wish to see.
>
> The expedition had now performed its functions. I saw that old father Nile without any doubt rises in the Victoria N'yanza, and as I foretold, that lake is the great source of the holy river which cradled the first expounder of our religious belief. I mourned, however, when I thought of how much I had lost by the delays in the journey which had *deprived me of the pleasure* of going to look at the northeast corner.[4]

Speke's esthetic disappointment exactly duplicates his logistical one. Obstacles block the view; the river's smooth flow, like the explorer's own movement, is interrupted. Behind the rocks, the falls and the hill, Lake Victoria N'yanza undoubtedly lies, as Lake Tanganyika did for Burton, "basking in the gorgeous tropical sunshine," but Speke cannot see it/(her) – yet only the seeing, and the writing of the seeing, can fully constitute the discovery. Locked into the rhetoric, and locked at the same time

The Ripon Falls—the Nile flowing out of Victoria N'yanza.

36 Ripon Falls, from John Hanning Speke's *Journal of the Discovery of the Source of the Nile* (1863).

into a public Oedipean battle with Burton, Speke displays his failure here even as he claims the achievement. The rhetoric uses him, and he it. Estheticization is reduced to the mundane categories of the interesting and attractive, not the sublime; neither metaphors nor adjectives nor European allusion provide density of meaning. The European's claim to mastery and will to intervention are also absent here. Speke writes the scene of fish, fishermen, livestock, and ferries as a complete whole that in no way belongs or even beckons to him. If anything, mastery resides with the Wasoga and Waganda fishermen, and Speke is one of the thousands of passenger-fish leaping hopelessly up the falls. And indeed, in the final paragraph, Speke moves out of the monarchic trope to find meaning for his act in a series of Oedipean images: old father Nile, his religious forbear Jesus, and the unmentioned, unforgiving father, Burton.

HYPHENATED WHITE MEN AND THE CRITIQUE FROM WITHIN

The solemnity and self-congratulatory tone of the monarch-of-all-I-survey scene are a virtual invitation to satire and demystification. Congo explorer Paul Du Chaillu, a contemporary of Speke and Burton, was one explorer-writer who accepted the invitation, writing a travel book in 1861 that wildly disturbed the esthetic-ideological matrix of art-and-empire. Du Chaillu was a Franco-American whose father had been in trade in West Africa. While the British sought to "win" the source of the Nile, Du Chaillu took on another enigma: the gorilla. Reports of a huge man-like animal had emanated from the Congo ever since anyone could remember, but western curiosity about the creature had been quenched by equally vivid reports of cannibalism throughout the region. Fever was also a major deterrent, as well as the inland African traders on the Congo, who seem to have been particularly adept at protecting their business from European encroachment. With the advent of evolutionary thinking and modern race theories in the 1850s, however, the possibility of the gorilla acquired extraordinary new significances (for instance as the lower beast to whom Africans would be more closely related than Europeans).[5] It became imperative for Europeans to confirm or discount the creature's existence. At about the same time, medical advances made African travel safer for Europeans. Though not everyone believed him, Du Chaillu did "discover" the gorilla and wrote it up in his popular and sensational *Explorations and Adventures in Equatorial Africa* (1861). It is a discovery so ideologically charged that westerners have had to re-enact it at regular intervals ever since. (A 1980s re-enactment took place in the film *Gorillas in the Mist*, based on the life of primatologist Dian Fossey.)

Du Chaillu's "discovery" of the gorilla made him famous, and his highly entertaining travel books gained him notoriety – as a satirist, a sensationalist, and a liar. Like Henry Morton Stanley, another hyphenated (in this case Anglo-) American who would soon turn up in the Congo, Du Chaillu challenged head on the literary decorum of the British gentlemen travelers and their legitimating rhetoric of presence, substituting it with what one might call a rhetoric of illegitimate presence. Consider, for instance, what happens to the monarch-of-all-I-survey scene in this excerpt from Du Chaillu's vivid exploration narrative. It begins like an echo of Burton, then evolves into parody:

> From this elevation – about 5000 feet above the ocean level – I enjoyed an unobstructed view as far as the eye could reach. The hills we had surmounted the day before lay quietly at our feet, seeming mere molehills. On all sides stretched the immense virgin forests, with here and there the sheen of a water-course. And far away in the east loomed the blue tops of the farthest range of the Sierra del Cristal, the goal of my desires. The murmur of the rapids below filled my ears, and as I strained my eyes toward those distant mountains which I hoped to reach, I began to think how this wilderness would look if only the light of Christian civilization could once be fairly introduced among the black children of Africa. I dreamed of forests giving way to plantations of coffee, cotton, spices; of peaceful negroes going to their contented daily tasks; of farming and manufactures; of churches and schools; and luckily, raising my eyes heavenward at this stage of my thoughts, saw pendent from the branch of a tree beneath which I was sitting an immense serpent, evidently preparing to gobble up this dreaming intruder on his domains.[6]

Again, many standard elements of the imperial trope are present: the mastery of the landscape, the estheticizing adjectives, the broad panorama anchored in the seer. But as soon as the explorer's eyes light on the "goal of his desires," an interventionist fantasy completely displaces the reality of the landscape before him and becomes the content of the vision. Unlike Burton and Grant's fantasies of adding a little something here and there to perfect the scene (a mosque here, a steamship there), Du Chaillu orchestrates a wholesale transformation unabashedly colonialist (and American) in character. Then along comes the serpent to ironize the guilty fantasy, and point to its guilt. Simultaneously a double of the dreamer and a symbol of the other, the serpent (not snake, mind you) has come directly from the Garden of Eden, bringing among other things the unwelcome (but also welcome) knowledge that the cozy pastoral-plantation fantasy is forbidden fruit likely to lead to expulsion from the garden. Who might know this better than an American in the aftermath of the Civil War?

In the face of the serpentine intrusion, Du Chaillu, the original sinner/
intruder, abandons his visionary role and grabs onto the fundamental material
instrument of the civilizing mission: "My dreams of future civilization
vanished in a moment," we read; "Luckily my gun lay at hand." That is
the end of the serpent ("my black friend," he calls it), but not the satire,
for now, "the Christian civilization of which I had mused so pleasantly a
few minutes before received another shock":

> My men cut off the head of the snake, and dividing the body into proper
> pieces, roasted it and ate it on the spot; and I poor, starved, but civilized
> mortal, stood by, longing for a meal, but unable to stomach this. So much
> for civilization, which is a very good thing in its way, but has no business
> in an African forest when food is scarce.[7]

The scene has all the overtones of a communion or last supper, except that
the Messiah is an outsider who will not share the meal, and could become
part of it. Far from sharing and reflecting the explorer's paradigms of value
and desire, "the party" in Du Chaillu's depiction act on values of their own
which, in a very overdetermined way, are incompatible with Du Chaillu's.
Throughout his book, Du Chaillu repeatedly tells us he does not eat snake or
gorilla. Why not? Symbolically, it seems, to eat snake ("my black friend") is
to eat Satan (alias the African as other), while eating gorilla raises the specter
of cannibalism (alias the self as African).

"Civilized" impractical practices anchored in "uncivilized" white suprema-
cist assumptions – so the imperial project is displayed by Du Chaillu. So
the imperial subject splits in his writing: Du Chaillu is now parodist,
now parodied; now dreamer, now demystifier of his own dream; now
Adam, now serpent; now provider of civilization, now deprived of it;
now hunter, now hunted. His discourse here achieves its semantic density
through the very contradictions of the European's presence in Africa.
This perverse perspective is very likely connected with the fact that Du
Chaillu is himself neither European nor African, but a Franco-American.
A hyphenated white man writing at the height of civilizing mission,
Du Chaillu is indeed an early serpent in the African imperial garden.
Thirty years later, it was right there in the Congo that the civilizing
mission unmasked itself in the sadistic, genocidal drama of the Congo
rubber boom. From their mountain retreats, the gorillas perhaps looked
on while Europeans became, and watched each other become, white
barbarians as wild and ruthless as those they had always imagined for
themselves in Africa. Relayed back to Europe through the intervention
of critical intellectuals, European barbarism in the Congo became one
of the great political scandals of the turn of the century. Among the
European witnesses were several hyphenated white men armed with pens
and paper: Henry Stanley, the Anglo-American who led the scramble
for Africa and transformed English exploration writing to fit the bill;

CROSSING A MANGROVE SWAMP, WITH THE TIDE OUT.

37 "Crossing a mangrove swamp, with the tide out," from Du Chaillu's *Explorations and Adventures in Equatorial Africa* (1861).

DEATH OF MY HUNTER.

38 "Death of my hunter," from Du Chaillu's *Explorations and Adventures in Equatorial Africa* (1861).

Roger Casement, the Anglo-Irishman who worked tirelessly to expose the horrors Stanley had set in motion; and Joseph Conrad, the Anglo-Pole who made the Congo debacle into the allegory of the failure of Europe. Each was a white man whose national and civic identifications were multiple and often conflicted; each had lived out in deep personal and social histories the raw realities of Euroexpansionism, white supremacy, class domination, and heterosexism. The hyphenated white men are principal architects of the often imperialist internal critique of empire. Later in this chapter I consider the continuity of that critique in the work of Franco-Algerian Albert Camus and Afro-American Richard Wright.

THE LADY IN THE SWAMP

It is hard to think of a trope more decisively gendered than the monarch-of-all-I-survey scene. Explorer-man paints/possesses newly unveiled landscape-woman. But of course there were explorer-women, like Alexandra Tinné and Mary Kingsley, who led expeditions in Africa, and explorer-wives like Florence Baker, who accompanied expeditions up the Nile. Like the social exploratresses discussed in chapter 7, these women, in their writings, do not spend a lot of time on promontories. Nor are they entitled to. The masculine heroic discourse of discovery is not readily available to women, which may be one reason why there exists so very little European women's exploration writing at all. Mary Kingsley's extraordinary *Travels in West Africa* (1897) is probably the most extensive instance that does exist. Through irony and inversion, she builds her own meaning-making apparatus out of the raw materials of the monarchic male discourse of domination and intervention. The result, as I will suggest below, is a monarchic female voice that asserts its own kind of mastery even as it denies domination and parodies power.

Kingsley went to West Africa around the age of 30 as an entomologist and ichthyologist mainly interested, or so she tells us, in the small-scale life forms that inhabit the vast and unexplored mangrove swamps of the Gabon. The domain she chose to occupy, then, could hardly contrast more starkly with the gleaming promontories her fellow Victorians sought out. Indeed, "her" swamps, as she calls them, are a landscape that the Africans themselves seem neither to use nor value, a place where they would never contest the European presence. Kingsley depicts herself discovering her swamps not by looking down at them or even walking around them, but by sloshing zestfully through them in a boat or up to her neck in water and slime, swathed in thick skirts and wearing her boots continuously for weeks on end. Her comic and self-ironic persona indelibly impresses itself on any reader of her book. Here she is in a famous passage, fresh out of the interior and hitching a ride to the coast in a small boat with a blanket for a sail, as usual the only European and the only woman in the party:

> As much as I have enjoyed life in Africa, I do not think I ever enjoyed it to the full as I did on those nights dropping down the Rembwe. The great, black, winding river with a pathway in its midst of frosted silver where the moonlight struck it; on each side the ink-black mangrove walls, and above them the band of stars and moonlit heavens that the walls of mangrove allowed one to see. Forward rose the form of our sail, idealised from bedsheetdom to glory; and the little red glow of our cooking fire gave a single note of warm colour to the cold light of the moon. Three or four times during the second night, while I was steering along by the south bank, I found the mangrove wall thinner, and standing up, looked through the network of their roots and stems on to what seemed like plains, acres upon acres in extent, of polished silver – more specimens of those awful slime lagoons, one of which, before we reached Ndorke had so very nearly collected me. I watched them, as we leisurely stole past, with a sort of fascination . . . Ah me! give me a West African river and a canoe for sheer good pleasure. Drawbacks, you say? Well, yes, but where are there not drawbacks? The only drawbacks on those Rembwe nights were the series of horrid frights I got by steering on to tree shadows and thinking they were mudbanks, or trees themselves, so black and solid did they seem. I never roused the watch, fortunately, but got her off the shadow gallantly singlehandedly every time, and called myself a fool instead of getting called one. . . . By daylight the Rembwe scenery was certainly not so lovely, and might be slept through without a pang.[8]

What world could be more feminized? There shines the moon lighting the way; the boat a combination bedroom and kitchen; Kingsley the domestic goddess keeping watch and savoring the solitude of her night vigil. Far from sharing her joy, the party, thank goodness, are asleep. The place is almost subterranean – like a mole, the traveler peers through roots and stems. Beauty and density of meaning lie not in the variety and color that unveil themselves, but in the idealization which the veil of night makes possible *in the mind of the seer*. By day, one sees not variety and density, but their opposite, monotony. Which is to say that Kingsley creates value by decisively and rather fiercely rejecting the textual mechanisms that created value in the discourse of her male predecessors: fantasies of dominance and possession, painting that is simultaneously a material inventory. She foregrounds the workings of her (European and female) subjectivity: the polished silver is the product of her own imagination at work on a mangrove swamp. Far from taking possession of what she sees, she *steals* past; far from imagining a civilizing or beautifying intervention, she contemplates only the silly possibility of "damaging Africa" in a collision that would doubtless damage her worse.

Estheticization in Kingsley is replaced by a relentlessly comic irony applied to herself and those around her. Pleasure is constant, but it lies in play, not in beauty: Africa is a rousing jolly good time. Above all, Kingsley's book owes its enduring popularity to this masterful comic irreverence. Masterful: that is just the thing. At the same time as it mocks the self-importance and possessiveness of her male counterparts, Kingsley's irony constitutes her own form of mastery, deployed in a swampy world of her own that the explorer-men have not seen or do not want. If the Nile explorers standing on their bright hilltops are kings, down below moving through the dark and the mud, Mary Kingsley is the Queen, Cleopatra on the Nile, perhaps, as alone at the helm as her counterpart back in England.

In imaging Mary Kingsley as a queen, I want to capture the fact that she did locate herself within the project of empire, however much she rejected the tropes of imperial domination. Indeed, as recent biographical work reminds us,[9] Kingsley participated very actively in the politics of expansion in Britain, on behalf of a particular political position. An imperialist but passionate anti-colonialist, she used her fame as a writer and explorer to lobby hard for the free-market view that expansionism and frontier relations were best left in the hands of traders. Colonial administrations, missionary operations, and big companies were all oppressive, destructive, and impractical (as indeed the Congo experience was proving in the 1890s). The Nile explorers of the 1860s were, of course, writing in the relatively innocent decades before the scramble for Africa unleashed European rivalries in a vicious territorial frenzy. By the time orphanhood freed Kingsley to travel, the scramble for Africa was well underway, and the civilizing mission very much open to question. Even as she wrote, other writers like Joseph Conrad and André Gide were transforming Africa from a sun-drenched promontory into the guilt-ridden heart of darkness where European lust for dominance met up with the impossibility of total control.

Rhetorically and politically, Kingsley seeks out a third position that recovers European innocence. Politically she argued for the possibility of economic expansion without domination and exploitation. In her rhetoric she seeks to separate mastery from domination, knowledge from control. "Not knowing" for her does not mean "needing to know"; "not seeing" does not mean "needing to see"; "not arriving" does not mean "needing to arrive." The bumbling, comic innocence of everyone in her writings, including herself, proposes a particular way of being a European in Africa. Utopian in its own right, her proposal seems expressly designed to respond to the agonies of the European who has landed in the swamp after falling from his promontory. How schematically Kingsley's utopian Rembwe scene (quoted above) contrasts with its counterpart in Conrad's *Heart of Darkness* (1900):

> The dusk came gliding into [the river] long before the sun had set. The current ran smooth and swift, but a dumb immobility sat on the banks. The living trees, lashed together by the creepers and every living bush of the undergrowth, might have been changed into stone, even to the slenderest twig, to the lightest leaf. It was not sleep – it seemed unnatural, like a state of trance. Not the faintest sound of any kind could be heard. You looked on amazed, and began to suspect yourself of being deaf – then the night came suddenly, and struck you blind as well. About three in the morning some large fish leaped, and the loud splash made me jump as though a gun had been fired. When the sun rose there was a white fog, very warm and clammy, and more blinding than the night.[10]

Night here threatens European subjectivity with destruction and annihilation. The heart of darkness revolves around a vortex of fear. In her utopian moment on the river, Kingsley expressly substitutes this fear with "a sort of fascination." The "horrid frights" she experiences are those she inflicts on herself by steering onto shadows and taking them for real perils. Only the need for certainty and control make uncertainty and vulnerability fearful, she suggests. These things can be forfeited. It is not only Kingsley's gender that enables her to forfeit them in her writing. Besides being a woman, she is a child in Africa as well, at play in the ego-centered non-Oedipean world Speke must have died longing for. Africa is her mother, and down those shimmering, dark and slimy pathways, Kingsley is getting herself born.

THE WHITE MAN'S LAMENT

In contemporary travel accounts, the monarch-of-all-I-survey scene gets repeated, only now from the balconies of hotels in big third-world cities. Here, like their explorer forbears, postcolonial adventurers perch themselves to paint the significance and value of what they see. Here is one example from a West African travelogue called *Which Tribe Do You Belong To?* (1972) by Italian novelist and essayist Alberto Moravia. It is the opening paragraph of the book:

> From the balcony of my room I had a panoramic view over Accra, capital of Ghana. Beneath a sky of hazy blue, filled with mists and ragged yellow and grey clouds, the town looked like a huge pan of thick, dark cabbage soup in which numerous pieces of white pasta were on the boil. The cabbages were the tropical trees with rich, trailing, heavy foliage of dark green speckled with black shadows; the pieces of pasta the brand-new buildings of reinforced concrete, numbers of which were now rising all over the town.[11]

A few years later in a popular account of a rail journey through Latin America

(*The Old Patagonian Express*, 1978), the Anglo-American novelist and travel writer Paul Theroux repeated the gesture in Guatemala City:

> Guatemala City, an extremely horizontal place, is like a city on its back. Its ugliness, which is a threatened look (the low, morose houses have earthquake cracks in their facades; the buildings wince at you with bright lines) is ugliest on those streets where, just past the last toppling house, a blue volcano's cone bulges. I could see the volcanoes from the window of my hotel room. I was on the third floor, which was also the top floor. They were tall volcanoes and looked capable of spewing lava. Their beauty was undeniable, but it was the beauty of witches. The rumbles from their fires had heaved this city down.[12]

The contrast between these grotesque, joyless cityscapes and the gorgeous, sparkling panoramas depicted by Burton, Grant, and the others could hardly be greater. Nevertheless, the three strategies I emphasized in Burton's text – estheticization, density of meaning, and domination – are still at work here, transposed into a very different historical moment and a different esthetic key. Burton's text, I suggested, created density of meaning through the plentiful use of adjectives, and a general proliferation of concrete, material referents introduced either literally or as metaphors. The Theroux and Moravia texts share these properties. Despite the fact that they too are on unfamiliar territory, these writers, like Burton, claim authoritativeness for their vision. What they see is what there is. No sense of limitation on their interpretive powers is suggested. And perhaps less explicitly than in Burton, relations of subordination and possession are articulated through metaphors. For Theroux, Guatemala City is on its back, in a position of submission or defeat before him, and with a threatened look. The image of a battered woman comes near to consciousness here. Moravia sees Accra as a plate of soup that Ghana seems to have prepared, pasta and all, for him to eat.

Estheticization we also have in these passages, except that where Burton found beauty, symmetry, order, the sublime, Moravia and Theroux find the esthetic opposites: ugliness, incongruity, disorder, and triviality. In reading beauty, order, and grandeur in his landscape, Burton constituted it verbally as a worthy prize, and then projected onto it a vision of an even more ordered and beautiful future under European guidance. Such is the heady optimism of incipient empire. Moravia and Theroux, on the other hand, are speaking from the 1970s, deep in the postcolonial era of "underdevelopment" and decolonization. Few pristine worlds remain for Europeans to discover, and the old ones have long since belied the myth of the civilizing mission. The impulse of these postcolonial metropolitan writers is to condemn what they see, trivialize it, and dissociate themselves utterly from it. It is as if there were no history tying the North American Theroux to Spanish America or the Italian Moravia to Africa, despite the fact that much of what they are lamenting is the depredations of western-induced dependency. There is perhaps a future implied in their texts, one of violence, by and against themselves. Theroux is threatened by female witch volcanos which could bring down the city, including his hotel (see below for Joan Didion's account of this very experience); Moravia's soup image calls to mind the cartoon missionary on the boil in the cannibals' pot.

While their cityscapes are constructed around ugliness, grotesquery, and decay, rural landscapes for Theroux and Moravia consist of scarcity of any meaning at all. The accounts of both the South American and African countryside complain of a kind of esthetic and semantic underdevelopment which both writers, in pure Euroimperial fashion, connect with the prehistoric. Here is a sample from Theroux, nearing his destination in Patagonia. Notice in this passage how the lack of meaning and lack of differentiation are first predicated of nature, then extended to the human world:

> The landscape had a prehistoric look, the sort that forms a painted backdrop for a dinosaur skeleton in a museum; simple, terrible hills and gullies; thorn bushes and rocks; and everything smoothed by the wind and looking as if a great flood had denuded it, washed it of all its particular features. Still the wind worked on it, kept the trees from growing, blew the soil west, uncovered more rock, and even uprooted those ugly bushes.
>
> The people in the train did not look out the window, except at the stations and only then to buy grapes or bread. One of the beauties of train travel is that you know where you are by looking out the window. No signboards are necessary. A hill, a river, a meadow – the landmarks tell you how far you have come. But this place had no landmarks, or rather it was all landmarks, one indistinguishable from the other – thousands of hills and dry riverbeds, and a billion bushes, all the same. I dozed and woke: hours passed; the scenery at the window *did not alter*. And the stations were interchangeable – a shed, a concrete platform, staring men, boys with baskets, the dogs, the battered pickup trucks.
>
> I looked for guanacos. I had nothing better to do. There were no guanacos.[13]

If Burton constructed the Victoria N'yanza description out of possession and ambition, Theroux constructs Patagonia out of paralysis and alienation. (If he knew Spanish, would he have had something better to do? Would everything have been less interchangeable?) The contrast could hardly be more pronounced – or more overdetermined. Here the normative categories are not beauty versus ugliness, but density versus scarcity of meaning. One of the conspicuous hallmarks of western commodity culture is precisely the proliferation of differentiations, specializations, subdivisions, games of taste. Differentiation is what is seen as lacking here – not just absent, but lacking. There is nothing for Theroux's powers of taste to work on.

Moravia's embarrassing introduction to something he generically calls "African landscape" has obvious similarities. Again the language is pervasively normative: the landscape *lacks* shape, finiteness, pattern, history. The possibility of limitations on the speaker's authority is never hinted at.

Thus a journey to Africa, when it is not a mere full excursion from one to another of those big hotels that the inhabitants of the Western world have strewn across the Black Continent, is a veritable dive into prehistory.

But what is this prehistory that so fascinates Europeans? First of all, it should be said, it is the actual conformation of the African landscape. The chief characteristic of this landscape is not diversity, as in Europe, but rather its terrifying monotony. The face of Africa bears a greater resemblance to that of an infant, with few barely indicated features, than to that of a man, upon which life has imprinted innumerable significant lines; in other words, it bears a greater resemblance to the face of the earth in prehistoric times, when there were no seasons and humanity had not yet made its appearance, than to the face of the earth as it is today, with innumerable changes brought about both by time and man. This monotony, furthermore, displays two truly prehistoric aspects: reiteration, that is, repetition of a single theme or motif to the point of obsession, to the point of terror; and shapelessness, that is the complete lack of limitation of the finite, of pattern and form, in fact.[14]

There is never an excuse for this dehumanizing western habit of representing other parts of the world as having no history. For a Southern European to make such an assertion about Africa (or a North American about South America) takes an extraordinary act of denial. To get away with it takes some very persuasive, well-crafted writing. Yet Theroux and Moravia willingly fall into open contradiction to sustain their normative and authoritative viewpoint. What does it mean for Theroux to assert, on the one hand, that "One of the beauties of train travel is that you know where you are by looking out the window," then add, on the other, that in Patagonia this did not work because the landscape "did not alter"? For Theroux, it means *Patagonia* is violating the esthetic norms of train travel, failing to provide the right kind of landmarks. The Patagonians, who do not look out the window, are failing to travel correctly on their own trains. In similar fashion, to establish the deviance of the "African landscape," Moravia finds himself arguing that the face of Africa as it is today does not resemble the face of the earth as it is today. Such are the logic and rhetoric of unexamined prejudice.

Theroux and Moravia, both widely read canonical writers, exemplify a discourse of negation, domination, devaluation, and fear that remains in the late twentieth century a powerful ideological constituent of the west's consciousness of the people and places it strives to hold in subjugation. It is the official metropolitan code of the "third world," its rhetoric of triviality, dehumanization, and rejection coinciding with the end of colonial rule in much of Africa and Asia, the rise of national liberation movements, and accelerated processes of modernization, industrializing, and urban growth in many parts of the world. No longer cornucopias of resources inviting the artful, perfecting intervention of the west, newly assertive, de-exoticizing places and peoples become in the eyes of the seeing-man repugnant conglomerations of incongruities, asymmetries, perversions, absence, and emptiness. Lament as they might, these seeing-men do not relinquish their promontories and their sketch books. Though the party can no longer be counted on to "join with them in joy," they are still up there, commanding the view, assigning it value, oblivious to limitations on their perceptual capacities, their relations of privilege perfectly naturalized. Or perhaps imperfectly naturalized, for by the 1960s and 1970s the seeing-man's dominion now comes accompanied by persistent fears of annihilation and violence. It is in this fear that the contemporary seeing-man records what has always been there: the returning gaze of others, now demanding recognition as subjects of history.

As even the two small examples I have given suggest, the white man's lament seems to remain remarkably uniform across representations of different places, and by westerners of different nationalities. It is a monolith, like the official construct of the "third world" it encodes. In contemporary metropolitan readers this discourse often produces an intense "effect of the real." In one undergraduate course I taught on travel writing, Theroux's *Old Patagonian Express* neutralized weeks of carefully nurtured critical reading. Students came in relieved and confident – this was it, this guy had *really* captured the way South America *really* was, you could just tell he knew what he was talking about. Theroux had fired their imaginations, empowered them to argue for his veracity by the very vividness of the writing, the richness and intensity with which their expectations, stereotypes, and prejudices had been confirmed. The students were carrying out, and being carried out by, the ideological project of third worldism and white supremacy. They were producing the metropolis's official ideologies as they had been taught to do. I was able to assure them they were in respected company. In a review of *The Old Patagonian Express*, published in that organ of official book culture, the *New York Times Book Review*, Paul Fussell praised Theroux for his "sharp eye, which is capable of such shrewd perception." Examples of shrewd perception included, for instance, the *aperçu* in Peru that "the Indians have a broad-based look, like chess pieces"; that the Andean altiplano looked, from the train window, like a "world of kitty litter." If this book is not so interesting as Theroux's earlier railroad odyssey in Asia, said Fussell, in a crescendo of arrogance, the fault is America's, not Theroux's:

> Europe and Asia are a richer venue for this sort of thing than Latin America, which by contrast lacks character, deep literary and historical

associations, and variety. For anyone experienced with Europe, it is desperately boring. Squalor in Mexico is identical to squalor in El Salvador [. . .] Illiteracy here is like illiteracy there [. . .][15]

and so forth. (The *Review* did not print the letters it received objecting to Fussell's review.)

The white man's lament is also the lament of the Intellectual and the Writer. It may be thought of in part as an attempt to drown out the chatter of another monolithic voice emerging in the same decades: the voice of mass tourism. The depth-creating powers of the travel writer must compete with the ten-day nine-night air-hotel package, tips included, and the glossy, disembodied fantasies of tourist propaganda. In the 1960s and 1970s, exoticist visions of plenitude and paradise were appropriated and commodified on an unprecedented scale by the tourist industry. "Real" writers took up the task of providing "realist" (degraded, countercommodified) versions of postcolonial reality. The "effect of the real" Theroux had on the class I taught was doubtless constructed in part out of students' own identification with "real" representation over and against commodified representations through which tourism, quite successfully, markets the world to them.

POSTCOLONIAL HYPHENS

Fifteen years before Moravia, another foreigner stood on a balcony in Accra and wrote about it in a book Moravia might well have read. Afro-American novelist and essayist Richard Wright made his first trip to Africa on the occasion of Ghanean independence in 1957. He related the experience in a travel book whose title, *Black Power*, announced the emerging forms of global identification and historical subjectivity so fearful to the masters of the white man's lament. Like the hyphenated white men before him, in *Black Power* Wright directly set himself to work parodying and reworking the inherited tropology. Consider, for instance, Wright's reconfiguration of the balcony scene in the account of his first day in Accra:

> I wanted to push on and look more, but the sun was too much. I spent the afternoon fretting; I was impatient to see more of this Africa. My bungalow was clean, quiet, mosquito-proof, but it had not been for that I'd come to Africa. Already my mind was casting about for other accommodations. I stood on my balcony and saw clouds of black buzzards circling slowly in the hazy blue sky. In the distance, I caught a glimpse of the cloudy, grayish Atlantic.[16]

The last two sentences provide a very reduced, vestigial instance of the conventional promontory scene. The panorama that is glimpsed is the Atlantic Ocean, which, unlike Lake Tanganyika, inspires no possessive or civilizing fantasies. Wright encodes it as evil and death, as well he might, for between the Afro-American and Africa the Atlantic is the place of death, the middle passage. At the same time, however, Wright explicitly declares dissatisfaction with the balcony convention and the balcony vantage point, from which he feels one can NOT see or judge adequately. Throughout his account, Wright is conspicuously at pains to acknowledge limits on his capacity as a seeing-man (here, for instance, he has to retreat from the sun). Probably a quarter of the sentences in his book are rhetorical questions. In the passage above there are almost no metaphors, and almost no negatives.

Wright's rejection of the balcony is predicated, like Mary Kingsley's, on an awareness of alternatives – alternative lodgings, to start with, but also alternative conventions of representation. Within the representative norms of Wright's travel book, one can only represent and judge what one is *in*. When he cannot be in the street in the passage quoted, Wright describes being in his room. Like Kingsley, he seems to be looking for ways to abdicate the a priori relation of dominance and distance between describer and described.

Outside the city, Wright depicts himself as almost as alienated from tribal and rural life as Moravia. However, in a fashion again reminiscent of Mary Kingsley, he finds himself at home in the night, when the alienation of the seer–seen relations is suspended. In the night an empowered subject is called forth for whom uncertainty, vulnerability, and the invisible bring joy, plenitude, and an expansion of self. Here is Wright's version of the jungle-at-night scene (my italics):

> Night comes *suddenly*, like wet black velvet. The air, charged with too much oxygen, drugs the blood. The scream of some wild birds cuts through the dark and stops *abruptly*, leaving a suspenseful void. A foul smell rises from somewhere. A distant drumming is heard and dies, as though ashamed of itself. An *inexplicable* gust of wind flutters the window curtain, making it billow and then fall limp. A bird chirps sleepily in the listless night. *Fragments* of African voices sound in the darkness and fade. The flame of my candle burns straight up, burns minutes on end without a single flicker or tremor. The sound of a lorry whose motor is whining as it strains to climb the steep hill brings back to me the world I know.[17]

In the dark the cult of the seeing-man dissolves (there is no "I" in the passage until the candle is named). Perception gets fragmented, but (western) consciousness and selfhood do not – as with Kingsley's womb-like cooking fire on the Rembwe, Wright's phallic candle burns steadily. The linguistically minded may have noticed how the fragmenting and abruptness of impressions is counteracted by a strong, continuous rhythm, and how the images become more innocuous as the text proceeds. Wright is trying to represent an experience of ignorance, disorientation, incomprehension, self-dissolution which does not give rise to terror or madness, but rather to a serene receptivity and intense eroticism. The lorry does not come to make a rescue; its task is not to bring Wright back to his world, but to bring his world back to him: the boundaries between the known and the unknown are permeable.

Permeable they are too in the writings of Franco-Algerian Albert Camus, a contemporary of Wright's and another extraordinary hyphenated subject of empire. Camus's fiction displays a deep and very specific engagement with the forms and discourse under discussion here. Much of it explores the contradictions of colonialism – a challenge western criticism has tried to reject by stubbornly reading Camus's narratives as decontextualized existential and moral parables.[18] One brief example will suffice to suggest alternatives. Camus's short story "The Adulterous Woman," in *Exile and the Kingdom* (1957), relates the experience of an Algerian-born Frenchwoman who accompanies her husband on a sales trip into the Algerian interior. There she finds, as she puts it, "nothing was as she expected it." Her own existential crisis in the story coincides with her recognition of the impotence of European colonial power in the inland regions. Not coincidentally, her two great moments of truth in the story take place when she stands alone atop the southernmost French fort looking out over the Sahara. They are fascinating reworkings of the monarch-of-all-I-survey scene. In the first of them, quoted below, the meaning-deficient "prehistoric" landscape so dear to western hegemonic thought is postulated and then rejected. Despite the promontory stance, reference is repeatedly made to things the seer cannot see or comprehend:

> From east to west, in fact, her gaze swept slowly, without encountering a single obstacle, along a perfect curve. Beneath her, the blue-and-white terraces of the Arab town overlapped one another, splattered with the dark red spots of peppers drying in the sun. Not a soul could be seen, but from the inner courts, together with the aroma of roasting coffee, there rose laughing voices or incomprehensible stamping of feet. Farther off, the pale grove divided into uneven squares by clay walls, rustled its upper foliage in a wind that could not be felt up on the terrace. Still farther off, and all the way to the horizon extended the ocher-and-grey realm of stones, in which no life was visible. At some distance from the oasis, however, near the wadi that bordered the palm grove on the west could be seen broad black tents. All around them a flock of motionless dromedaries, tiny at that distance, formed against the gray ground the black signs of a strange handwriting, the meaning of which had to be deciphered. Above the desert, the silence was as vast as the space.[19]

An undifferentiated, timeless, empty landscape is posited in terms similar to those of the white man's lament, but almost immediately its "perfect curve" is interrupted, by multicolored, irregular shapes and uneven squares – the Arab town. Farther off, the dead "realm of stones" proves to be populated by tents and dromedaries, a society written on the landscape in language the colonial protagonist cannot read. More important, she recognizes she cannot read it, and here she, the Euro-African, parts ways with the European seeing-man. For the seeing-man rarely suffers such perplexities; in his books, he is "author"-ized not only to read what he sees, but to write over it in roman letters. Camus's colonial protagonist, reliable as far as she goes, everywhere spots things – human things – going on that she cannot decipher. She has done so all her life.

"The Adulterous Woman" culminates with a climactic nocturnal scene at the same fort when, alone in the dead of night, the woman experiences an orgasmic momentary fusion with the "desert kingdom" that "can never be hers," then returns weeping to her joyless matrimonial bed. This momentary permeation of the colonialist boundaries between Euro-African and Africa constitutes the adultery referred to in the story's title, a kind of cultural adultery. The adulterous woman is the only female protagonist in Camus's fiction. The fluid boundaries of female subjectivity provide the means for imagining what a decolonization of self might mean. Camus constructs a glimpse, and no more, of an agonized relinquishing that is also an emancipatory release, and then pulls back. His colonial exploratress returns from the interior not in triumph like the Nile heroes, but in hopelessness and loss. Like her, Camus himself belonged to the "third category" of the Euro-African, a category whose mediating potential was to be lost in the polarity of colonial warfare.

Camus's "Adulterous Woman" and Wright's *Black Power* were both written in the mid-1950s, when colonial conflicts in many parts of Africa were moving rapidly toward violent confrontation. Both were written in direct connection with specific moments in the struggles for decolonization. Camus's stories date from the onset of the brutal Franco-Algerian war that Fanon studied as a paradigm for the horrors of modern colonial violence. One Algerian in six would die before independence was won. Wright was witnessing the founding of the independent nation of Ghana, formerly Britain's Gold Coast, an event that became a paradigm for the peaceful unraveling of colonial apparatuses. A hyphenated Frenchman and a hyphenated American, the two wrote twenty years before Theroux and Moravia, before the advent of the white man's lament. The black power and cultural adultery they imagine in their 1950s African nights bear witness to openings in the structures of western domination and colonialist ideology *within* the metropolis, openings into which the literature and thought of third-world liberation movements flowed in the 1960s and 1970s. In those dramatic decades, the white man's lament deployed itself in contact with contestatory voices that were increasingly seizing the word. In certain white writers of the 1970s the bitter nostalgia for lost idioms of discovery and domination is a response to that challenge, as well as to the depravity of "development" and the tastelessness of tourism.

THE LADY IN THE AIRPORT

The very brevity of Joan Didion's *Salvador* (1983) suggests a dead end to all of this, or at least the wish for one. An account of a trip to El Salvador motivated by the Central American political crises of the 1980s, Didion's book hinges not on the category of "underdevelopment," but on *terror*, a key ideological matrix of the 1980s. Didion goes to El Salvador to see terror in its officially recognized forms: state terror, paramilitary death squad terror, and terrorist insurrection. She writes a travel book of barely a hundred pages that reads above all like an attempt to finally dismantle the genre, to crumple it under the weight of realities grown grimmer than Paul Theroux found or even wished for. In a discourse generated neither by beauty and plenitude nor by ugliness and lack, Didion seems to reject the estheticizing project of travel writing altogether. She erects nothing, paints nothing, masters nothing. She quotes a lot. The one landscape panorama in the book is a miniature that parodies the discovery trope. Looking down from the plane as she arrives, Didion recalls that El Salvador "is smaller than some California counties . . . the very circumstance that has encouraged the illusion that the place can be managed."[20] So the grand aspirations of the imperial powers reduce here to a bureaucratized wish simply for "management." Welcome to the 1980s!

The voice and authority of the metropolitan subject attenuate in *Salvador* to the point not of dissolution, but of disillusionment. Being there produces a sense neither of dominance (as in Burton and Theroux) nor self-realization (as in Kingsley and Wright). Repeatedly Didion depicts herself as seeing less than she expected, or averting her eyes when the expected unexpectedly occurs. The account is deliberately polyphonic. No integrated subjectivity, no steadily burning flame of a self takes charge of the long quotations of embassy officials, human rights advocates, journalists, creative writers. Their conflicting official discourses to a great extent speak for themselves, often giving an impression of pastiche. The whole seeing project is destabilized – quite literally so, in fact. The one hotel-balcony scene in the book takes place during an earthquake: "I recall crouching under a door frame in my room on the seventh floor," says Didion, "and watching, through the window, the San Salvador volcano appear to rock from left to right."[21] What Theroux feared in fantasy from Guatemala City's volcanos finally takes place.

Perhaps that is no coincidence, for Didion invokes Theroux specifically as her predecessor in El Salvador. At one point she quotes his description in *The Old Patagonian Express* of an alienating experience lecturing at the University of El Salvador. By the time she got there, we are told, things were much worse. The University had long been closed and "a few classes were being held in storefronts around San Salvador."[22] The white man's lament for a (merely) fallen world can no longer master the situation. Stereotypes of underdevelopment break down. Observing the affluent, metropolitan clientele in a luxury supermarket, Didion realizes that she is (my italics) "*no longer* much interested in this kind of irony, that this was a story that would not be illuminated by such details, that this was a story that would perhaps not be illuminated at all, that this was perhaps even less a "story" than a true *noche obscura*."[23] With her "no longer," Didion seems to inaugurate (discover?) a new phase requiring different forms of understanding, altered relations between western observers and their chosen observees – and at this exact point, as if throwing in the towel, her language leaps back into the old vocabulary of darkness and light that constitutes the very discourse she is "no longer much interested in."

What is a "true *noche obscura*"? Why must it be named in another language? Because in contrast with Conrad, Didion in fact identifies her subject matter as inaccessible to her western and female self. Terror, based on the unseen, unsaid, unknown, becomes the source of a plenitude the visitor does not witness or create, one she cannot deploy in the density of description. While terror constructs the authoritative standpoint from which the whole panorama makes sense, readers are spared any effort to imagine or comprehend its workings. Didion experiences terror only as a disempowering state, to quote the book's opening arrival scene, "in which no ground is solid, no depth of field reliable, no perception so definite that it might not dissolve in its reverse. *The only logic is that of acquiescence*"[24] (my italics). Like the hapless Speke, Didion does not succeed in occupying that standpoint, but she winds up letting her readers believe that it is there. Thus, while her book aggressively and lucidly sought to abdicate the authority of the seeing-man, that authority was warmly restored to her on the reception end. The official organs of metropolitan culture eagerly welcomed her as a discoverer returned from a Source. In a dozen cover blurbs the *New York Times*, the *Washington Post*, *USA Today*, and *People* magazine hailed *Salvador* for the very things it rejects: vividness, truthfulness, perceptiveness, accuracy, all the mastery of the seeing-man. "El Salvador has truly become the heart of darkness," exulted the *Atlantic Monthly*. At last we know! Madness and terror are not in ourselves, but in El Salvador! So the "logic of acquiescence" leads as ever to a dead end relieved to discover itself as such.[25]

This logic must be very western. In San Salvador Didion visits the Metropolitan Cathedral, site of a notorious political massacre in 1980. She sees red paint spilled on the stairs outside, while inside "here and there on the cheap linoleum" she spies "what seemed to be actual blood dried in spots, the kind of spots dropped by a slow hemorrhage, or by a woman who does not know or does not care that she is menstruating."[26] Imaginary women have always served as national icons. This one, carelessly, tastelessly, *unconsciously* shedding her own blood, seems to be Didion's icon of El Salvador, brought into being by a metropolitan perspective of masculinist dominance.

But Didion's bleeding woman is imaginary. If a Salvadoran woman were there, and if she spoke, she would probably point out that for her the differences between paint and blood, or between menstruation and slow hemorrhage, are not at all matters of oblivion, indifference, or acquiescence. She would probably point out that terror, for her, consists of more than the merely unseen and unsaid. Such clarifications have indeed been occurring as the women in the cathedral have made their way into metropolitan communicative circuits in the last decade and a half through political movements and collaborative media like oral history, *testimonio*, interviews, film, video. The epigraph at the beginning of this chapter, for example, quotes from the *testimonio* of Bolivian rural labor activist Domitila Barrios de Chungara, recounting one of numerous imprisonments and interrogations at the hands of her government. The moment the blindfold is lifted from her eyes, Barrios claims authority to make an explicitly politicized picture of the contact zone from the perspective of a dominated/resistant historical subject.[27] Such a viewpoint seems inaccessible in *Salvador*, even at the level of the imagined. Historically speaking, Didion's abdication of authority stands adjacent to Barrios's claim to it – whether the one is conditional on the other remains to be seen.[28]

Notes

1 INTRODUCTION: CRITICISM IN THE CONTACT ZONE

1 Guaman Poma de Ayala, *Nueva Coronica y buen gobierno*, ed. John Murra and Rolena Adorno, Mexico, Siglo XXI, 1980, manuscript p. 372.
2 The best source introduction to Guaman Poma's work in English is Rolena Adorno, *Guaman Poma de Ayala: Writing and Resistance in Colonial Peru*, Austin, Texas UP, 1986.
3 I first heard this term in a comment by Gayatri Spivak, whom I thank for it and for many other insights. See her essay collection *In Other Worlds*, London, Methuen, 1989.
4 "Transculturation" was coined in the 1940s by Cuban sociologist Fernando Ortiz in a pioneering description of Afro-Cuban culture (*Contrapunto Cubano* (1947, 1963), Caracas, Biblioteca Ayacucho, 1978). Uruguayan critic Angel Rama incorporated the term into literary studies in the 1970s. Ortiz proposed the term to replace the paired concepts of acculturation and deculturation that described the transference of culture in reductive fashion imagined from within the interests of the metropolis.
5 Ron Carter, "A Question of Interpretation: An Overview of Some Recent Developments in Stylistics," in Theo D'haen, ed., *Linguistics and the Study of Literature*, Amsterdam, 1986, pp. 7–26.
6 I have made this argument at greater length in "Linguistic Utopias," in Nigel Fabb, Derek Attridge, Alan Durant, and Colin McCabe, eds., *The Linguistics of Writing*, Manchester, Manchester UP, 1987, pp. 48–66.
7 In her dissertation on early Chicana writers, Gloria Treviño discusses the folkloric writings of Josefina Niggli, Jovita Gonzalez, and Maria Cristina Mena (Stanford University, 1981).
8 See Martin Bernal's controversial study *Black Athena*, New Brunswick, NJ, Rutgers UP, 1987.

PART I SCIENCE AND SENTIMENT, 1750–1800

2 SCIENCE, PLANETARY CONSCIOUSNESS, INTERIORS

1 Quoted in Peter Gay, *The Enlightenment: An Interpretation, Vol. II*, The Science of Freedom, New York, W. W. Norton, 1969, p. 126. The reference is to Voltaire's *Correspondence*, vol. IV, 48–9.

2 Captain Betagh, *Observations on the Country of Peru and its Inhabitants During his Captivity* in John Pinkerton, ed., *Voyages and Travels in all Parts of the World*, London, Longman et al., vol. 14, 1813, p. 1.

3 M. Frézier, *A Voyage to the South Sea and along the Coasts of Chile and Peru in the Years 1712, 1713, and 1714*, translated from the French, London, Jonah Bowyer, 1717, Preface.

4 Alonso de Ovalle, *An Historical Relation of the Kingdom of Chile* (1649), in Pinkerton, op. cit., vol. 14, pp. 30–210.

5 Betagh, op. cit., p. 8.

6 My discussion here makes use of Victor Von Hagen, *South America Called Them*, New York, Knopf, 1945; Hélène Minguet, Introduction to La Condamine, *Voyage sur l'Amazone*, Paris, Maspero, 1981, pp. 5–27; Edward J. Goodman, *The Explorers of South America*, New York, Macmillan, 1972.

7 Charles-Marie de la Condamine, *A Succinct Abridgement of a Voyage made within the Inland Parts of South-America*, London, E. Withers, 1748, p. iv. This is the first English translation of his *Relation abrégié d'un voyage fait dans l'intérieur de l'Amérique meridionale* (1745).

8 Pierre Bouguer, *An Abridged Relation of a Voyage to Peru* (1744), in Pinkerton, op. cit., vol. 14, pp. 270–312.

9 La Condamine, op. cit., p. 24.

10 ibid., p. 51.

11 It still is, of course. At this writing, the most recent re-enactment of the Amazon quest is Joe Kane's *Running the Amazon*, New York, Random House, 1989.

12 John Adams, Preface to Ulloa's *Voyage to South America* (1747), in Pinkerton, op. cit., vol. 14, p. 313.

13 Von Hagen, op. cit., p. 300.

14 Louis Godin des Odonais, Letter to M. de la Condamine, July 1773, appended to La Condamine's *Abridged Narrative* in Pinkerton, op. cit., vol. 14, pp. 259–69.

15 Frézier, op. cit., p. 10.

16 Adams, op. cit., p. 314.

17 Messrs. Saugnier and Brisson, *Voyages to the Coast of Africa* (1792), New York, Negro UP, 1969. This is an English translation of the 1792 French original *Relation de plusieurs voyages à la côte d'Afrique*.

18 Alexander von Humboldt, *Personal Narrative of a Voyage to the Equinoctial Regions*, trans. Helen Maria Williams, London, Longman et al., 1822, vol. I, p. vii.

19 This discussion of Linnaeus and natural history is informed by the following sources: Heinz Goerke, ed., *Linnaeus*, trans. Denver Lindley, New York, Scribner's, 1973; Tore Frangsmyr, ed., *Linnaeus: The Man and his Work*, Berkeley, California UP, 1983; Gunnar Broberg, ed., *Linnaeus: Progress and Prospects in Linnaean Research*, Pittsburgh and Stockholm, 1980; Daniel Boorstin, *The Discoverers*, New York, Random House, 1983; Henry Steele Commager, *The Empire of Reason*, New York, Doubleday, 1977; P. J. Marshall and Glyndwr Williams, *The Great Map of Mankind*, Cambridge, Harvard UP, 1982; Edward Dudley and Maximilian E. Novak, eds., *The Wild Man Within*, Pittsburgh Pittsburgh UP, 1972; Michel Foucault, *The Order of Things*, New York, Pantheon, 1970; Gay, op. cit. In 1956 the British Museum published a facsimile edition of the 1758 edition of *The System of Nature* under its Latin title *Caroli Linnaei Systema Naturae*.

20 Foucault, op. cit., p. 136.

21 Boorstin, op. cit., p. 16.

22 Quoted ibid., p. 444.

23 Sten Lindroth, "Linnaeus in his European Context," in Broberg, op. cit., p. 14.

24 Gunnar Eriksson, "The Botanical Success of Linnaeus. The Aspect of Organization and Publicity," in Broberg, op. cit., p. 66.
25 Foucault, op. cit., p. 136.
26 ibid., p. 132.
27 ibid., p. 136.
28 ibid., p. 132.
29 Quoted in Marshall and Williams, op. cit., p. 48.
30 This is not to say, of course, that there were no women naturalists – there certainly were, though their participation in the professional aspects was limited, and they did not initially number among the disciples sent to carry the mission abroad. See chapters 6 and 8 below for discussion of some women travel writers in relation to the scientific mission.
31 Quoted in Gay, op. cit., pp. 152–3.
32 Quoted in Foucault, op. cit., p. 148.
33 Barbara Stafford, *Voyage into Substance*, Cambridge, MIT Press, 1987, p. 10.
34 La Condamine, op. cit., p. 37; my italics.
35 Lindroth, op. cit., p. 25.
36 Barbara Stafford, in a puzzling statement, converts the innocence into a fact of nature, arguing that "The popularity of the nonfiction travel account [in the late eighteenth century] hinged in part on the genetic desire of the explorers and the public to return to an almost mythic apprehension of the earth as it might have been or as it unfolded before human consciousness appeared in it" (op. cit., p. 441).
37 Commager, op. cit., p. 7.
38 John G. Burke, "The Wild Man's Pedigree," in Dudley and Novak, op. cit., pp. 266–7.
39 Adams, op. cit., p. 310.
40 Quoted in Stafford, op. cit., p. 22.
41 Review of Hasselquist's *Voyages and Travels in the Levant*, in *Monthly Review*, New Series, vol. 35, 1766, pp. 72–3.
42 Anders Sparrman, *A Voyage to the Cape of Good Hope*, London, G. and J. Robinson, 1785, p. xiii.
43 For a detailed study focused on the nineteenth century, see Harriet Ritvo, *The Animal Estate*, Cambridge, Harvard UP, 1987.
44 Gay, op. cit., p. 4. Gay conspicuously works *within* the ideology of the Enlightenment, without seriously questioning what it saw as its "improvements."
45 Lindroth, op. cit., p. 11.
46 Foucault, op. cit., p. 141.
47 Lindroth, op. cit., p. 10.
48 Nicos Poulantzas, *State, Power, Socialism*, London, Verso, 1978, p. 17.

3 NARRATING THE ANTI-CONQUEST

1 For materials on South African history, I am indebted to the following sources: Chinweizu, *The West and the Rest of Us: White Predators, Black Slavers and the African Elite*, New York, Vintage, 1975; Philip Curtin, Steven Feierman, Leonard Thompson, and Jan Vansina, *African History*, Boston, Little, Brown, 1978, especially chapters 9 and 10; D. K. Fieldhouse, *The Colonial Empires: A Comparative Survey from the Eighteenth Century*, London, Macmillan, 1982 (orig., 1965); Vernon S. Forbes, *Pioneer Travellers of South Africa: A*

Geographical Commentary upon Routes, Records, Observations and Opinions of Travellers at the Cape, 1750–1800, Cape Town, A. A. Boekema, 1965; Mary Gunn and L. E. Codd, *Botanical Exploration of Southern Africa*, Cape Town, A. A. Boekema, 1981; George M. Theal, *History and Ethnography of Africa South of the Zambesi*, vols. II and III (to 1795), London, Allen & Unwin, 1897, rpt. as *History of South Africa before 1795*, Capetown, C. Struik, 1964.

2 I have chosen here to follow the nomenclature used by Curtin et al. (see note 1), which refers to African peoples by names of indigenous origin, rather than by European colonial nomenclatures. Thus, except for quotations, people referred to in the European literature as "Hottentots" are here called Khoikhoi; "Bushmen" are here referred to as !Kung; "Kaffirs" are here referred to as Nguni; for the most part the traditional term "Boer" has been replaced by the contemporary term "Afrikaner."

3 Curtin et al., op. cit., p. 295.

4 Theal, op. cit., vol. III, rpt. 1964, p. 68.

5 Monomotapa turned out to be a real place. In the thirteenth and fourteenth centuries, a large gold-mining state, which modern historians call Great Zimbabwe, had consolidated in the Zambezi Valley and entered into longterm conflict with the gold-seeking Portuguese in the sixteenth and seventeenth centuries, when it went into decline. Its survivors regrouped in the valley of a tributary of the Zambezi, where they also mined gold. Their rulers were known as Mwene Mutapa, thus the Europeanized "Monomotapa" (Curtin et al., op. cit., chapter 9).

6 Peter Kolb (or Kolben), *The Present State of the Cape of Good Hope*, vol. 1, trans. Mr. Medley, London, W. Innys, 1731, rpt., New York, Johnson Reprint Corporation, 1968.

7 ibid., p. 56.

8 ibid., p. 172.

9 ibid., p. 37.

10 J. M. Coetzee, *White Writing: On the Culture of Letters in South Africa*, New Haven, Yale UP, 1988, p. 32. Coetzee seems here to bump up against the limits of his own conceptual framework as well. The alternative view of "idleness" he seems to suggest in this essay is that of Adam before the Fall, a paradigm whose idealization and Eurocentrism he clearly recognizes.

11 As is often observed, such readings of non-European societies seem to reflect Europeans' own anxieties over the rapid institutionalization and rationalization of their own societies. Again, western self-understanding functions only by inventing a projected other whose other is the European self.

12 Kolb, op. cit., p. 23.

13 James Turner, *The Politics of Landscape: Rural Scenery and Society in English Poetry 1630–1660*, Cambridge, Harvard UP, 1979, p. 10.

14 Kolb, op. cit., pp. 362–3.

15 Michel Foucault, *I Pierre Rivière, having Slaughtered my Mother, my Sister and my Brother*, New York, Pantheon, 1975.

16 Curtin et al., op. cit., p. 298.

17 Forbes, op. cit., p. 46.

18 Anders Sparrman, *A Voyage to the Cape of Good Hope*, London, G. and J. Robinson, 1785, vol. I, rpt., New York, Johnson Reprint Corporation, 1971.

19 Forbes, op. cit., p. 81.

20 Lt. Guillaume Paterson, *Relation de quatre voyages dans le pays des Hottentots et dans la Caffrerie*, trans. M. T. M****, Paris, Letelier, 1790. Unfortunately, I have not had access to the English original of Paterson's narrative; translations from the French are mine. In 1980, a luxurious edition of Paterson's original manuscript (uncovered in the 1950s) was published in Johannesburg. Prepared

by Vernon S. Forbes and John Rourke (*Paterson's Cape Travels 1777–79*, Johannesburg, Brenthurst Press, 1980), the volume includes meticulous notes, maps, introductory and supplementary materials, and many of the original color plates. In its unedited state, the manuscript differs a great deal from the published *Narrative*, hence my choice to rely on the 1790 French text.

21 Paterson, op. cit., p. 5.
22 Sparrman, op. cit., p. vi.
23 ibid., pp. xv–xvi.
24 Paterson, op. cit., p. 23.
25 Sparrman, op. cit., p. 128.
26 Paterson, op. cit., p. 196.
27 Throughout the eighteenth and nineteenth centuries, and into the twentieth, the genitalia of the "Hottentots" were a subject of endless, usually pornographic, discussion and debate all over Europe. The central issue – and fantasy – came to be the question of whether Khoikhoi women possessed an "extra" genital part which came to be called the "Hottentot apron." "Eyewitnesses" on both sides of the issue abound, and the debate represents easily one of the most sordid chapters in the history of Europe's dehumanized colonial imaginings. Sander L. Gilman studies some aspects of this sexual mythology in "Black Bodies, White Bodies: Toward an Iconography of Female Sexuality in Late Nineteenth-Century Art, Medicine, and Literature," in Henry Louis Gates, ed., *Race, Writing, and Difference*, Chicago, Chicago UP, 1986. Gilman's article has been rightly criticized for reproducing the very pornographic dimension he is seeking to condemn. See, for instance, Houston Baker's response to Gilman and others in the same collection.
28 Sparrman, op. cit., p. 265.
29 ibid., p. 202.
30 ibid., p. 61.
31 ibid., p. 63.
32 ibid., p. 65.
33 I thank Elizabeth Cook for bringing this example to my attention.
34 Paterson, op. cit., p. 5.
35 Curtin et al., op. cit., pp. 301ff.
36 John Barrow, *An Account of Travels into the Interior of Southern Africa in the Years 1797 and 1798*, London, Cadell and Davies, 1801, rpt., New York, Johnson Reprint Corporation, 1968, pp. 190–1. A sequel to the *Travels* appeared in 1804 as a second volume. Unless otherwise indicated, all quotations are from vol. I.
37 Barrow retains his self-effacement even when narrating moments of great drama and personal danger that could make dramatic high points. In recounting an escape from a grassfire, he has the wagons, oxen, dogs, and terrain register the crisis, while human experience is barely alluded to:

> We turned a little out of the way towards the quarter from whence the smoke proceeded; but being to leeward of it, and the wind encreasing, the waggons were in the midst of the fire before we perceived it; and the smoke was so thick and acrid, that it was impossible to see the length of the team. The oxen, being burnt in the feet, became unmanageable and galloped off in great confusion, the dogs howled, and there was a general uproar. The smoke was suffocating; the flames blazed up on each side of the waggons, which, to those especially that contained a quantity of gunpowder, was very alarming. . . . The face of the country for several miles was a sheet of fire, and the air was obscured with a cloud of smoke.
>
> (Barrow, op. cit., p. 195)

So suppressed is the human presence, that the syntax makes the wagons

alarmed by the flames rather than the people who are in danger of being blown up!
38 Barrow, op. cit., p. 165.
39 Barrow, *Travels*, vol. II, p. 3.
40 Barrow, op. cit., pp. 125–6.
41 ibid., pp. 132–7.
42 ibid., p. 310.
43 ibid., pp. 76–7.
44 Coetzee, op. cit., p. 32.
45 Barrow, op. cit., p. 78.
46 cf. Coetzee, op. cit., p. 27. Barrow's second volume, written after the Cape had been returned to Dutch control, continues the attack on the Afrikaners at considerably greater length.
47 Barrow, op. cit., p. 17 and p. 1 respectively.
48 ibid., pp. 283–4. Barrow's book also includes lengthy ethnographic portraits of the Khoikhoi (Hottentots) and Nguni (Kaffir) peoples.
49 Johannes Fabian, *Time and the Other: How Anthropology Makes its Object*, New York, Columbia UP, 1983, p. 35.
50 I thank Harriet Ritvo for this observation.
51 Barrow, op. cit., pp. 241–2.
52 ibid., p. 272.
53 ibid., p. 291.
54 Curtin et al., op. cit., p. 311.

4 ANTI-CONQUEST II: THE MYSTIQUE OF RECIPROCITY

1 Quoted in Christopher Lloyd, *The Search for the Niger*, London, Collins, 1973, pp. 13–14.
2 E. W. Bovill, ed., *Missions to the Niger*, Hakluyt Society, Series II, vol. 123, p. 2.
3 ibid., p. 4.
4 The Frenchman René Caillié proved to be the first modern European to survive a journey to Timbuktu and back. When he returned in 1828 to claim the 2,000 franc reward offered for this feat by the French Geographical Society, he reported that the fabled city was, "at first view, nothing but a mass of ill-looking houses, built of earth" (quoted in Lloyd, op. cit., p. 73.).
5 Mungo Park, *Travels in the Interior of Africa*, Edinburgh, Adam & Charles Black, 1860, p. 3. Subsequent references will be to this edition.
6 Michel Adanson, *A Voyage to Senegal*, in John Pinkerton, ed., *Voyages and Travels in all Parts of the World*, London, Longman et al., vol. 16, 1814, pp. 598–9. The translation (1759) is by "an English gentleman, who resided some time in that country." Christopher Lloyd in *The Search for the Niger* quotes Lord Chesterfield in the early years of the eighteenth century telling his son that "The Africans are the most ignorant and unpolished people in the world, little better than the lions and tigers and leopards and other wild beasts, which that country produces in great numbers" (Lloyd, op. cit., p. 17).
7 Paul Erdman Isert, *Voyages en guinée et dans les îles caraibes en Amérique*, Paris, Marandan, 1793, p. 305 (my translation). The French original reads:

Mais, disent les défenseurs de l'esclavage, les nègres sont naturellement paresseux, obstinés, adonnés au vol, a l'ivrognerie, a tous les vices. . . .

Je n'ai autre chose à répondre à ces Messieurs, sinon que s'ils veulent sincèrement être guéris de leurs préjugés contre les Nègres, ils n'ont qu'à se donner la peine de faire un tour dans l'intérieur de l'Afrique, ils y observeront par-tout, l'innocence, la simplicité des mœurs, la bonne-foi. Là, seulement sont en vogue ces pratiques d'enfer, où leurs rudes agens, les Européens, avec leurs productions, ont introduit les appétits qui les y excitent.

A visitor on the Guinea coast, Isert was thrilled to be invited inland by a woman (whom he describes as a princess) who sought medical advice for a relative. As with most of his contemporaries, Isert's abolitionism did not make him an egalitarian. To replace slavery, he proposed moving the plantations to Africa, where the Africans would continue to work them through wage labor or indentured servitude (ibid., p. 307).

8 Quoted in Wylie Sypher, *Guinea's Captive Kings: British Anti-Slavery Literature of the XVIIIth Century*, Chapel Hill, North Carolina UP, 1942, p. 152.

9 My summary of Park's expedition and its African context have relied on the following sources: Philip Curtin, *The Image of Africa: British Ideas and Action, 1780–1850*, 2 vols., Madison, Wisconsin UP, 1985; Lloyd, op. cit.; Kenneth Lupton, *Mungo Park, the African Traveler*, Oxford UP, 1979; Peter Brent, *Black Nile*, London, G. Cremonesi, 1977; Richard Owen, *Saga of the Niger*, London, R. Hale, 1961; Ronald Syme, *I, Mungo Park*, London, Burke, 1951.

10 Park, op. cit., p. 177. The observation that the Niger flowed eastward proved deceptive in the end, for it eventually turns sharply to the south and back west, giving out into the Bight of Benin on the western coast of the continent. This unexpected course was not documented by European explorers until the 1820s by Richard Lander.

11 Preface to Park, op. cit., p. ix.

12 Bovill, op. cit., p. 48.

13 Park, op. cit., p. 2.

14 On the death of Cook, see Marshall Sahlins, *Islands of History*, Chicago, Chicago UP, 1985; on the Caribs, see Peter Hulme, *Colonial Encounters*, Cambridge UP, 1987.

15 For a recent source in English on the Andean revolt, see Steven J. Stern, ed., *Resistance, Rebellion and Consciousness in the Andean Peasant World, 18th to 20th Centuries*, Madison, Wisconsin UP, 1987; on the Surinam maroons, see Richard Price, *First-Time: The Historical Vision of an Afro-American People*, Baltimore, Johns Hopkins UP, 1983; on the Santo Domingo revolution, see C. L. R. James's classic *Black Jacobins: Toussaint L'Ouverture and the Santo Domingo Revolution*, New York, Vintage, 1963.

16 Bovill, op. cit., p. 48.

17 Preface to Park, op. cit., pp. viii–ix.

18 Hulme, op. cit., p. 229.

19 Park, op. cit., p. 107.

20 ibid., p. 160.

21 ibid., p. 225.

22 M. L. Pratt, "Fieldwork in Common Places," in James Clifford and George Marcus, eds., *Writing Culture*, Berkeley, California UP, 1987.

23 Park, op. cit., pp. 104–5. This description recalls Leo Africanus' description of Timbuktu as inhabited by "people of a gentle and cheerful disposition, who spend a great part of the night singing and dancing through the streets."

24 John Barrow, *An Account of Travels into the Interior of Southern Africa in the years 1797 and 1798*, London, Cadell and Davies, 1801, rpt., New York, Johnson Reprint Corporation, 1968, p. 192.

25 Park, op. cit., p. 180.
26 ibid., p. 234.
27 ibid., p. 109.
28 ibid., p. 49.
29 ibid., p. 119.
30 I owe this term to my colleague Martin Evans, who uses it to speak of the cultural dialogue between the United States and Europe. See his *America: The View from Europe*, Stanford Alumni Association, 1976.
31 Park, op. cit., p. 91.
32 ibid., p. 291.
33 ibid., p. 240.
34 ibid., p. 182.
35 ibid., p. 47.
36 See, for example, Preface, ibid., pp. viii–ix.
37 Philip Curtin, *The Image of Africa*, Madison, Wisconsin UP, vol. II, p. 207. In a similar vein, Christopher Lloyd deems Park not "the sort of man capable of throwing a romantic colouring over his adventures, because he was temperamentally incapable of padding out his story with verbose descriptions" (op. cit., p. 47).
38 Hulme, op. cit., p. 147.
39 Karl Marx, *Capital* (1867), trans. Ben Fowkes, New York, Vintage, 1976, vol. I, p. 280. For critical discussion of this passage see Don L. Dorham, *History, Power, Ideology*, Cambridge UP, 1990, pp. 198ff.
40 In addition to Mungo Park's *Travels*, the exploration literature on the Niger includes the following: E. Denham, H. Clapperton, and W. Oudney, *Narrative of Travels and Discoveries in Northern and Central Africa* (1828); René Caillié, *Travels through Central Africa to Timbuctoo* (1830); H. Clapperton, *Journal of a Second Expedition into the Interior of Africa* (1829); Richard Lander, *Records of Captain Clapperton's Last Expedition in Africa* (1830); R. and J. Lander, *Journal of an Expedition to Explore the Course and Termination of the Niger* (1830); Macgregor Laird and R. A. Oldfield, *Narrative of an Expedition into the Interior of Africa by the River Niger* (1837); H. D. Trotter, W. Allen, and T. R. H. Thompson, *Narrative of the Expedition to the River Niger in 1841* (1848); Samuel Crowther, *Journal of an Expedition up the Niger and Tshadda* (1855); W. B. Baikie, *Narrative of an Exploring Voyage up the Rivers Kwora and Binue in 1854* (1856); Heinrich Barth, *Travels and Discoveries in North and Central Africa* (1857–8). Richard Lander's 1830 account is one of the best examples of picaresque travel writing I know of. Samuel Crowther was probably the first African to lead a European exploration mission.

5 EROS AND ABOLITION

1 *Monthly Review*, New Series, vol. 21, 1759, p. 453.
2 There was, of course, a body of sentimental travel writing written within Europe about Europe which worked along many of the same lines I consider here.
3 *Monthly Review*, New Series, vol. 34, 1766, pp. 72–3.
4 ibid., p. 74.
5 *Monthly Review*, New Series, vol. 21, 1796, p. 1.
6 John Hawkesworth, ed., *An Account of Voyages undertaken by order of his Present Majesty for Making Discoveries in the Southern Hemisphere*, 4 vols., London, W. Straham, 1773–85, vol. I, p. v. The first-person format, says Hawkesworth, "would, by bringing the Adventurer and the Reader nearer

together . . . more strongly excite interest, and consequently afford more entertainment" (ibid.).

7 *Monthly Review*, New Series, vol. 44, 1771, p. 421.

8 François Le Vaillant, *Voyages de F. Le Vaillant dans l'intérieure de l'Afrique 1781–85*, edited and abridged by Jacques Boulanger, 2 vols., Paris, Librairie Plon, 1931, vol. I, p. 52. The original French reads:

> Nous quittames aussitôt le bois pour aller nous établir plus haut, en rase campagne. Je voyais avec le plus amer chagrin qu'il n'était pas possible de sortir de l'endroit où nous nous trouvions circonscrits. Ces petits ruisseaux, qui auparavant nous avaient paru si agréables et si riants, s'étaient changés en torrents furieux qui charriaient les sables, les arbres, les éclats de rochers; je sentais qu'à moins de s'exposer aux plus grands dangers, il était impossible de les traverser. D'un autre côté, mes bœufs harassés, transis, avaient désertée de mon camp; je ne savais pas où et comment envoyer après eux pour les ratrapper. Ma situation n'était assurément point amusante; je passais de tristes moments. Déjà mes pauvres Hottentots, fatigués et malades, commençaient a murmurer.

9 The presence of Varon has occasioned frequent veiled homophobic allusions to Le Vaillant's possible homosexuality. The latter's narcissism and dandyism (a tendency to dress flamboyantly while en route in Africa, for instance) are alluded to in similar critical fashion. "He treasured in his waggon a dressing case of powders, perfumes and pomatums," writes Vernon Forbes in 1965. Whatever Le Vaillant's sexual preferences, such reactions suggest the extent to which the figure of the scientific explorer was bound up with heterosexual paradigms of masculinity.

10 Le Vaillant, op. cit., pp. 113–14.

11 Le Vaillant also recounts, without embellishment, a visit with a white woman who had become chieftain of an African village, having inherited that office from the African man she had married – an instance of a kind other writers report only as hearsay, if at all.

12 The venerable Vernon Forbes, while recognizing that the "romantic sentiments and flowery verbiage" of Le Vaillant's books "apparently recommended them to many of his contemporaries" (*Pioneer Travellers of South Africa, 1750–1800*, Cape Town, A. A. Boekema, 1965, p. 117), nevertheless finds him "wearisome in his adulation of the simple Hottentots" (ibid., p. 5), and concludes that "vanity was the fatal weakness that led to his numerous fanciful exaggerations and fabrications. . . . It is regrettable that he did not realise how enduringly his reputation would have stood if only he had been content to set down the simple truth of all he had seen and done" (ibid., p. 127). Le Vaillant's standing has been redeemed somewhat since the discovery in 1963 of a set of 165 watercolor drawings made by Le Vaillant or at his instruction depicting his South African travels. Apart from their esthetic contribution, the drawings demonstrate that Le Vaillant did indeed visit some of the places whose description he had been accused of fabricating (ibid., p. 127).

13 As Wylie Sypher notes in *Guinea's Captive Kings: British Anti-Slavery Literature of the XVIIIth Century* (Chapel Hill, North Carolina UP, 1942, chapter 1), social commentators of the period frequently register the creole presence in the elite society of Europe's capitals, usually in a very disparaging fashion; West Indian heiresses are stock characters in eighteenth- and nineteenth-century fiction. Intellectual and political history has perhaps been less honest on this score. Throughout Le Vaillant's lifetime, European political spheres were animated by representatives of the independence and anti-independence movements of the

Americas, lobbying the European powers for influence and support. Creole sons were as present in intellectual and educational milieux as heiresses in social circles. On both sides of the anti-slavery debate much of the intellectual and political leadership came from Euroamericans: Quakers on the one side and West Indian slaveholders on the other.

14 As it happens, few travel books have received the quality of scholarly and editorial attention Stedman's (deservedly) has, as well. One is fortunate to have the benefit of the recent edition and commentary by R. A. J. van Lier (Barre, Massachusetts, Imprint Society, 1971), which I will be using here, and Richard Price and Sally Price's recent edition of Stedman's original manuscript (Baltimore, Johns Hopkins UP, 1988), accompanied by their valuable historical commentary.

15 John Gabriel Stedman, *Narrative of a Five Years' Expedition against the Revolted Negroes of Surinam* (transcribed from the original 1790 manuscript), ed. Richard Price and Sally Price, Baltimore, Johns Hopkins UP, 1988, p. xxi. To avoid confusion, in what follows I will refer to this source as Price and Price.

16 John Gabriel Stedman, *Narrative of a Five Years' Expedition against the Revolted Negroes of Surinam*, 2 vols., ed. R. J. van Lier, Barre, Massachusetts, Imprint Society, 1971, p. xvii. To avoid confusion, in what follows I will refer to this source as Stedman.

17 I am relying here on the Introductions to Price and Price and Stedman.

18 Stedman, op. cit., p. 2.

19 See Price and Price, op. cit., pp. lxxiii–lxxxiii for a summary of the many editions, translations, and adaptations of Stedman's text.

20 Stedman, p. 59. Price and Price contrast this passage with what Stedman wrote in his original manuscript: "Good God; I flew to the Spot in Search of poor Joanna and found her bathing with her Companions in the Garden" (Price and Price, op. cit., p. lx) There follows a voyeur's poem reminiscent of Le Vaillant in Africa, celebrating the beauties of the unsuspecting beloved.

21 Stedman, op. cit., p. 59.

22 ibid., p. 62.

23 ibid., p. 440.

24 Isert, op. cit., p. 241. "Le conseil voit avec plaisir de pareilles alliances, parce qu'un Européen qui se porte à cette démarche ne sera pas probablement tourmenté bien vite de la maladie de son pays." To refer to Stedman's relation with Joanna as concubinage is not to say that Stedman's attachment to Joanna was not as real and deep as he had to any woman. When he remarried back in Europe he named his daughter after her, and their son did join him, as the book recounts. In fact, according to Price and Price, Stedman's editor toned down his professions of commitment to Joanna in the book.

25 Referred to in Price and Price, op. cit., p. xxxiii.

26 Stedman, op. cit., p. 426.

27 Hulme, op. cit., p. 249.

28 ibid., p. 141.

29 According to Hulme (op. cit., pp. 225ff), this story first appeared in print in 1734 in the *London Magazine* and proliferated in many versions between 1754 and 1802. Mary Wollstonecraft used it for a narrative model; Goethe proposed a play.

30 See discussion of this motif in Sypher, op. cit., especially ch 3.

31 Stedman, op. cit., p. 52.

32 Hulme, op. cit., p. 253.

33 Baltimore, Johns Hopkins UP, 1983.

34 Anna Maria Falconbridge, *Narrative of Two Voyages to Sierra Leone*, London, L. I. Higham, 1802, rpt., London, Frank Cass, 1967, p. 24.

35 ibid., p. 33.

36 ibid., p. 38.

37 ibid., p. 150.

38 ibid., p. 66.

39 ibid., p. 169.

40 ibid., p. 186. While Falconbridge's book was undoubtedly motivated, if not sponsored, by pro-slavery campaigns in England, the author also reveals a personal motive in publishing her letters, a most unsentimental private vengeance (again, the political is personal): the Company has persistently refused to pay her monies left owing to her husband. Her vendetta, like Joanna's decision to remain in America, points from within at the limits of ideologies of romantic love and humanitarianism. Despite her pro-slavery stance, Falconbridge's critical empowerment, as well as the anti-moral life story she tells, align her to a degree with late eighteenth-century feminism. Historians of women in the bourgeois era often regard the two decades following the French Revolution as a critical juncture in which European feminists struggled to consolidate openings for radical change in the gender system, while other forces sought to close them, through such devices as laws restricting women's political participation. Late eighteenth-century radicalism, so the account goes, was largely defeated in the early decades of the nineteenth century, coopted by ideologies of domesticity and republican motherhood, or contained in clearly oppositional movements like Fourierism. See Joan Landes, *Women and the Public Sphere in the Age of the French Revolution*, Ithaca, Cornell UP, 1988.

41 *The Tour of Africa*, selected and arranged by Catherine Hutton, 3 vols., London, Baldwin, Cardock and Joy, 1819, vol. I, p. 1.

42 Mrs. R. Lee (formerly Mrs. T. Edward Bowdich), *Stories of Strange Lands and Fragments from the Notes of a Traveller*, London, Edward Moxon, 1835. In its opening words, the first story, "Adumissa," assigns Lee the authority of a mediator, anchored in that quintessential domestic drama of the contact zone, her dialogue with her African manservant: "'That was Adumissa's house,' said my servant one day, when he attended me in a walk through the town of Ogwa. 'And who was Adumissa?' I asked. 'What, missy, you no hear of Adumissa, who pass all woman handsome that black man ever saw?'" (p. 1).

43 ibid., p. xiv.

44 The passage quoted in note 42, for example, comes accompanied by an ethnographic footnote to the effect that "Adumissa was what is generally called on the western coast of Africa, a red-skinned woman; that is, her complexion was of a rich and warm brown, and which certainly renders more distinct the play of feature, and the emotions passing within, than the jet-black skin . . ." (ibid., p. 19). This nineteen-page story is followed by twelve pages of notes on everything from flowers and fruits to architecture and the uses of elephant tusks.

45 ibid., p. xiv.

46 Materials on Victorian women travelers include Leo Hamalian, *Ladies on the Loose: Women Travellers of the 18th and 19th Centuries* (1981); Herbert M. van Thal, ed., *Victoria's Subjects Traveled*, London, A. Barker, 1951; Dea Birkett, *Victorian Women Explorers*, London, Basil Blackwell, 1990; Marion Tinling, *Women Into the Unknown: A Sourcebook on Women Explorers and Travelers*, New York, Greenwood, 1989. Beacon Press has recently begun publishing a series of travel books by women which includes a number of Victorians. For discussion of the now legendary Mary Kingsley, see chapter 9 below.

PART II   THE REINVENTION OF AMERICA, 1800–50

6   ALEXANDER VON HUMBOLDT AND THE REINVENTION OF AMERICA

1 Hanno Beck, "The Geography of Alexander von Humboldt," in Wolfgang-Hagen Hein, ed., *Alexander von Humboldt: Life and Work*, translated from the German by John Cumming, Ingelheim am Rhein, C. H. Boehringer Sohn, 1987 (German original 1985), pp. 221, 227.

2 Quoted in Douglas Botting, *Humboldt and the Cosmos*, New York, Harper & Row, p. 213.

3 Simón Bolívar, Letter to A. von Humboldt, Nov. 10, 1821, my translation.

4 The term *mestizo* refers to a person of European and Amerindian parentage; *mulato* to a person of African and European parentage; *zambo* to a person of African and Amerindian parentage. The term *pardo*, like English "colored," is sometimes used to refer to all these groups. These terms only touch the surface of racial classification in Spanish colonial society.

5 Leaders of the revolt in Peru issued a proclamation accusing the Spanish crown of "unbearable taxes, tributes, 'piezas,' 'lanzas,' customs duties, sales taxes, monopolies, 'cadastros,' tithes, military drafts, viceroys, high courts, chief magistrates and other ministers, all equal in their tyranny who, together with the court clerks of the same ilk, sell justice by auction . . . abusing the natives of the kingdom as if they were beasts, putting to death all those from whom they are unable to steal . . ." From Boleslao Lewin, *Tupac Amaru*, Buenos Aires, Siglo Veinte, 1973, Appendix I, p. 153. Translated by Jan Mennell.

6 John Lynch, *The Spanish American Revolutions 1808–1826*, New York, W. W. Norton, 1986 (2nd edition), pp. 190–1.

7 ibid., p. 194. I am indebted throughout to Lynch's lucid and detailed account.

8 Simón Bolívar, "Reply of a South American to a gentleman of this island [Jamaica]," Sept. 6, 1815. English translation from Harold A. Bierck, Jr., ed., and Vicente Lecuna, comp., *Selected Writings of Simón Bolívar*, New York, Colonial Press, 1951, vol. I, p. 110.

9 Unlike most other travel writers considered in this book, Humboldt has been the subject of significant academic scholarship, largely honorific and based chiefly in Germany. Basic sources in German include Hanno Beck's two-volume *Alexander von Humboldt*, Wiesbaden, Franz Steiner, 1959; Heinrich Pfeiffer, ed., *Alexander von Humboldt: Werk und Weltgeltung*, Munich, R. Piper, 1969; Kurt Schleucher, *Alexander von Humboldt: Der Mensch, Der Forscher, Der Schriftsteller*, Berlin, Stapp, 1988. One of the best recent sources, the beautifully illustrated essay collection *Alexander von Humboldt: Leben und Werken* (Ingleheim am Rhein, C. H. Boehringer Sohn, 1985), edited by Wolfgang-Hagen Hein, appeared in 1987 in English translation by John Cumming. The essays and bibliography are excellent. In French, a basic source is Charles Minguet's encyclopedic and uncritical *Alexandre de Humboldt, Historien et géographe de l'Amérique espagnol, 1799–1804*, Paris, Maspero, 1969. Minguet also edited the Biblioteca Ayacucho edition of Humboldt's *Cartas Americanas* (Caracas, 1980) with translations by Marta Traba. As ever, the Ayacucho edition provides an enormously useful Chronology. Among more popular works, Douglas Botting's *Humboldt and the Cosmos* (New York, Harper & Row, 1973) is lively and useful; Pierre Gascar's *Humboldt l'explorateur* (Paris, Gallimard, 1985) contributes little new, except for some frankness about Humboldt's homosexuality. Among Spanish

American sources on Humboldt, I have made particular use of Oscar Rodríguez Ortiz, ed., *Imágenes de Humboldt*, Caracas, Monte Avila, 1983. Professor Kurt Müller-Vollmer of Stanford University has recently uncovered a large collection of Humboldt manuscripts and correspondence in Germany, which will likely affect future discussion of Alexander's impact on the work of his brother Wilhelm.

10 Pierre Bertaux, Preface in Hein, op. cit., p. 7. As this quotation suggests, Humboldt's homosexuality continues to be treated by his commentators in a gentlemanly fashion, which is to say, as a dirty secret. He lived in a virtually exclusively male world of colleagues, disciples, friends, and companions, and was sustained by a series of enduring intimate relationships. One longtime companion was the young Ecuadorian aristocrat, Carlos Montúfar, who met Humboldt in Quito in 1802 and accompanied him, with Bonpland, for the remainder of their American travels and back to Europe. In France, Montúfar seems to have been replaced in Humboldt's life by Louis Gay Lussac, famed as a physicist and a balloonist, with whom Humboldt traveled and lived for several years. Perhaps best known of all is Humboldt's passionate attachment to the astronomer François Arago, with whom he met every day for fifteen years. Like many European travelers of the last century and this, Humboldt's wanderlust undoubtedly consisted in part of a need to escape the heterosexist and matrimonialist structures of bourgeois society. The history of travel and science is significantly shaped by the fact that they were legitimate contexts for same-sex intimacy and exclusively male society.

11 In fact, Humboldt visited Spanish American naturalists wherever he found them on his travels – even female ones, such as Manuela Santamaria de Manrique, whose collection he visited in Bogotá. Humboldt's encounters and relations with women naturalists barely register in the official European literature. My source here, for example, is *La mujer en la sociedad moderna* by the nineteenth-century Colombian feminist Soledad Acosta de Samper (Paris, Garnier, 1895, p. 298).

12 After South America, Aimé Bonpland followed the Linnaean career path and became keeper of a royal garden: the garden of none other than the creole Empress Josephine, at her retreat near Paris. After her divorce he became her beloved confidant and was with her when she died. Heartbroken, it seems, he returned to South America, where he took up residence in Paraguay and was eventually imprisoned for several years by the notorious dictator Dr. Francia. Humboldt, who for years had seen to it that Bonpland's pension was forwarded to him, appealed to Simón Bolívar on Bonpland's behalf and helped secure his release. Bonpland died in Paraguay in 1858.

13 Ortiz, op. cit., p. 10.

14 Bonpland's expertise was in botany, and that is where he made his contribution as an author. Desk work held little appeal for him, however, and it is primarily his data rather than his authorship that these title pages acknowledge.

15 In what follows I will be quoting standard English translations of Humboldt's writings. For *Ansichten der Natur* I will be quoting E. C. Otte and Henry G. Bohn's translation, London, Henry G. Bohn, 1850. For *Vues des Cordillères* I will be quoting the 1814 translation, *Views of the Cordilleras and Monuments of the Indigenous Peoples of America* by Helen Maria Williams (the well-known English radical), 2 vols., London, Longman et al. For the *Relation historique* I will also be quoting Helen Maria Williams' translation, *Personal Narrative of Travels to the Equinoctial Regions of the New Continent*, London, Longman et al., 1822.

16 Antonello Gerbi, *La disputa del nuovo mundo: Storia di una polemica* (Milano, R. Ricciardi, 1955). Revised and enlarged edition translated by Jeremy Moyle as *The Dispute of the New World: The History of a Polemic*, Pittsburgh, Pittsburgh UP, 1983. See also Gerbi's *La natura delle indie nove* (Milano, R. Ricciardi, 1975), also

translated by Jeremy Moyle as *Nature in the New World*, Pittsburgh, Pittsburgh UP, 1985. Astonishingly, in the English translation of this work, Alexander von Humboldt's name is substituted in the index with that of his brother Wilhelm. The confusion, which happens frequently, attests to the way in which in the twentieth century Alexander's reputation has been eclipsed by that of his brother. In his account of sixteenth- and seventeenth-century chronicles of the Americas Gerbi draws extensively on Humboldt's encyclopedic review of this material in the *Examen critique de l'histoire de la géographie du nouveau continent*, an extraordinary work almost entirely lost in official accounts of Humboldt's contributions.

17 Gerbi, *Dispute*, op. cit., pp. 411, 416.
18 Robert van Dusen, "The Literary Ambitions and Achievements of Alexander von Humboldt," *European University Papers*, Bern, Herbert Lang, 1971, p. 45.
19 Humboldt, *Views of Nature*, op. cit., p. 3.
20 ibid., pp. 7–8.
21 Quoted in Hein, op. cit., p. 56.
22 Humboldt, *Views of Nature*, op. cit., p. ix.
23 ibid., p. 154.
24 ibid., p. 16.
25 In *Views of Nature* the jungle is the subject of "Cataracts of the Orinoco" and "Nocturnal Life of Animals in the Primeval Forest"; the snow-capped mountains are the theme of views on the famous ascent of Chimborazo and several essays on volcanos in *Views of the Cordilleras*; the Venezuelan *llanos* are the theme of the classic "On Steppes and Deserts."
26 Humboldt, *Views of Nature*, op. cit., p. ix.
27 Christopher Columbus, Letter of March 14, 1493, in *Four Voyages to the New World: Letters and Selected Documents*, ed. and trans. R. H. Major, New York, Corinth Books, 1961, pp. 4–5.
28 The "view" opens through the eyes of a hypothetical "mariner" who "on approaching nearer to the granitic shores of Guiana . . . sees before him the wide mouth of a mighty river, which gushes forth like a shoreless sea." Humboldt, *Views of Nature*, op. cit., p. 206.
29 Though a lifelong admirer of Mungo Park and his *Travels*, Humboldt saw Park's dramatic personal writing as an endearing "relic of a former age" identified with sixteenth-century Spanish chronicles (Preface, *Personal Narrative*).
30 Williams, Preface to Humboldt's *Personal Narrative*, op. cit., vol. I, p. viii.
31 Humboldt, *Personal Narrative*, op. cit., vol. III, pp. 73–4.
32 ibid., vol. I, p. li.
33 Quoted in Hein, op. cit., p. 74.
34 Botting, op. cit., p. 202.
35 Humboldt, *Views and Monuments*, vol. I, pp. 39–40.
36 ibid., vol. II, p. 45.
37 ibid., vol. I, p. 9.
38 ibid., p. 44.
39 See discussion in Michael Adas, *Prophets of Rebellion: Millenarian Protest Movements against the European Colonial Order*, Chapel Hill, North Carolina UP, 1979.
40 These figures and these histories continue to be intensely meaningful in the Andes today: a contemporary Peruvian guerrilla movement now bears Tupac Amaru's name, as did the Uruguayan Tupamaros in the 1960s; the Bolivian counterparts Tupac Katari and Bartolina Sisa have both been adopted as symbols by Bolivian peasant movements.
41 Humboldt, *Personal Narrative*, op. cit., vol. III, p. 178. The *corregidor* is a

position roughly analogous to a district officer; its holders were commonly loathed by those over whom they held sway.

42 This clumsy term is coined on analogy with the term "addressee." As the latter means the person addressed by a speaker, "travelee" means persons traveled to (or on) by a traveler, receptors of travel. A few years ago literary theorists began speaking of "narratees," figures corresponding to narrators on the reception end of narration. Obviously, travel is studied overwhelmingly from the perspective of the traveler, but it is perfectly possible, and extremely interesting, to study it from the perspective of those who participate on the receiving end.

43 Johannes Fabian has written an interesting monograph on heteroglossia in East African travel accounts of the nineteenth century, looking in particular at where Swahili words turn up in European texts: *Language and Colonial Power: The Appropriation of Swahili in the Former Belgian Congo, 1880–1930*, New York, Cambridge UP, African Studies Series no. 48, 1986. Formal linguistic interpretation in the west normally assumes the perspective of the party in power.

44 On the basis of his contact with the Mexican intelligentsia, Humboldt continued research on the history of European writings on the Americas, and produced a five-volume *Examen critique de l'histoire de la géographie du nouveau continent* (*Critical Examination of the Geography of the New Continent*). Here is yet another extraordinary work largely disregarded by Humboldt's official legacy. Humboldt reviews in encyclopedic fashion the huge corpus of sixteenth- and seventeenth-century chronicles on the Americas. Antonello Gerbi relies heavily on Humboldt's account of this material in his *Nature in the New World* (op. cit., 1985).

45 Quoted by John Brenkman in *Culture and Domination*, Ithaca, Cornell UP, 1988, p. 64.

46 Teresa de la Parra, *Memorias de Mama Blanca*, in *Obras completas*, Caracas, Biblioteca Ayacucho, 1982, p. 329.

47 Benedict Anderson, *Imagined Communities: Reflections on the Origins and Spread of Nationalism*, London, Verso, 1983.

48 The *mita* was colonial Spain's most hated form of mass forced labor: villages were required to provide labor quotas to work in mines and elsewhere. The mortality rate of *mita* workers was very high.

49 Gerbi, *Dispute*, op. cit., p. 408.

50 Simón Bolívar, Letter to General Paez, August 8, 1826. English translation from Bierck and Lecuna, op. cit., vol. II, p. 628.

51 Pascual Venegas Filardo, *Viajeros a Venezuela en los siglos XIX y XX*, Caracas, Monte Avila, 1973, p. 14. Gabriel García Márquez has referred to Humboldt's writings as a source of his "magic realist" view of South America.

52 The fact that the *arpillera* originated in Peru as commercial or export art locates it, in my view, outside the realm of what the metropolis calls "authenticity." It could not be analyzed, that is, as "pure" Andean expression or self-expression. In making this assumption, I realize I am circumventing important and difficult issues in art history and the anthropology of art.

53 Michael Taussig, *Shamanism, Colonialism and the Wild Man: A Study in Terror and Healing*, Chicago, Chicago UP, 1987, p. 305.

7 REINVENTING AMERICA II: THE CAPITALIST VANGUARD AND THE *EXPLORATRICES SOCIALES*

1 John Rowe, "Movimiento nacional Inca," *Revista Universitaria de Cuzco*, no.

107, 1955, p. 12. Quoted by Teresa Gisbert, *Iconografía y mitos indígenas en el arte*, La Paz, Gisbert and Co., 1980, p. 204.

2 For detailed commentary on this pictorial tradition see Gisbert, op. cit., p. 132.

3 W. B. Stevenson, *An Historical and Descriptive Narrative of 20 Years Residence in South America*, 3 vols., London, Hurst, Robinson and Co., 1825, vol. I, p. vii. Stevenson was accused of being an English spy, which he possibly was, and spent several months of his visit in captivity.

4 John Mawe, *Travels in the Interior of Brazil, particularly in the Gold and Diamond Districts . . .*, Philadelphia, M. Carey, 1816, Introduction. Mawe also wrote *The Linnean System of Conchology* (1823) and a treatise on precious stones.

5 Stevenson, op. cit., vol. I, p. viii.

6 See, for example, Jean Franco, "Un viaje poco romántico: Viajeros británicos hacia sudamérica, 1818–28," *Escritura* no. 7, 1979 (Caracas), pp. 129–42; Noe Jitrik, *Los viajeros*, Serie "Los Argentinos," Buenos Aires, Editorial Jorge Alvarez, 1969; Michael J. Taussig, "On the Indian's Back: The Moral Topography of the Andes and its Conquest," in *Shamanism, Colonialism and the Wild Man*, Chicago, Chicago UP, 1987; and Kristine L. Jones, "Nineteenth Century British Travel Accounts of Argentina," *Ethnohistory*, special issue on travel literature, ethnography, and ethnohistory, vol. 33 no. 2, 1986, pp. 195–211.

7 Jitrik, op. cit., p. 13. My translation.

8 Letter to Santander, 1826, quoted in John Lynch, *The Spanish American Revolutions 1800–1826*, New York, W. W. Norton (2nd edition), p. 343.

9 Captain Joseph Andrews, *Journey from Buenos Aires . . . to Santiago de Chili and Coquimbo in the years 1825–26*, London, John Murray, 1827, p. i.

10 Stevenson, op. cit., vol. I, p. i.

11 John Miers, *Travels in Chile and La Plata*, London, Baldwin, Cardock and Joy, 1826, vol. I, p. 91. Miers also authored a botanical treatise.

12 Mawe, *Travels*, op. cit., p. 121.

13 This negative esthetic did not originate with the capitalist vanguard. It is found, for instance, in the writings of eighteenth-century Spanish commentators, especially critics of colonial policy. Prominent among these critics were La Condamine's erstwhile companions Antonio de Ulloa and Jorge Juan, who, in addition to their public writings had produced an in-house critique, the *Noticias secretas de America*. This work became available in English only in 1807, when it caused a sensation.

14 Robert Proctor, *Narrative of a Journey across the Cordillera of the Andes and of a Residence in Lima*, London, Archibald Constable, 1825, p. 79.

15 Lieutenant Charles Brand, *Journal of a Voyage to Peru: A Passage Across the Cordillera of the Andes in the Winter of 1827 . . .*, London, Henry Colburn, 1828, p. 57.

16 Captain Charles Stuart Cochrane, *Journal of a Residence and Travels in Colombia during the years 1823 and 24*, 2 vols., London, Henry Colburn, vol. I, p. vii.

17 Gaspar Mollien, *Travels in the Republic of Colombia in the years 1822–23*, London, C. Knight, 1824, p. 57.

18 Stevenson, op. cit., vol. I, p. i.

19 Joseph Andrews, quoted by Franco, op. cit., p. 133.

20 Mawe, *Travels*, op. cit., p. 32.

21 Mollien, op. cit., p. 89.

22 Miers, op. cit., p. 30 and passim.

23 Brand, op. cit., p. 182.

24 Miers, op. cit., p. 31.

25 It was a familiar discourse within Europe as well, applied by metropolitans to rural and peasant peripheries.

26 For a rich diatribe on this practice, and other aspects of this literature, see Taussig, op. cit.

27 Miers, op. cit., p. 32.

28 Brand, op. cit., p. 74.

29 Captain F. B. Head, *Rough Notes taken during Some Rapid Journeys across the Pampas and among the Andes*, London, John Murray, 1826, p. 224.

30 ibid., p. 228.

31 Aimé Bonpland was also a family friend. The family's links with Bolívar were well known enough to lead to speculation that he was Flora Tristan's biological father. Evidently, there was a need to find a genetic explanation for her revolutionary activities . . .

32 The technicality was that Flora's parents had been married in Spain, but their marriage was not legally registered in France. The family had long been involved in Peruvian colonial affairs. As Tristan herself recounts, Pío Tristan, who inherited leadership of the family on the death of Flora's grandmother in 1831, had a long career in the Spanish army and had been governor of Cuzco. He was considering seeking the Peruvian presidency when she met him.

33 Jean Hawkes, Translator's Introduction to Flora Tristan, *Peregrinations of a Pariah, 1833–34*, Boston, Beacon Press, 1986, p. xiii.

34 José Valenzuela D., Translator's Introduction to Maria Graham, *Diario de mi residencia en Chile in 1822*, Santiago, Editorial del Pacífico, 1956, p. 18.

35 Best known were *Little Arthur's History of England* and *Little Mary's Ten Days*.

36 Maria Graham, *Journal of a Residence in Chile during the year 1822*, London, Longman et al., and John Murray, 1824, p. 115.

37 Tristan, op. cit., pp. 98–9. See also the description of her convent cell "like a Parisian boudoir," p. 194. This is the first English translation of Tristan's book. Like most, it has been substantially abridged from the 600-page original. The 1979 French edition by Maspero is cut by about one-fourth. The full edition I consulted was the 1946 Spanish translation by Emilia Romero, Lima, Editorial Antártica, 1946, republished in 1971 by Moncloa-Campodonico, also in Lima.

39 Marie-Claire Hoock-Demarle, "Le Langage littéraire des femmes enquêtrices," in Stéphane Michaud, ed., *Un fabuleux destin: Flora Tristan*, Dijon, Editions Universitaires, 1985. See also Magda Portal et al., *Flora Tristan: Una reserva de utopía*, Centro de la Mujer Peruana Flora Tristan, 1985; Dominique deSanti, *Flora Tristan, la femme révoltée*, Paris, Hachette, 1972; Jean Baelen, *La Vie de Flora Tristan: Socialisme et féminisme au 19e siècle*, Paris, Seuil, 1972; Rosalba Campra, "La imagen de América en *Peregrinations d'une paria* de Flora Tristan: experiencia autobiográfica y tradición cultural," in *Amérique Latine/Europe*, special issue of *Palinure*, Paris, 1985–6, pp. 64–74.

39 Tristan, op. cit., p. 121.

40 Graham, op. cit., p. 271.

41 Tristan, op. cit., pp. 122–3. Graham, by contrast, finds "potatoes of the very first quality. Cabbages of every kind; lettuces inferior only to those of Lambeth . . ." and so on (op. cit., p. 132).

42 Hoock-Demarle, op. cit., pp. 105–6.

43 Tristan, op. cit., p. 281.

44 ibid., pp. 282–3.

45 Graham, op. cit., p. 115.

46 Tristan, op. cit., p. 28.

47 Graham, op. cit., p. 141.

48 ibid., p. 143.

49 ibid., p. 139.
50 ibid., pp. 153–4.
51 Graham, op. cit., p. 301.
52 Tristan, op. cit., p. 206.
53 ibid., p. 180. Maria Graham also speaks of the *rabonas* when she visits an orphanage in Santiago that houses children who have lost both parents on the battlefield. Apart from these references, neither Tristan nor Graham gives significant attention to indigenous and mestizo society in Peru or Chile.
54 ibid., p. 269.
55 ibid., p. 270.
56 ibid., pp. 274–5.
57 Lady Mary Montagu, *Embassy to Constantinople: The Travels of Lady Mary Wortley Montagu*, ed. and comp. Christopher Pick, Introduction by Dervla Murphy, London, Century Hutchinson Ltd., 1988, p. 111.
58 Graham, op. cit., p. 158.
59 ibid., p. 160.
60 ibid., p. 352.
61 Tristan, op. cit., p. 294.
62 ibid., p. 295.
63 *Blackwood's Magazine*, Edinburgh, W. Blackwood, 1828, p. 621.

8   REINVENTING AMERICA/REINVENTING EUROPE: CREOLE SELF-FASHIONING

1 Andrés Bello, "Prospectus," *El Repertorio Americano*, vol. 1, October, 1826, London, Bossange, Barthes, and Lowell. The Venezuelan government published a facsimile edition of *El Repertorio Americano* in 1973, Caracas, Ediciones de la Presidencia de la República, 2 vols.
2 Pedro Grases, Introductory Note, in *Antología de la poesía de Andrés Bello*, Madrid, Seix Barral, 1978, p. 48.
3 Andrés Bello, "Silva a la agricultura en la zona tórrida," lines 1–15. I have used the 1952 edition of Bello's *Obras Completas*, Ministerio de Educación, Caracas, vol. 1, pp. 65–74.
4 Andrés Bello, "Alocución a la poesía," op. cit., p. 43. The lines in question, from the opening stanza, read:

> tiempo es que dejes ya la culta Europea
> que tu nativa rustiquez desama,
> y dirijas el vuelo adonde te abre
> mundo de Colón su grande escena.

5 Alexander von Humboldt, Introduction, *Personal Narrative of Travels to the Equinoctial Regions of the New Continent*, trans. Helen Maria Williams, London, Longman et al., 1822, vol. I, p. li.
6 Pedro Henríquez Ureña, *Seis ensayos en busca de nuestra expresión*, Buenos Aires, Babel, 1927, pp. 27ff. Henríquez Ureña sees the "*afán europeizante*" as coexisting with the *criollista* momentum in Spanish American letters. The discussion of literary texts which follows does not attempt anything like a full-fledged reading of the independence period in South America letters, nor does it engage current debates within literary criticism. The aim is the much narrower one of discussing certain points of contact with, and extrapolation from, European travel writing.

7 The mestizo general San Martín, one of the leaders of the independence movement, whose mother belonged to the Inca nobility, favored a monarchic system of government for South America after independence. Possibilities included crowning Bolívar emperor, following the example of Napoleon, or restoring the Inca dynasty.

8 Such challenges and aspirations were shared to a great extent by white elites in North America as well. What I have to say here about postcolonial creole esthetics and ideology in South America has many parallels with developments in the United States, where the term "creole" is not commonly used but probably should be.

9 Andrés Bello, "Silva," op. cit., lines 203ff.

10 ibid., lines 351ff.

11 ibid., lines 302ff. Atahualpa and Moctezuma were the rulers of the Inca and Aztec empires, respectively, at the time of first contact with the Spanish.

12 ibid., lines 227–35. The Spanish reads:

> Mírola ya que invade la espesura
> de la floresta opaca; oigo las voces,
> siento el rumor confuso; el hierro suena,
> los golpes el lejano
> eco redobla; gime el ceibo anciano,
> que a numerosa tropa
> largo tiempo fatiga;
> batido de cien hachas, se estremece,
> estalla al fin, y rinde el ancha copa.

13 Simón Bolívar, "Mi delirio en Chimborazo," *Escritos fundamentales*, ed. German Carrera Damas, Caracas, Monte Avila, 1982, p. 235.

14 ibid., p. 236.

15 ibid., p. 237.

16 Jose María Heredia, "En el teocalli de Cholula," lines 1–5. The Spanish original reads:

> Cuanto es bella la tierra que habitaban
> los aztecas valientes! En su seno
> en una estrecha zona concentrados,
> con asombro se ven todos los climas
> que hay desde el polo al ecuador.

17 ibid., lines 5–16.

> Sus llanos
> cubren a par de las doradas mieses
> las cañas deliciosas. El naranjo
> y la piña y el plátano sonante,
> hijos del suelo equinoccial, se mezclan
> a la frondosa vid, al pino agreste,
> y de Minerva al arbol majestuoso.
> Nieve eternal corona las cabezas
> de Iztaccihual purísimo, Orizaba
> y Popocatepec; sin que el invierno
> toque jamás con destructora mano
> los campos fertilísimos.

18 José Martí, "Palabras sobre Heredia," *El Economista Americano*, New York, July

1888, in Marti, *Obras completas*, Editorial de Ciencias Sociales, La Habana, 1975, vol. 5, p. 136.

19 ibid., pp. 136–7.

20 Esteban Echeverría, *La cautiva*, Buenos Aires, Editorial Huemul, 1974, pp. 22–3. The Spanish original reads:

> Entonces como el ruido/ que suele hacer el tronido cuando retumba lejano/ se oyó en el tranquilo llano sordo y confuso clamor:/ se perdió . . . y luego violento, como baladro espantoo/ de turba inmensa, en el viento se dilató sonroso/ dando a los brutos pavor.

21 ibid., pp. 23, 24. The lines in Spanish are:

> ¿Quién es? ¿Que insensata turba/ con su alarido perturba las calladas soledades/ de Dios? . . .
> ¿Dónde va? ¿De dónde viene?/ ¿De qué su gozo proviene? ¿Por qué grita, corre, vuela . . . ?

22 The figure of Facundo has come vividly back to life since 1989 through the Peronist president, Carlos Menem, who was from La Rioja province, just as Facundo Quiroga was. Despite his own background as a Lebanese immigrant and a Muslim, Menem draws heavily on the Facundo legacy, most noticeably by wearing thick sideburns like those that adorn Facundo in the portraits found in all Argentine schoolbooks.

23 These lines are from *Cantos del peregrino*, the poem by José Mármol quoted in the epigraph. The lines read "América no puede ser libre todavía,/porque su herencia ha sido de bastarda oscuridad." *Cantos del peregrino*, ed. Juan Mármol, Buenos Aires, Félix Lajouane, 1889.

24 Domingo Faustino Sarmiento, *Facundo o civilización y barbarie*, Prólogo Noé Jitrik, Caracas, Biblioteca Ayacucho, 1977, p. 23. Curiously, Sarmiento attributes the epigraph to Francis Bond Head, probably by mistake, though at least one Argentine critic, Ricardo Piglia, suggests the misattribution might be intentional and parodic. An English translation of *Civilización y barbarie* appeared under the title *Life in the Argentine Republic in the Days of the Tyrants* (New York, Collier Books, 1961). The translator is Mary Mann, who with her husband Horace Mann had a longstanding dialogue with Sarmiento on educational policy. Translations here are my own.

25 Sarmiento, *Facundo*, op. cit., p. 23.

26 ibid., p. 28.

27 Simón Bolívar, Letter to Santander, quoted in John Lynch, *The Spanish American Revolutions 1808–1826*, New York, W. W. Norton, 1986, p. 250.

28 Domingo Faustino Sarmiento, *Viajes*, Prólogo de Roy Bartholomew, Colección Clásicos Argentinos, Buenos Aires, Editorial de Belgrano, 1981, p. 22.

29 ibid., p. xiv. My translation. The original 1849 title was *Viajes en Europa, Africa y América*. Sarmiento's contemporary Juan Bautista Alberdi also wrote of his travels to Europe in 1843–4, in a series of shorter pieces collected under the title *Veinte dias en Genova (Twenty Days in Genoa)*. Like Sarmiento, he, too, wrote of travels within South America, on visits to the Paraná and Tucumán. While of considerable interest, Alberdi's travel writings are not of comparable scope to Sarmiento's, and I have left their consideration for a future occasion. See Juan Bautista Alberdi, *Viajes y descripciones*, Serie Grandes Escritores Argentinos, ed. Alberto Palco, Buenos Aires, Ediciones Jackson, n.d. I am indebted to Elizabeth Garrels for details on Alberdi's travel writing.

30 Sarmiento, *Viajes*, op. cit., p. xviii.

31 ibid., p. 9.

32 ibid., p. 22.
33 ibid., p. 10.
34 ibid., p. 112.
35 ibid., p. 116.
36 ibid., pp. 114–15.
37 ibid., p. 112.
38 ibid., p. 266.
39 ibid., p. 270.
40 ibid., p. 33.
41 For this reason, the epic-scale *Poema de Chile*, written in the 1930s and 1940s by the great Chilean woman poet Gabriela Mistral, constituted such a radical innovation.
42 The novel in question is titled *Sab* (1841). Avellaneda's poetry includes several poems with titles identical to texts by Heredia. Both wrote odes to the sea, to Washington, to Niagara, to the sun, for example. In some cases, such as the Niagara poem, Avellaneda explicitly alludes to the Heredian antecedent.
43 "El viajero americano," in Gertrudis Gómez de Avellaneda, *Antologiá poetíca*, ed. Mary Cruz, Editorial Letras Cubanas, La Habana, 1983, pp. 156–8.
44 Juana Manuela Gorriti, *Sueños y realidades*. The most recent edition of this work is from Buenos Aires, La Nacion, 1907.
45 Alejo Carpentier, "Problemática de la actual novela latinoamericana," *Tientos y diferencias*, Montevideo, Editorial Arca, 1967, pp. 24–5.
46 Alejo Carpentier, *The Lost Steps* (*Los pasos perdidos*, 1953), trans. Harriet de Onís, New York, Knopf, 1956, p. 129.
47 Humberto Toscano, ed., *El Ecuador visto por los extranjeros*, Puebla (Mexico), Ed. Cajica, 1959, p. 553.
48 Pascual Venegas Filardo, *Viajeros a Venezuela en los siglos XIX y XX*, Caracas, Monte Avila, 1973, p. 15.
49 Toscano, op. cit., p. 43.
50 Jean Baudrillard, *America*, London, Verso, 1988; and *Simulations*, New York, Semiotext(e), 1983.

PART III   IMPERIAL STYLISTICS, 1860–1980

9   FROM THE VICTORIA NYANZA TO THE SHERATON SAN SALVADOR

1 Richard Burton, *The Lake Regions of Central Africa: A Picture of Exploration* (1860), New York, Horizon Press, 1961, vol. II, p. 43.
2 The spring of 1990 saw the release of a heroic Hollywood version of Burton and Speke's adventure, titled *The Mountains of the Moon*. Carrying out a trend that developed in the 1980s (*Out of Africa*; *The Jewel in the Crown*; *A Passage to India*; *Lord Greystoke*, etc.), imperialist nostalgia provides a cultural response to the absolute failure of western-style modernization in Africa.
3 James Augustus Grant, *A Walk Across Africa or, Domestic Scenes from my Nile Journal*, Edinburgh, 1864, p. 196.
4 John Hanning Speke, *Journal of the Discovery of the Source of the Nile*, Edinburgh: Blackwoods, 1863, p. 466.

5 Donna Haraway has produced a monumental study of the many-faceted significances of primates in western ideologies. See her *Primate Visions*, New York, Routledge, 1989.

6 Paul Du Chaillu, *Explorations and Adventures in Equatorial Africa*, New York, 1861, p. 83.

7 ibid., p. 84.

8 Mary Kingsley, *Travels in West Africa*, London, Virago Press, 1982, pp. 338–9. First edition, London, Macmillan & Co., 1897.

9 Deborah Birkett, "West Africa's Mary Kingsley," *History Today*, no. 37, May 1987, pp. 10–16. The secondary literature on Kingsley is now very extensive.

10 Joseph Conrad, *Heart of Darkness and Other Stories*, New York, Houghton Mifflin, 1971, p. 213.

11 Alberto Moravia, *Which Tribe Do You Belong To?*, trans. Angus Davidson, New York, Farrar, Straus, and Giroux, 1972, p. 1.

12 Paul Theroux, *The Old Patagonian Express*, Boston, Houghton Mifflin, 1978, p. 123.

13 ibid., p. 397.

14 Moravia, op. cit., p. 8.

15 Paul Fussell, Review of Theroux, *The Old Patagonian Express*, *New York Times Book Review*, August 26, 1979, p. 1.

16 Richard Wright, *Black Power*, New York, Harper, 1954, p. 154.

17 ibid., p. 263.

18 See M. L. Pratt, "Mapping Ideology: Gide, Camus and Algeria," *College Literature*, vol. 8, 1981, pp. 158–74.

19 Albert Camus, "The Adulterous Woman," in *Exile and the Kingdom* (1957), trans. Justin O'Brien, New York, Vintage Books, 1957, pp. 22–3.

20 Joan Didion, *Salvador*, New York, Washington Square Press, 1983, pp. 40–1.

21 ibid., p. 60.

22 ibid., p. 81.

23 ibid., p. 36.

24 ibid., p. 13.

25 ibid., quoted on the book jacket.

26 ibid., p. 79.

27 Domitila Barrios de Chungara with Moema Viezzer, *Let Me Speak*, trans. Victoria Ortiz, New York, Monthly Review Press, 1978. Spanish original is *Si me permiten hablar . . . Testimonio de Domitila, una mujer de las minas de Bolivia*, Mexico, Siglo XXI, 1977. For an introduction to the category of "resistance literature," see Barbara Harlow, *Resistance Literature*, New York, Methuen, 1987.

28 Perhaps Didion does as much as a travel book can honestly do with terror, and perhaps that is her challenge to her readership: How can westerners know terror and the contact zone without trying to master them? Anthropologist Michael Taussig bears witness to that challenge in his remarkable book *Shamanism, Colonialism and the Wild Man: A Study in Terror and Healing* (Cambridge, Harvard UP, 1987). Analyzing the "culture of terror" around the turn-of-the-century rubber boom in the Putumayo region of Colombia, Taussig suggests that when one tries to comprehend the practices and semiotics of terror one finds that they are constructed not only out of what is NOT seen, said, known, but also out of what people do see, say, and know AND what people do not see but hear others say they have seen; on what people do not hear said, but hear or read others who say they have heard it said; on what people did not do themselves but heard others say they saw done, and so on. The cultural and ideological engine of terror, argues Taussig, runs not just on the (distorted) conceptions each side holds of its enemy, but on the distorted conceptions each side holds about the distorted conceptions

its enemy holds about it. Equally important, Taussig pairs terror in his title with healing, insisting that the two may be found together, that where there is terror there healing will also be found – in the powers of shamans, for example. Didion would perhaps agree that once entered into, the workings of terror call for a long stay, and a long book (as Taussig's is) that tells readers more than they care to know (as Taussig's does). She might also argue that Taussig's *tour de force* rests on a kind of one-man omnipresence she refuses.

Index